Frederick Denison Maurice

Sermons preached in country Churches

Frederick Denison Maurice
Sermons preached in country Churches
ISBN/EAN: 9783743341524
Manufactured in Europe, USA, Canada, Australia, Japa
Cover: Foto ©Lupo / pixelio.de

Manufactured and distributed by brebook publishing software (www.brebook.com)

Frederick Denison Maurice

Sermons preached in country Churches

SERMONS

PREACHED IN COUNTRY CHURCHES

BY

FREDERICK DENISON MAURICE

SECOND EDITION

London
MACMILLAN AND CO.
1880

The Right of Translation and Reproduction is reserved

PREFACE.

THE title of these Sermons exactly expresses what they are. Mr. Maurice frequently took duty in some quiet village during the summer vacation. He found more rest in ministering to the poor and in speaking to them, than in visits to English watering-places or in foreign travel. The poor "heard him gladly." They understood his teaching, and crowded to hear him. It is thought that words which went home to the hearts of many simple and ignorant people may be blessed to others, though unaccompanied by the voice and the face which made them so precious to those who heard them spoken.

GEORGINA F. MAURICE.

CONTENTS.

SERMON	PAGE
I.—The Pool of Bethesda	1
II.—The Gift of Hearing	10
III.—The Spirit of Love	18
IV.—Waiting for Christ	29
V.—St. Peter's Conversion	40
VI.—The Sick of the Palsy	50
VII.—The Marriage Feast of the King's Son	62
VIII.—The Redemption of the Body	72
IX.—The Spirit the Help to Prayer	80
X.—The Law of Inheritance	88
XI.—The Deliverer from Crime	98
XII.—St. John Baptist's Day	110
XIII.—The Transfiguration	121
XIV.—The Publican	131
XV.—The Spirit and the Flesh	139
XVI.—Man's Dominion	148
XVII.—God and Mammon	157
XVIII.—The Glory of the Cross	165
XIX.—The Widow of Nain's Son	172
XX—Justification	179
XXI.—Truth	190
XXII.—Ministers of Christ	197
XXIII.—The Light of the World	206
XXIV.—The Lord of the Winds and Sea	214

SERMON	PAGE
XXV.—The Man of Sorrows	222
XXVI.—St. Matthew's Day	229
XXVII.—Michaelmas Day	236
XXVIII.—God's Visitations	243
XXIX.—The Eternal Weight of Glory	250
XXX.—The Grace of God	258
XXXI.—The New Covenant	269
XXXII.—The Last Supper	277
XXXIII.—The Law of Liberty	284
XXXIV.—The Sure and Certain Hope	291
XXXV.—The Baptism of Repentance	297
XXXVI.—God's Covenant with the Nations	305
XXXVII.—Life and Raiment	313
XXXVIII.—The House of God	320
XXXIX.—St. John the Evangelist's Day	332
XL.—Suffering and Glory	342
XLI.—Repentance and Conversion	350

SERMONS

PREACHED IN COUNTRY CHURCHES.

SERMON I.

THE POOL OF BETHESDA.

Preached at Clyro, 8th Sunday after Trinity, July 17, 1853.

"Jesus saith unto him, Rise, take up thy bed, and walk."
ST. JOHN v. 8.

You have heard in the second lesson this morning where our Lord spoke these words. There was a pool near the sheep-market in the city of Jerusalem. The people of the city believed that the water of this pool could heal sick people. They did not think it could heal at all times, but only when there was some stir in it. They thought that an angel or messenger of God caused it to stir. They, therefore, who had anything ailing them lay in crowds about this pool waiting for the moving of the water. It was so one Sabbath day when Jesus was walking in Jerusalem. We are not told that He spoke to the sick people generally;

but He fixed His eyes on one who had been ill for thirty-eight years. He said to him, " Wilt thou be made whole?" The man said he could not reach the pool in time to get any good from it. When it began to move numbers pushed forward and bathed. He was very weak, and others were quicker than he was, and there was no one to lift him in. " Jesus saith unto him, Rise, take up thy bed, and walk. And immediately the man was made whole, and took up his bed, and walked."

I have said that the people of Jerusalem thought that there was some advantage to be gained from bathing in this pool. No doubt they had reason for thinking so. St. John speaks as if they had. One and another had found good from the water, and therefore all of them thought that they might. They were just such men as we are. One tells another of some medicine that has been serviceable to him. Those that are ill and long to be well, desire to try whether it may not serve them also. And if they observe that the benefit comes at one season rather than another, then they wish to seize the very moment, and if they fail, they often fancy they should have been quite cured, if it had not been for some unfortunate accident, or some person who was in the way, and hindered them. The people of Jerusalem believed also that the good which was in the pool did not come from the pool itself; but that it was God's gift. His angel stirred it. He put the healing power into it. This belief, too, was on the whole a right one. They might have foolish fancies that they saw the angel going down into the pool at certain moments; just as people in our country have had, and may have still. But they were not wrong that everything which is healthful comes from the Giver of all good, they were not wrong in saying, It must be some power from Him which makes any one well who has been sick; able to walk, who has been fixed to his bed and helpless.

Jesus did not come to the couch of that poor man who had been ill for thirty-eight years, to tell him that this was not so. He wished him to believe it more than he had ever believed it before. And yet, you see, He did not assist to put him into the pool; He did not say, Wait a little, and the angel will stir it again, then you may profit by it as others have done. But He said at once, "Rise up and walk." The poor cripple must have wondered. He who spake these words looked like another man. He spoke with a voice like his voice; He had not any signs of being greater than those about Him. The rulers of the Jews thought nothing of Him. And yet He took upon Him to do what the Angel could not do. He addressed the man as if He were his master; as if He knew him thoroughly; as if He understood exactly what his weakness was; as if the power to make him a healthy living man was in Him. And we are told that the impotent man felt it was in Him. The word did not fall dead upon his ears. It gave him what he wanted. He rose, took up his bed, and walked.

It was a good thing for that poor cripple, doubtless,

that, after thirty-eight years' illness, he should be able to feel his limbs again, and do his work freely and usefully. But what is it to us? Why should it be put down in this Gospel of St. John? Why should it be a Gospel or good news to us who live eighteen hundred years since this man has been dead, in a country thousands of miles from his? It could not be good news to us to tell us that there was at that time in Jerusalem a pool which had now and then some healing power; for Jerusalem is altogether changed, and we hear of no such pool now; and, if there were such, what could it concern the poor and sick people of England and Wales? It could not help us much to hear reports of other waters nearer to us that might sometimes be useful to one or another. For they might not do us good in *our* diseases; or we might not be able to reach them at the right time, as this poor man was not, though he was so close to the spot, and took so much pains. And it could be no great good news to us that there were kind angels who sometimes took an interest in poor mortals, and sent them aid; for we should say to ourselves, What are they against the multitudes of dangers and evils that are besetting us continually? But if we could be told of one who is always alive and always at hand, who is the same to us as He was to the people of Jerusalem, or to any one of those people; one who is not here to-day and gone to-morrow, strong now and weak at another time, kind for a little while, and then hard or indifferent; but who *is* at hand when we think least of

Him, and is mighty when we are least able to help ourselves; and, best of all, who has the same mind to us, however changeable our minds may be; if we could be told of such an one, and that He has tried His strength with our enemies and has prevailed against them, this would be good news; this would be news that every one everywhere might care to hear.

And it is just this news which the lesson to-day preaches to us. It does not tell us that Jesus Christ had a special regard for that man who had been ill thirty-eight years, and was lying beside the Pool of Bethesda, and that therefore He cured him. But it gives us this instance, and a number of other instances, that we may know who it is that is the Lord and Master over our bodies and our spirits, and the bodies and spirits of all men that are living now, and that have ever lived, who it is from whom we get strength when we are strong, who it is that restores strength to us when we are weak, who gives wisdom to every physician, and virtue to every spring and to every medicine, who it is that raises every sick man from his couch, and enables him to do his work again after he has been tied hand and foot. This lesson says to us, You are not to depend upon one place or another; upon this favourite remedy or another; no, nor upon the gifts of God's angels. All gifts come from your Lord, all angels are His servants; and therefore it is to Him, and not to them, you are to look in all hours of weakness and suffering. What you want in these hours is not merely some one to cure you, but some one to understand what you feel, and to feel with you. If you find a fellow-creature, a sister or a wife, who can do that, you are more glad than even of some relief from the pain. It is a relief from the pain to have some one who can enter into it. Now, the great Lord of all is He who has borne our weaknesses and carried our sicknesses; who knows what they are, not by report, but by experience; and those secret troubles which you cannot tell to the nearest and dearest companion, that which makes you suffer what other people, perhaps, would not suffer, though they had the same sickness and pain: these He knows of. You can be sure that there is One who has the most entire acquaintance with all your bodily sufferings, and with all that is in your hearts too, with all the weakness, and folly, and sin that is there.

Yes, but that is what we shrink from! We might be glad of a healing pool, glad of a kind physician, or a kind sister, or a kind angel. But should we like one who knew all that we were doing, and wishing, and thinking: all the strange things that are going on in our hearts; all that ever has gone on in them ever since we were born? Should not we say, Oh, hide me from that look! Do not let all the dark desires I have had, and all the bad words I have spoken, and the acts I have committed—do not let my dearest friend know them. I could not bear it; he would certainly turn away from me. Brethren, it is a most natural feeling; it is one which we all of us have had.

And when people have told us how righteous Jesus Christ is, and how hateful all evil is to Him, we have thought that He was the very last person before whom we should like to be laid open. But let us remember it well, brethren, He who is to heal us must be acquainted with all that has made us sick; and He cannot do that if He does not know us, our own selves, and all that we have done, and all that we have been. Be assured, too, that there is such an one. You know that there is. Your consciences speak of Him. When words you have spoken, and deeds you have done, and thoughts you have thought years ago, come out clear and fresh before you, as they often do; that is a proof that there is some one near you who is acquainted with you, not only with what has happened to you—with what other people have said to you, or done to you—but with all that has ever been in you, right or wrong, fair or foul, good or evil. I know it is a thought that frightens us at first very much indeed, and it ought to frighten us; but we must face it, because it is true. We cannot shrink from this searcher of hearts. We cannot get out of His way. When we try to forget Him, He shows that He remembers us. When we have lost ourselves in all kinds of nonsense and vanity, He comes to us and shows us to ourselves, and makes us tremble.

But who is He? I have told you, it is that Lord Jesus Christ who said to the man who had been sick thirty-eight years, "Rise up and walk." It is He of whom we read in all the Gospels that He went about doing good, healing the sick, and casting out devils. We know, too, what manner of being He is, for He has made Himself known. We know what He would do to each of us. We know certainly that He is the healer; and that He would heal us of our infirmities, and that He can do it. We cannot tell, indeed, that He will cure the bodily ailments of any particular man at once. Of all that were round the Pool of Bethesda at that time, this is the only one who rose up and walked. But we know for certain that His purpose to every man is to make them right, and to reverse whatever makes them wrong. We know for certain that if He lets a man remain sick, it is because there is something else in him that needs to be cured besides, something which must be cured if he is to be a sound man. And this, brethren, is the cure of those most secret evils of our hearts, of that which puts everything else in us out of order. When we find out that we have this friend, this healer, this life-giver, so close to us, and that we may turn to Him and confess all that is oppressing us —all the evil of other men, yes, and all our own—all that we are most ashamed of in the past part of our lives—all that we are most ashamed of in ourselves now;—when we believe that He is such an one, and that He can understand us, and that He can heal us, then our lives become altogether different; then we can become simple, honest, brave men, who do not want to hide anything from our Maker; then we can come boldly to Him every day to ask Him to make us true when we feel false, and brave when we feel cowardly, and strong to act when we feel as if we could do nothing. So this is a lesson for us who are going about the world, as much as for those who are on sick beds. We want healing—continual healing—just as they do. We want strength as much as they do; strength to be right and to do right; strength for the work that we have to do each day.

And this is part of the lesson which we ought to remember. It was the Sabbath-day on which our Lord healed the impotent man. The Jewish rulers were angry; they thought our Lord ought not to have healed on the Sabbath-day. But He declared that the Sabbath-day was the very day for healing: that God means it to be a day of healing and blessing to all His creatures. We come here on Sundays because it is so. We come to Church not to say a few prayers, or to hear a few words from the pulpit, but to learn who the great healer is, and how we are to be healed. We come that we may get strength to walk during the week, to go through the business of it truly and heartily; as if we were God's children, sent into the world by Him to till the earth and subdue it, and to be like Him, loving and just, and lowly, as His well-beloved Son Jesus Christ was on earth and is in heaven. May He enable us to be so this week by His good Spirit, and then we shall feel that Christ heals on the Sabbath as He did of old.

SERMON II.

THE GIFT OF HEARING.

Preached at Clyro, 12th Sunday after Trinity, August 14, 1853.

"And they were beyond measure astonished, saying, He hath done all things well; He maketh both the deaf to hear, and the dumb to speak."—ST. MARK vii. 37.

IN the Epistle to-day St. Paul tells us that he was a minister of the New Testament, or of God's new Covenant. At first we may not understand what that means; but he explains it to us himself. He says that the children of Israel in the old time had a law given them which was written on stones. It was a good law, a blessed law. God gave it to them. It declared His will to them. But, though it declared His will, it could not make them do His will. It was said on the stone that men were not to worship idols, or kill, or steal. But they did worship idols, and kill, and steal. They did it though the law said it was death to do so. How was this? Could not God's law, then, be obeyed? Was it only given to torment men and make them know what a bad state they were in, and what misery was in store for them?

So many men thought; at one time St. Paul himself thought so. He had tried hard to keep the law, he fancied he had kept it. But he found that he did not love it, that his mind was against it; that, if he did not break it, he wished to break it. He found that, though the law said, "Thou shalt not covet," he did covet; nay, it seemed to him as if he coveted more because he was forbidden to do it. He found, therefore, that his mind and God's mind were at variance.

This made him very miserable. He saw that God's law was good, very good, and yet he felt as if he must hate it. He honoured it, and yet he would have been glad if he had never heard of it. Then it was shown him that God does not merely give a law upon stones, but that He promises to write this law on our hearts, to put the love of it into them; to make our minds like His. This he learnt was God's new covenant or Testament. This was what He promised He would do for men when His Son came into the world. And this He had done. For Jesus, the Son of God, loved His Father's law, and delighted to do it. This law was in His heart. He fulfilled it altogether, and bore all that it laid upon Him.

And now that God has given His Son to take our flesh and to die for us, He deals with us as sons. He says, I will send the Spirit of my Son into your hearts, that you may be like Him. I make a New Testament or covenant with you in His blood. And it is this—You shall love the things which I love, and hate what I hate.

Now, St. Paul says that he was a preacher of this New Testament or covenant. He is very thankful, and proud of that office. He thinks it the most glorious that a man could have. For he says, I am not sent to tell men of what they must do, but to tell them how they can do it. I am not sent to say, you will die if you do not keep these commandments. But I am sent to say, God gives you His own life, His own Spirit, that you may be able to keep His commandments. I am a minister of Righteousness, not of condemnation; of the Spirit, not of the letter; of the law in the heart, not of the law on stones.

He might well rejoice and wonder that he had such a trust. And yet he knew also, and he tells us in this Epistle, that there were people to whom his Gospel was hid, who did not heed it at all. It is not, he says, that there is any veil over God's countenance, Christ has taken that away. But it is that there is a veil over them, over their own hearts, and that they will not turn to God that this veil may be taken away. It is in vain I tell them of His love; of His sending His Son to make them one with Him; of His sending His Spirit to write His laws in them. They do not know what such words signify; they do not acknowledge there is anything in them that wants to be made right; they are content to be as they are.

Brethren, this same New Testament ministry exists in the world now. God sends His message to you as much as He did to the people of Corinth or Ephesus, to whom St. Paul preached. He tells you, every one of you, that He is your Father, and that He has sent His Son to die for you, and that He has reconciled you to Himself, and that His Spirit is ready to come and dwell with you, that His laws may be written in your hearts, and you may keep them. And you come here every Sunday because it is so, and you pray these prayers, and hear the Lessons and the Epistle and Gospel read, because it is so. All these are ministers to you of the New Testament. They tell you what God has done for you, and is doing for you; how He has taken the veil off His face, and is showing it to you in His Son—full of grace, and beauty, and love; and how He would make you after His own image, gracious and loving as He is.

But, if this is so, how comes it that so few people hear this Word? that it goes so little way with them? that it seems to be caught away and vanish almost as soon as it has been spoken? Oh! brethren! that we would ask ourselves how this comes to pass! Because, if we did, this great and terrible disease might be cured; this deafness might be taken away from us; we might be enabled to receive God's words into our inmost souls, and His words might bring forth fruit there unto life eternal.

And that is the reason, I think, why this Gospel

about Christ's curing the deaf and dumb man is joined to the Epistle about the ministry of the New Testament. It says very plainly to those who feel how hard it is for them to take in the New Testament message, how dull, and deaf, and stupid, they are. Yes, but that need not continue. There is a Physician at hand. There is one who doeth all things well, who maketh both the deaf to hear and the dumb to speak.

I have told you before that the stories of Christ in the Gospel, whether they be of His healing the man at the Pool of Bethesda, or of His promising to draw men to Him on His Cross, or of His being shown to the Jews as their King, are all written for us. I have said that He is just as much among us as He was among the Jews in the city of Jerusalem, and that these words are to tell us what He is doing for some, and would be doing for us all.

First, then, I say that it is Christ who enables any one of us to hear any of the common sounds that enter into our ears as we walk out on an August day like this. If you have heard the singing of the birds or the running of the stream, or the voices of children as you came to church, then recollect it was Christ who caused you to hear them. He fills the earth and air with all melodies, and He gives to men the power of taking them in. By giving back hearing to this man who had lost it, He declared this; He said, I am the giver of hearing; the power comes from me. Think how wonderful that is. I suppose none of us have thought of it seriously till we have been reminded by seeing deaf people, or by becoming more or less deaf ourselves, what the blessing of sounds is; what it is to have them shut out.

But I say again: if this trial comes to anyone of you in any degree, and then the power of hearing has been restored to you again, be sure that that was as much Christ's blessing to you, as it was His to the man we have read of this morning, over whom He sighed and said, "Ephphatha, be opened." It is not less His because you do not see Him before you, or because these words are not spoken. Whatever any physician does for you, is done by His power: it is His work. Be sure you confess that it is; and then you will love all that act as His servants to your bodies or your spirits, for His sake.

And now, then, I come back to what I spoke of before. I say that there is another kind of deafness besides that which cannot take in sounds. We may hear sounds, and yet the words that are within the sounds may never reach us. They may float about us, and seem as if they were coming unto us. And then we may feel just the same as if they had never been uttered; as far as we are concerned, we might as well have been a hundred miles away. But if they are words of health and life, words that come from the good God; words that are to make us right and true men; words that are to make all that is past fresh and new to us; and what is now going on around us good and not evil; and what is to be hereafter through all ages blessed; it is a very sad thing, is it not, that they should be all lost upon us? A very sad thing that we cannot stop them, and hold them fast; a very sad thing that a man should have to remember some other day, on a death-bed, 'They were proclaimed to me; I was told they were intended for me, but I did not mind them; and now it seems as if I and they had nothing to do with each other any more.' But must it be so; shall it be so with any of us? What, when it is written, "He maketh the deaf to hear!" When we can say, Lord, Thou hast sent us these words; they are Thine. Thou didst come from heaven, and live and die on earth, that they might be ours. And Thou who dost give the ear to hear, and the heart to understand—and Thou who dost desire that we should hear and should understand—wilt not Thou heal us; wilt not Thou help us? Thou didst not care more for that poor deaf man, on the coast of Tyre and Sidon, than Thou dost care for me. Thou didst not die for him more than for me. And my ears are even more stopped, and stopped in a worse way than his were. Oh, once more say Ephphatha! be opened, to me and to all who have not received the good news of Thy New Testament into their hearts.

It is said, moreover, that the string of this man's tongue was loosed, for like most people who are born deaf, he was dumb also. So Christ declared Himself to be the Lord of speech as well as of hearing. He does not only fill the world with sweet sounds, and give us the power to enjoy them, He also enables us to tell what we enjoy, and what we have seen and heard, and what is going on within us, to our fellow-men. Mighty power of speech! who can tell what that is? Why, what treasures of silver and gold are like that treasure? The greatest gift which the richest man in the world has, is that which the poorest has likewise. Words can do more than all the money and all the swords in the universe; money and swords are only their servants. But what mischief can they do as well as good! What curses can they spread abroad! How they can make neighbourhoods miserable; how they can overturn whole countries! Oh, what need have we of some one to rule over our tongues, to guide them, and to make them sources of health and not of pain!

Dear brethren, Christ is the master of them; he is called the Word in Holy Scripture; it is He who alone can command our words, so that they shall be good as He would have them be; so that they shall be mighty for His purpose. May He ever command yours and mine. And may the words of His New Testament break through all barriers that hinder them from entering into us, and be to us instruments of God's righteousness, of God's own Spirit.

SERMON III.

THE SPIRIT OF LOVE.

Preached at Clyro, 13th Sunday after Trinity, August 21, 1853.

"Which now of these three, thinkest thou, was neighbour to him that fell among the thieves? And he said, He that shewed mercy upon him. Then said Jesus, Go, and do thou likewise."—
ST. LUKE x. 36, 37.

I SPOKE to you last week of the law that was written on stones, and of the law that is written on men's hearts. There is more to be said about this matter yet. I think the Gospel to-day may make it clearer to us. Be sure that you remember who it is that causes the deafest ear to hear, and then you will ask Him that you may take in His own wonderful words.

On a certain day, St. Luke says, Jesus was telling His apostles that their eyes and ears were blessed, for that they saw things which prophets and kings had desired to see and had not seen, and to hear and had not heard.

The apostles, you know, were fishermen, poor men. What could it mean that they were better off than all the great men of their own country and of other countries who had lived before them? They must have been pondering this thought in their minds, when one of the learned men of the Jews came up to Jesus, and said, "Master! what shall I do that I may inherit eternal life?" This lawyer thought he had kept the commandments; he did not remember that he had ever committed any great offence. But he supposed that was not enough to get eternal life; he must do something very special to please God, if he was to win such a prize as that. He had heard that Christ spoke of eternal life, and told His disciples that they might possess it. The lawyer asked Him, How can I get this life? What shall I do to please God, and obtain a reward which other men have not?

Our Lord did not answer him as he expected. He did not say, I know a secret which men in general do not know. I can tell you a new way of gaining this life which you have never heard. But He said, "What is written in the Law?" 'You are a lawyer; you are reading in the law continually. Has that told you nothing about eternal life?' Then the lawyer bethought him of some words in the book of Deuteronomy, where it is written, "Thou shalt love the Lord thy God with all thy heart and with all thy soul, and with all thy mind: and thou shalt love thy neighbour as thyself." He had often read these words, and it came into his mind that perhaps the answer to his question might be there. If he loved God and loved his neighbour, he might have the reward he wanted; all that any man could have. Our Lord told him he was right; if he did that, he would live.

But the lawyer was not satisfied; I suppose that he was never less satisfied.

For the thought struck him, Have I ever done this? Can I do this? If I had been bidden to bear some heavy burden; to torture myself in some strange way; even to kill myself, I could have done that. But when I am commanded to love—that is another thing altogether. Am I more loving because I have been told that it is right to be so? If I can only obtain eternal life at this price, shall I ever obtain it? I fancy these thoughts must have been in his mind first, but then came another. Was the law clear enough? It talked about his neighbour, but it did not say who his neighbour was. St. Luke says he was wishing to justify himself; not that anybody had found fault with him, but that some one was saying to him in his heart, 'Learned lawyer as thou art, thou hast not kept the law;' and he wanted to silence that voice, it tormented him.

But he had asked Jesus, Who is my neighbour? and he was to have his answer. The Lord told him a story. Again it was not what he supposed it would be. It was the story of a poor man—a Jew—who went down from the chief city of Judæa to Jericho. That was a very dangerous road, and the man fell among thieves. He was stripped of his raiment, and he was left half dead. A priest—the most holy man among the Jews—one who offered sacrifices to God for the people, one who blessed the people in God's name, came travelling that way. The wounded man was there—one of his own countrymen—one of those for whom he presented prayers and sacrifices, and whom he was to bless. But the priest did not think this man was his neighbour. He went on and left him. Then came a Levite, one of the same tribe of the Jews with the priest. His business was especially to interpret the law to the people—that law which said, "Thou shalt love thy neighbour as thyself." He looked at the wounded man, but he did not think that he was his neighbour; he passed by on the other side. Not long after a Samaritan rode by. The man was not his countryman; he was not one of his friends; he belonged to a people with whom his people had no dealings. Moreover, the Samaritan was not considered a holy or religious man by the Jews at all; quite the contrary: they thought him a man whom God abhorred; one who could not possibly have eternal life. But this Samaritan *did* look upon the wounded man as his neighbour; he stopped his journey to help him. He poured oil and wine into his wounds; he set him on his own beast; he took him to an inn, and bade the landlord take care of him; and he said, as he went away, that whatever more was spent upon the poor traveller, when he came again he would repay.

The lawyer had to listen to this tale. And then he was asked—

"Which now of these three—the priest, the Levite,

or the Samaritan, was neighbour to him that fell among thieves?" He did not quite like to say the Samaritan; that would have been too hard a word for him to speak. But he said, "He that shewed mercy on him;" and then our Lord bade him go and do like the man whom he thought most meanly of, and whom he regarded as God's enemy.

Now let us think of this story. You see that the priest and the Levite knew the law, which was written in a book, perfectly. They had nothing to learn about that. The words of it rose at once to their lips; they could confound any one who disputed it. And yet when they were called to fulfil this law—when their neighbour lay on the ground needing their help, they did not remember it at all. It was a long way from them. They were to love their neighbour as themselves, no doubt. But who was their neighbour? Not this poor creature, though he was a Jew, a son of Abraham, an heir of the covenant. They owed him nothing; they were going on their own errands; what was he to them? That is to say, they had the law of love upon tables, but they had it not written on their hearts. They were serving God for hire; they could do things which they thought would profit them, and avoid things which they thought would injure them, but they did nothing because they had God's mind; they did nothing because they felt to men as He feels towards them.

But this Samaritan, though he had never studied the words of the law as they had; though he had not a hundredth part of the blessings which belonged to them; though he had probably a great many mistakes and confusions in his head, from which they were free, had this law of love in his heart, and showed that he had; God had written it there. And, therefore, he did not ask whether this poor half-dead traveller by the roadside belonged to his village, or his town, or his country, or his religion. He had nothing to do with any of these questions, supposing there was any one able to answer them. This was his neighbour, for he was a man. That was quite enough, and therefore he at once did what his neighbour wanted, what he would have had another do to him.

Here was a lesson for the lawyer; one which he might be learning day by day, which would last him as long as he remained on earth, and long after that. If he would keep God's commandments, he must give up his pride as a lawyer, his pride as a Jew; he must become simply a man, just like this poor despised Samaritan. He must understand that God cared for men, and therefore he must care for them. He must ask God continually to show him how He cared for them, and to give to him that will, that spirit, which is in Himself, otherwise he would continue hard as the stones on which the commandments were written; otherwise he might have the highest reputation among men, and yet be abominable in the sight of God; otherwise he might be trying to win eternal life, and really be sinking deeper and deeper into death.

And now you will understand, I think, why the eyes and ears of the disciples, fishermen as they were, had a blessing which did not belong to all the great men and wise men that had been in the world before them. Some of those great and wise men had had this law proclaimed to them in direct words, and had seen it written in letters. But that was not enough for them. They knew it was to be obeyed; they felt they could not obey it while it was outside of them. They wanted to have it in them, and to be governed by it altogether. But the more they wanted this, the more they felt how unlike their mind was to God's mind; how short they fell of the love which was in Him, and which He wished to be in them. There were others who had never heard the law in words, or seen it in letters, yet God had written it in their hearts, and it had come forth in such acts as this of the good Samaritan; but they cried and sighed like the others over the selfishness which they found in themselves and in the world; they asked, 'When will God's will be done on earth as it is in heaven? when will there be one to do it perfectly?'

Both, therefore, those to whom the law came outwardly, and those to whom it came only within, cried for the same person. They cried for a Son of God who should show them what God's truth and charity is; they cried for a son of man who should show them how a man may be the perfect image of God; they cried for a king who should reign over their hearts, and make them like Himself. And now, says our Lord to His disciples, 'Blessed are your eyes, for they see that Son of God who can show you what the Father is; that Son of Man who perfectly delights to do His Father's will, and to finish His work; that King who can govern you according to His pleasure. Blessed are your ears, for He is speaking to you, and commanding you.' Long afterwards they will have recollected how the lawyer's question, and our Lord's parable, came in just when they had been considering what their blessing was. And they will have said to themselves, 'Yes, truly, blessed are our eyes, for we have seen Him who has met with us all lying sick and wounded and half dead; who has gone about healing men and restoring them without asking whether they were His friends or His enemies, but caring for them all as His brethren. Blessed are our eyes, for we have seen Him who was called a Samaritan by the Jews; whom they despised, because He mixed with publicans and sinners; whom they cast out as a blasphemer. Blessed are our ears, for we have heard Him speak God's words; we have heard Him bid us go and do as He has done; and suffer as He has suffered. He has made us content to be called Samaritans, or worse names than that, if we can but pour oil and wine into the wounds of men that are perishing. Blessed are we, for we know what eternal life is now, since we have seen Jesus Christ, and have perceived what life there was in Him. This was the life which He received from the Father. This was the life which He has bestowed upon us. We are not to do something great, that we may obtain it. He gives it us without money and without price. But when He has given it us, when He has poured His own Spirit upon us, it works within us. It stirs us up to act as if men were our own neighbours, our brethren as well as His.'

This was what the disciples thought long afterwards; but they did not think these things—they scarcely knew what our Lord meant—they never got the blessing which He said was theirs till He was gone out of their sight. Then it was, when He had ascended on high, that they began to feel who had been with them, and who was with them still; then they began to preach to all men, 'He is your king as well as ours, He is with you as well as with us; He has given us His Spirit, His life of love, He will give it to you.' Then they began to treat all men—Jews, Samaritans, heathen—as brethren; then they could say boldly to their hearers, "Go, and do you likewise." And, therefore, brethren, I say, you and I have all the blessing they had, and the only question is whether we will use it or cast it away. That is a very serious question indeed for us, one and all. It is a very serious one for us who are, like the Levites of the Jews, called to teach you about God's laws, and, like the priests, to lead you in your prayers, and to present the perfect sacrifice of Christ for you to God, and to direct you unto the witnesses of His love, and to bless you in Christ's name. For we may become just as tough and hardhearted as these Jewish priests and Levites became. If we are left to ourselves we shall be harder and colder than all people, because those who are in the habit of using holy words and doing holy acts, are more in danger of losing the sense of them, and becoming stupid and indifferent, as if they meant nothing, than those who are less familiar with them. It is a terrible fact but it is a fact. And, therefore, we must pray to God that He will not leave us to ourselves; that He will not let us sink down into hardness and carelessness about our fellow-creatures; that He will stir us up to think of them; that He will quicken us with His own Divine love; that He will make us true witnesses for Him by our acts as well as our words, and then what we say and what we do will not only be for ourselves, but for you. If we want to get eternal life for ourselves as the lawyer did, we shall not get it; if we are willing to receive it from Christ that others may share it with us, He will give it us abundantly, and then the very humblest of us will be able to go and do like the man whom we have heard of to-day. He was merely an ordinary person with very few advantages, as I have told you; people who thought highly of themselves thought meanly of him. But, because he had been taught to think of men as his brethren, the sons of one Father, he did an act which Christ owned. Christ said, 'That was my act; God himself inspired it.' And let each one of us say to himself, 'Christ the Son of God died and rose again for me, and for all who dwell about me, for all my neighbours and kinsfolk, for every stranger that comes in my way, and for all sick and wounded people, and for all sinful people; Christ died and rose again for them, and He is their Lord and their brother as well as mine. And His will is to do them good; and His will is that we should work with Him to do them good, to raise them out of the dust, to heal their wounds, to give them rest. He commits them to us, and He will come again to see whether we have fulfilled our trust or not. And when He comes He will say—for he has told us so—" Inasmuch as ye did it to one of the least of my brethren, ye did it unto me."'

SERMON IV.

WAITING FOR CHRIST.

Preached at Clyro, 18th Sunday after Trinity, September 25, 1853.

"Waiting for the coming of our Lord Jesus Christ, who shall also confirm you unto the end, that you may be blameless in the day of our Lord Jesus Christ."—1 CORINTHIANS i. 7, 8.

You have heard of people out on the hills at night who have been overtaken by a snowstorm and have lost the track by which they went up. You have heard of people—perhaps it may have happened to yourselves—who have been tossing all night on their beds in a fever. What do you think was the chief thought in the minds of both of them? It was surely this, 'Oh, that the sun would come forth! Oh, that he would not remain so long hidden from us! We know he is there. The morning must come; but oh, that it would break out now—that it would scatter this terrible darkness.'

These men know what it is to expect the coming forth of the sun,—what it is to long that he would lift up the veil that hides him from them. But we all do expect him, and wait for his rising. We should all be miserable if we were told by some one we believed, 'He will not appear to-morrow.' That would not be a message of grief and horror only to people on the hills and to the sick. It would be a message of grief and horror to the whole earth. Nothing else could make up for it. There may be ten thousand beautiful things on the earth, but that would be gone which enables us to see their beauty. In a little time the beauty itself would all be withered and dead. Each man might have hoarded treasures of his own; but when the common sun was withdrawn, all his particular blessings would be worth nothing to him. He would find that he and his poorest neighbours were on a level, alike in misery and desolation.

What has this to do with the words of St. Paul? Much, I believe. He speaks to the Corinthians, one and all, as to men waiting for the coming or the unveiling of Christ. They bore Christ's name, they were signed with the sign of His cross; they believed Him to be the Source of Light, Peace, Healing, to them and to the whole world. Must they not then desire that He should be fully revealed to them and to the world? Must not that be the great hope of their hearts? Those who felt what confusion there was in their minds for want of His clear light, might long for it more than others; those that were sick at heart might long for His healing more than others. But would it not be a miserable thing to tell any man, 'He will not appear;' 'He will never be revealed'?

Brethren, I am sure this would be the most horrible news that any one could have brought to the Corinthians. I am sure it would be the most horrible news that I could bring to you. I will tell you first why I say this about them, then I will tell you why I say the same about you.

St. Paul had found the Corinthians in great darkness of mind, worshipping many different gods, of whom they had different fancies and notions, worshipping the Goddess of Pleasure above all. They had a dream of some God, some Father, some Friend; at times they fancied these gods to whom they were doing homage were likenesses of Him, His children to whom He had given power in various places and over various things.

But then it seemed to them that there was more evil than good in the world, and that these powers must oftener mean evil to them than good, and that He from whom they got their powers must be harder and sterner than they were, and must design worse and more terrible mischiefs to the creatures He had formed.

They knew that they had done wrong; they felt as if He who had the government of the world must mean to punish them for the wrong; they thought they must try hard to persuade Him not to punish them; the more they tried, the more hopeless they were of escaping.

St. Paul came to these men, saying, 'God, who created all things, hath sent forth His only begotten Son, the express image of His person, into this world of ours, to deliver it, and them who dwell upon it, from the enemies which are tormenting it. You are not mistaken; the evils of the world are as great as you take them to be. They are about you, tormenting you every hour. You do need to be set free from them. And you are not mistaken that these evils, the very worst of them, come from yourselves. You have committed evil, the desires which led to this evil are in your hearts. And you are not mistaken that God is a righteous Being, and that all these evils are sins against Him. But because that is so, He hath sent His Son to set you free from these plagues above all others. While He was on earth He was freeing men from plagues of body, hunger, leprosy, palsy, fever, and their minds from plagues of rage and madness, and confusion.' All these, he said, were proofs that an evil spirit, a tyrant, had got dominion over men, and that they were acknowledging his dominion.

These things were not the will of His Father, they were contrary to His will. He came to do His Father's will by making His creatures straight and well, by breaking the yoke of the oppressor. And now, St. Paul said, He has proved Himself the conqueror. He died the death of the Cross. His love showed itself stronger than death. He rose from the dead, He ascended on high. He ascended, not because He was going to leave men or forget them, but that He might do good to the whole universe. Not merely to one here and one there; that He might be the king over all; that He might send His Spirit into the hearts of men, to teach them of Him and of His Father; to make men who had hated each other brethren in Him: to reconcile all to His Father: to fill up the gulf that separated the world after death from the world before death; to bring all things into one.

The Corinthians had believed the Apostle's gospel; they had renounced their idols. They had been baptized into the name of the Father, and the Son, and the Holy Ghost; they met together to eat that bread and drink that wine which declared that they were members of one body in Christ, and that Love had triumphed over sin and death and hell. The more earnestly they believed this to be true, the more they found it true. They found that there was a love stronger than the evil that was in them, stronger than the evil that was in their brethren—one which could convert the most rebellious to itself. But still the world was full of misery. There was this tyranny of the Roman Empire established over the greatest part of it; in each particular country and neighbourhood there were crimes, divisions, oppressions.

Besides believing, then, the Corinthians had need to hope and to wait. What had they to hope and wait for? That He who had been declared to be the deliverer of the world—who had proved Himself so by dying for it—who was proving himself so in their hearts—would come forth, would declare Himself to be the King of kings and Lord of lords, would put down the wrong, would establish the right. To work for this, to wait for this, the Apostle tells them, was the best thing possible for them, one and all. This kept their heads above water, when they had the strongest current against them, and they found it hardest to strive against it; this helped them to strive against the sin that most easily beset them; against their pride, and their divisions, and their distrusts. This kept them together, because one was not looking for this end, and another for that; but all had the same end before them. Christ was He whom all alike were expecting.

Now I compared this expectation to the looking out for the sun, which I said would certainly shine out in due time, however long the night might seem. But is not there a great difference? The Corinthians waited for Christ—were they not disappointed? Did He come as the sun comes, out of the dark night? After eighteen hundred years has He ever yet appeared? Brethren, the Corinthians were *not* disappointed? They found more, not less, than they looked for. He whom they believed to be the King of the world proved Himself to be the King of the world. The Jewish nation, which had said, "We will not have this man to reign over us," was broken in pieces. He who was rejected by it was He who had held it together, without Him it had no life. That breaking up of the nation was an unveiling of Jesus Christ—a clear manifestation of His dominion over men, of His presence in the midst of them. It had been no cunningly-devised fable they had believed. He who was called the carpenter's son, He who suffered under Pontius Pilate as a malefactor, was the head of all principalities and powers. He was ruling amidst the powers of heaven and amidst the inhabitants of the earth.

But what, you may say, were the Corinthians the better for this? Did this knowledge save them from dying? Had they not to suffer just what their fathers had suffered before them? Had not some of them to bear even harder and more intolerable deaths than their fathers? Even so! Their threescore and ten years came to an end. Some of them breathed out their souls on their beds, some on crosses, some in the fire. They did not escape what the only-begotten Son had endured. And what then? They had learned who it is that governs in both worlds. They had learned that Christ is there as He is here. They had learned that as He is veiled from men here, there He is unveiled. They had learned that death is not a barrier which separates from Him, for He has borne it. They had learned all these lessons; and therefore could wait for the sun with perfect confidence that it would appear. They could be sure that if it shone on them, it would shine on multitudes besides. They could bid all people look for this universal sun. They could tell them that it was a miserable thing not to be expecting the light, and a miserable thing to be loving darkness, rather than light. They could encourage all to come to the light, to walk in it, and live in it, that when it broke out in its full glory they might rejoice that now they had all which they had dreamed of, and waited for; all that was needful to make them thoroughly blessed.

II. So was it with the Corinthians. Why is it to be different with us? We are baptized, as they were, into the name of the Father, and the Son, and the Holy Ghost. We have heard, as they heard, that Christ is the great deliverer and king. We have had more proofs than they had that He is actually reigning in this country of ours. We have proofs of it in our own consciences. Every sin of which our heart condemns us, is a witness of a righteous Lord who is the enemy of sin. We have the witness of it in the world about us. Every event that has happened in any nation of the earth; any great judgment that has befallen it; any great deliverance that has been wrought for it, has been a day of the Lord, an appearing of Christ; a proof that He is in deed and not in name only our sovereign. If we do not receive it as such, the reason is that our eyes are darkened, that we do not see things as they are. The saints in light, who must perceive in whatever befell them on earth, in whatever befalls the kinsfolk and friends whom they have left behind, sure tokens that He is in the midst of us teaching, guiding, reproving, blessing us; they must wonder at their own blindness, that they did not confess this to be so always. And they must expect with confidence the full revelation of the Son of God, to finish all that He has begun, to establish peace where there is war, and freedom where there is tyranny, and order where there is injustice and confusion. They are sure that He will work out all His purposes, that He will accomplish all His Father's will. 'How long, O Lord,' they cry; 'how long, O Lord, holy and true, dost Thou not judge and avenge our blood? How long dost Thou wait before thus making the earth a place where men may dwell together in love, and where God may dwell with them, and be their God?'

And, oh, brethren, we sinners upon earth may join in that cry of theirs; we may join our hopes and longings with those of the men who have washed their robes and made them white in the blood of the Lamb, and are for ever before the Throne. 'What,' some of you may say, 'must not I who have so many dark thoughts in me, must not I tremble to meet my Lord? Can I desire to see Him whose eyes are as a flame of fire—who looketh into the thoughts and intents of the hearts—must not I shrink and quail, when He appears?' It is a good question. Would to God any of you are asking it in your hearts; then I could give you the answer, and it is this:—Be sure, brethren, that Christ will appear, and that every eye shall see Him; and that the thoughts of every heart will be made manifest before Him. There is no more doubt of that than there is that the sun will rise out of this coming night, and will make all things clear and plain that are hidden in the darkness, or confused in the twilight. And if you have hidden thoughts that you do not wish to be revealed, seeing that they must be laid bare then, oh, let them be laid bare now! Christ's light is about you at this moment; you need not wait for that till another day; you may come to it, you may ask Him to scatter the darkness that is in you now. It is a miserable thing to have that within us which we are ashamed of; it becomes worse when Christ says, 'I will deliver you from it, I will take it out of you, I will give you a clean heart and a right spirit.' Well, then, I say: if you seek for this day by day; if you beg Christ to separate you from the evil that is in you, and to make you right, you are expecting Him; you are waiting for Him. And instead of looking at it as a thing to be dreaded that He should appear at last in His full glory, and put out this darkness in you altogether, that is the very thing of all others you must wish for; you can be content with nothing short of that. And let not any of us, dear brethren, be content with less than that, for Christ promises us no less; and our folly and our misery is, that we do not ask Him and trust Him to fulfil His promises. They exceed all that we can ask or can think. He is willing to make us pure; He is willing to make this earth pure. In a little time, when this world and its fashion have passed away from before our eyes, we shall find that it is so. We shall find that we had Him with us all through our pilgrimage; that He was every moment speaking to us, and moving us to do right; every moment warning us of the wrong. We shall find that we erred in hoping not too much, but far, far too little ! If we had hoped more, we should have been freer, and purer, and more loving. We have despaired of God's goodness, therefore it has been far from us.

But let us despair no longer. For the will of our Father in heaven is to do us good, to save us, to bring us to the knowledge of His truth. His will is that we should receive the blessings He has given us, and wait for the blessings He has in store for us.

SERMON V.

ST. PETER'S CONVERSION.

Preached at Clyro, 1853.

"The God of our Fathers raised up Jesus whom ye slew and hanged upon a tree; Him hath God exalted with His right hand to be a Prince and a Saviour, for to give repentance to Israel and forgiveness of sins."—ACTS v. 30, 31.

THESE are the words of St. Peter. Do you remember some other words of his, when he was sitting with our Lord the night before His crucifixion? He said then, "Lord, I will go with thee to prison and to death." And Jesus answered, "Verily, I say unto thee, the cock shall not crow twice till thou hast denied me thrice." As He spoke, so it came to pass. Jesus was standing before the judgment-seat. One and another person said to Peter, "Thou wast one of His disciples." "Did I not see thee in the garden with Him?" "Thou art a Galilean; thy speech betrayeth thee." But he said to each, "I know not what thou sayest," or, "I know not the man."

Some three or four months had passed away since

that time, and here is the same Peter. Those people before whom he was afraid to confess that he knew Christ were men-servants and maid-servants. Now he was before the rulers and elders of the Jews, the men whom he had been taught to fear as the greatest in his country, ever since he was a child. He had not often seen them, for they lived in the chief city of Judæa, and he had been brought up in the upper part of the land. Those who came from his country were despised by the South people, and he had passed his life as a fisherman on the lakes; yet hear how he answers a council of the most learned and powerful men in Jerusalem: "We ought to obey God rather than men. The God of our fathers raised up Jesus, whom ye slew and hanged on a tree. Him hath God exalted at His own right hand to be a Prince and a Saviour for to give repentance to Israel and forgiveness of sins. And we are His witnesses of these things. So also is the Holy Ghost, which God hath given to them that obey Him."

You see the coward has become the bravest of men: he who could not acknowledge his dearest friend, when he had just been sitting and eating with Him, is ready indeed to go to prison and death for Him, now that he sees Him no more. How has this happened? What is the cause of this mighty change which has since come over him?

I believe it concerns us much to know, brethren; for we may find out secrets which have as much to do with us as with Simon Peter.

While St. Peter and the Apostles were walking day by day with Christ, seeing the wonders that He did, hearing Him utter parables to the people, asking Him in private to explain them, receiving power from Him to go and heal the sick themselves—while all this was going on, they felt as if they were His especial favourites, those whom He had chosen to receive blessings which other people had not. And He did not tell them they were wrong. On the contrary, He said He had chosen them to be His ministers, to sit and rule and judge with Him in His kingdom: and that kingdom, He said, was the kingdom of heaven, the one to which all others must bow. But He explained to them also, that He who was the chief in this kingdom had come to be the servant of all; and that if they reigned with Him, they must be servants too. They could not understand this. If they were the chosen companions of a king, must not they some day or other be admitted into a palace, and have servants to wait on them? Must they not look down upon those, who had looked down upon them? They thought it *must* be so; they often questioned among themselves which of them should have the choicest place—which of them should be the greatest, and sit nearest to the king. That dispute they were busy with even at the Last Supper, when He was saying, "One of you shall betray me;" and when His soul was troubled "even unto death." You will think, then, how they must have been upset and bewildered when they saw Him who was to be a king Himself, and who was to make them kings, led out to be tried, and mocked, and crucified. You will think how their hopes must have withered up; they must have felt like men who had tumbled from a great height, and had not yet reached the bottom. It seemed as if they had been in a sleep ever since they left their father's ship, and had been dreaming a long dream, which had passed away when the morning came. No doubt Christ had told them often that He should be rejected by the chief priests and elders, and given up to the Romans and put to death. But they could not believe Him; they thought it was impossible, and they felt as little prepared for these events as if the words had never been spoken. They were not the least false men when they said they were sure they loved Him, and would cling to Him in life and death. They thought so in their very hearts; but they became utterly helpless and stupefied. Their strength was gone from them, so they all forsook Him; and he that was boldest, denied Him.

What could raise him out of this depth? First, we are told, "Peter went out and wept bitterly" for what he had done. Then he began to know more of Christ and of His power than he had ever known all the three years he had been with Him before. His heart had been fast bound; now it was loosened, and all the streams poured forth from it. Who had caused them to flow? When the cock crew "the Lord turned and looked upon him;" Peter felt how mighty He was then when they were binding and scourging Him. Yes, he felt Him to be more mighty than when He was feeding five thousand, and saying to the winds, "Peace, be still!"

This, then, was the first step in Peter's change. He had had many good gifts before, but this one thing he had not had—a broken and contrite heart. He had thought highly of his Master, but he had thought more highly still of himself; that is to say, he thought of his Master chiefly for himself. He thought of what He would give him and do for him. How great a thing it was to be called by Him, and to be set above others, and to have such blessings in store for him afterwards. Now, he knew that he was good for nothing; all his proud fancies of what he was, and of what he might be, melted away together. He saw that as the earth is very warm and bright because the sun shines upon it, so his goodness had all come from Christ, and not from himself, and that if he was separated from Him he was the poorest wretch alive.

If this time of sorrow and darkness had not come first, the news which he heard afterwards from the women who went to the sepulchre on the third day—"Jesus Christ is risen"—would not have been the wonderful news it was. And, even when he heard it, and when he went himself to the tomb and saw the linen clothes and the napkin, he could not believe it. That Christ should die was amazing and terrible; but that He should rise—how could that be? Who could think that something had taken place in their day which had never taken place since the creation of the world? The women must be mistaken. But Jesus himself stood among them, and said, "Peace be unto you." And it was not merely that He wished them peace; the peace really came to them. They felt that He was the giver of it. And when He showed them His hands and His side, they were sure that these were the signs and pledges of peace with God, and peace with each other. They were sure that He was the same now as He had been before His crucifixion, the same as He had been before He took flesh and dwelt amongst men.

They saw Him only now and then during the forty days after He rose from the dead. And when He had appeared to them for a little time, He again vanished away. It was a strange intercourse. Did not they sometimes long for the time to come back again when He was with them, journeying with them whole days and weeks? No; they were beginning to have such high thoughts of Him, that it was impossible for them to wish to recover that time.

He had known death; He had been in the dark world. They wondered that He could converse with them at all; that they could touch Him and eat with Him. They looked at Him, and touched Him, and yet doubted. He ascended on high out of their sight. How was it then? Was He not gone quite away from them? They did as He commanded. They waited in an upper room near the Temple at Jerusalem. There they found He was nearer than He had ever been; and they were sure that He had some great work for them to do, and that in due time they should have power to do it.

The power came. The Spirit of God descended upon them as they were gathered together at a great feast of the Jews. They felt that this Spirit was master of their words and their thoughts. They spake with other tongues, as He gave them utterance. St. Peter stood forth before the multitude, and said that this Spirit was given as a sign and proof that Jesus whom they crucified was raised up to be a Prince and Saviour, and that by His strength they were to tell those who had rejected Him that He was their King. Those who heard were pricked in their hearts, and said, "Men and brethren, what shall we do!" And three thousand were baptized in the name of Christ, as the Son of the Living God, and the Spirit of the Father and the Son came upon them.

Here, then, was the cause of the mighty change which came on Peter in those two or three months. He had thought of Jesus of Nazareth as his mighty friend and teacher; now he knew Him to be a *prince*, in the full meaning of the word. Not a person seated on a high throne, or in a great palace, that people could gaze at; but One who could rule and govern the thoughts of men's hearts; whose throne was over them; whose palace was in them. He knew that this was the way in which Christ had proved Himself a king over him, when he had feared to confess Him, and when his heart had been tied and chained by his pride. He had laid him low; He had given him repentance; and now that He had left the world, and was exalted to His Father's right hand, it was that He might do for others what He had done for him. For now, instead of dreaming of Christ as one who favoured him more than others, he delighted to think that He was the Friend and Saviour of men; that he had taken their flesh and died their death. He entered into the mind of Christ. He began to see that it was His joy to do His Father's will, by breaking the bonds which held His creatures in slavery; that it was His joy not to exalt Himself, but to be abased; not to be the chief of all, but the servant of all. St. Peter understood that he was sitting and reigning with Christ when he was witnessing to men of His love for them and His dominion over them—when he was showing them by his own example what forgiveness there was in Him, and how He could turn those who had erred most, and grieved Him most, to Himself.

Why, then, should he fear chief priests and rulers? He was sent to tell them of One who was their king as well as his. He was sent to tell them of One who was their Saviour as well as his. He could not fear them, for he knew how much stronger Christ was than they were. He could not hate them, for he knew that Christ had died, and risen, and ascended on high, because He cared for His enemies. St. Peter had learnt that he was the most contemptible of all in himself; he had learnt that he had the same evil nature with those chief priests and rulers who had put Christ to death; he had learnt that there was One who could subdue that evil nature in them and in him, who could rescue both from the evil spirit who had held them captive.

And now you see why I said the secret which concerned Peter, and which was made known to him, concerns us, and is declared to us in his words. He was a fisherman, as poor a man as any of you; he was a sinner, like each of us; he was an apostle—a herald of Christ's kingdom to all men. He speaks of Christ being raised up to give repentance to Israel, because he was addressing Israelites, rulers of Israel, those who had committed the heaviest of all crimes; and, therefore, there is not one syllable or letter of that message of his which is not intended for any man, everywhere. It was for the publicans, and harlots, and outcasts of the Jews; it was for the rich men, and scholars, and doctors. All wanted repentance; all wanted to have a right and true heart given to them, to have their proud and selfish heart broken down in them. St. Peter says, Christ is raised up on high that He may do this for them all; that He may give them repentance; and that He may send away their sins; may relieve them from that heavy burden. He does not say, 'If you will repent,' 'If you will put away your sins,' then such and such good things will come to you. But he says, the Son of God and Son of Man has died and risen and ascended, that you may be able to repent; that your sins and you may be put asunder; that you may know they are your enemies, and that they have been vanquished.

And that is the good news which St. Peter preached, and which we are to preach to you. Repentance is far too hard a thing for man to accomplish; any man who has tried to repent knows that. But Christ is revealed as a prince over our hearts, to turn them according to God's good and gracious will. Our sins cling too close to us for you and me to tear them off. But Christ has claimed us for members of His body, that He may do that for us which we cannot do. Christ gives us His spirit that He may make us free, in spite of all our inclination to continue slaves of a cruel tyrant. Let us believe this, brethren. And then you will desire that same Holy Spirit, who, when He had converted Simon Peter, made him a witness to his brethren, and a strengthener of them, to give you power by your lips to declare to all you meet, that Christ is their prince and Saviour; that He has been raised from the dead to give them repentance and remission of sins.

SERMON VI.

THE SICK OF THE PALSY.

*Preached at Welsh Hampton, 19th Sunday after Trinity,
September 28, 1856.*

" That ye may know that the Son of Man hath power upon earth to forgive sins; then saith He to the sick of the palsy, Arise, take up thy bed, and go to thine house."—St. Matthew ix. 6.

You know to whom these words were spoken, and who spoke them. In the town of Capernaum there was a man whose limbs were palsied. He could not go himself to see if there was any one who could cure him. He was fixed to his bed. But his friends heard that Jesus, who had been absent, had returned to this town, and that He had healed many people who were sick of different diseases. They thought He would do something for this poor man, who belonged to His own neighbourhood. Four of them brought him on his bed. St. Luke says that there was such a crowd about the house that they could not come through the door, and therefore they let him down by the roof. They must have had great trust in the power of Jesus to do that. They must have had great trust that He was willing to use His power for the good of a suffering man.

At first it appeared as if they had not gained their ond. Jesus saw the bed. He took notice of the man who was stretched upon it. He spoke to him in a kindly affectionate voice. He called him "Son." But He said nothing about the palsy. He must have seen that the man could not move; that he was in pain; that he had no use of his limbs. Instead of setting this right, He said, "Son, thy sins be forgiven thee."

The friends who had brought him must have been surprised. That was not at all what they had looked for. There were some present—learned men who had come from the city of Jerusalem—who were not only surprised but shocked. This, they said, is a strange power, indeed, for a man to take to himself! Sins are offences against God. He only can forgive them and put them away. For any one who has a mortal body, who speaks with a human voice, to do that is blasphemy.

Well, this was the judgment of the bystanders. But what do you think the poor man felt about it himself? I suppose he wanted to recover his strength, and to be able to do as he had been used to do, as much as his friends. Do you think, then, he was disappointed, as most likely they were? No; he found that this person who spoke to him knew thoroughly what was the matter with him; that He saw into the very heart of him.

There was something in him which he could not tell any one of; which he could not explain to any doctor. There was a palsy upon him, upon his own very self, which was harder to bear than the palsy upon his limbs. He could not have described it, I am sure; he had felt it, but perhaps he had never thought about it till then. But Jesus had discovered it. He understood the man better than he understood himself. And when He said to him, "Son, thy sins be forgiven thee," the man became a free man. A secret chain which had been binding him was taken off from him; he could look up into the face of Jesus and be certain that He was the Deliverer.

But he lay on his bed still, apparently he was as helpless as before. But when the learned men from Jerusalem began to murmur that Jesus had taken God's power to Himself, Jesus spoke again. He said, "That ye may know that the Son of Man hath power on earth to forgive sins, I say unto thee, Arise, take up thy bed and walk." And the man found that the Deliverer had not done a half work. He had had power over him altogether. The palsy was gone from his limbs as well as from his heart. He could do what he was bidden. He rose up in the presence of them all. And the people marvelled that God had given such power to a man.

And that is the point I want to speak to you of. We have gone through the story. Now let us consider the reason that Jesus gives us for what He did. I will take each part of it separately, for it is the way to understand His words.

1st. You see He says that He healed the man "That you may know." It was not done only for his sake, though it was done for his sake. It was done for those who were sitting around, for those who were believing in Him, and for those who were disbelieving. All of them wanted to know whether the Son of Man had this power or no; whether he was a blasphemer, as the Scribes said, or whether he was speaking truth and acting truth. It was even for our sakes who are reading it here in this church to-day. You and I now just as much want to know whether the Son of Man has this power, as this palsied man did, or his friends, or the Scribes, or the people generally. If He had it not then He has it not now. If He had it then, He has it now. If they wanted that He should use it for them, we want that He should use it for us. So let us give heed.

He speaks of Himself, you see, as the *Son of Man.* What does that mean? Jesus was actually standing in that room in Capernaum in a body such as the people about him had; He spoke with such a voice as theirs. He looked in all respects like them. He was verily and indeed a man. And He showed that He was by knowing what was in man. He felt for this particular man. He understood what was going on in him. He knew the sin that was in him.

You will say, 'But was not He a man in some other way than we are men?' If you mean were there not some things which belong to man that He had not, were there not some things in men which He did not enter into? I answer no; absolutely, no. He has everything which belongs to a man. He enters into everything which there is in every man. And that is the reason He is called the Son of Man. He is *The* Man; the Head Man, the King of Men. But if you go on to say, 'What! was there, indeed, sin in Him, then?' I answer, no, verily; for He would not have been able to understand every man, He would not be truly and perfectly a man if there had been. Sin is what separates us from each other. Sin is what prevents us from understanding each other. Sin is what every man hugs in himself, and which keeps him away from other people. The Son of Man had no sin, and therefore He felt for all, and cared for all. The Son of Man has no sin, therefore He feels for all and cares for all. But, as you see by the story I have read to you, the Son of Man can feel for men that have sin in them, all the more because He is without it; He knows what a burden it is, as we that have so much of it do not know. He cares to set men free from it, as we do not care.

Now, brethren, the great and blessed thing of all is to know and believe assuredly that He is such a Son of Man as this.

That was the message which Jesus brought to the poor people of Galilee and Judæa, to the fishermen and the publicans. He made them feel and understand that there was a King of Men, a Lord of Men, who cared for them, for every one of them; who loved them, every one of them; who would deliver them, every one of them, from that which was separating him from his neighbour, and making him at war with himself. The Scribes and learned men did not believe this. They could not make it out. They had a notion of a God, a Being very far off from man, who punished their offences against Him, and sometimes, perhaps, might be persuaded to forgive them. But they did not know what was meant by a Son of Man. They did not think there was such a person. What was the consequence? They knew nothing of God, though they talked of Him and pretended to fear Him; they merely dreamed of Him; they made a God out of their own dark fancies and wicked thoughts. Jesus, the Son of Man, came to show us who the true God is. He came, as He said, from God, to do the works of God. He said that God was not a tyrant, but a Father; and that in Him they might see the Father. And it is in Him, brethren, that you and I must see the Father, and only in Him. If we try to think of God without thinking of the Son of Man, we shall get all astray, and suppose Him to be another Being altogether from what He is. But if we think what this Jesus, the Son of Man and the Son of God was, if we think that He is now what He was always, then we shall begin to know what God is; then we shall begin to know something of His goodness, and truth, and love; then we shall desire to be like Him, and we shall believe that He would have us to be like Him. So take in well this thought of Jesus the Son of Man, and feed upon it, then you will understand what follows.

2. The Son of Man has *power* even to forgive sins. What power that must be! Think how it worked with this poor palsied man. He had been out, I daresay, in great storms. He had seen the lightning and heard the thunder. Was not there power there? Yes, but it had never come nigh to him. He had never felt that the thunder or the lightning were his lords, or that they could make him another man. But this Son of Man said, "Son, thy sins be forgiven thee," and these words went down into the very heart of him. He was sure, 'These do come from my Lord and Master. He has found me. He is speaking to me now.' And remember, dear brethren, that is the power we need for ourselves. It is a power that can speak to us; that can get the mastery over our own selves. No other will do for us. And remember there is such a power near you and near me at every moment; it is the power of this Son of Man. It is the power of Him who is the true Lord of each one of us. The Son of Man did not exercise power over the palsied man by looking at him or touching him; He spoke to the heart within him. And every time that there comes any twinge in our consciences, every time that any one of us wakes up and says, 'I have been doing wrong,' His voice has been speaking to us; and every time that any one of

us has said, 'I will try to be a better and truer man,' His power has been used over us.

3. He goes on, "The Son of Man has power *on earth* to forgive sins." The Scribes thought that perhaps God would forgive men's sins after they left the earth, if they tried to please Him and make up with Him here. Many of us thus think. But our Lord speaks a different language; He does not speak of what is to be done hereafter, but of what is to be done here. It is on earth that our sins plague us and torment us, and plague and torment our neighbours; it is on earth we want to get quit of them. And, therefore, Christ's first word to this palsied man was, "Son, thy sins be forgiven thee now." And that is a sign and pledge of what He had power to do, and will to do, for those who were on earth then, and for those who are on earth now.

4. But, then, mind what this word *Forgive* means.

Does it mean less than the Scribes thought it meant? less than men commonly think it means? No, verily, but a great deal more. The Scribes thought that if a man had committed a great many sins, God would perhaps pass them by, and not punish them, if certain sacrifices and offerings were made to Him. People now often say, 'Well, I am a little given to drinking; I am a little more covetous than I ought to be; I am not quite just and fair in all my dealings, but I do hope God will forgive me.' Yes! He is ready to do that. The Son of Man came from His Father to tell us so.

But He is not so hard and cruel a King and Friend as to forgive a man for being a drunkard, and to leave him a drunkard; to forgive a man for being covetous, and to leave him covetous. Why, is not a sot the most miserable wretch and slave? Is not his drink his lord and master? Does it not make him into the vilest thing? Is not the covetous man sold to his money? Does it not hold him in prison and put him to tortures every day? Do you think the Son of Man would leave us in such accursed bondage as that? No, to forgive means to *send away*. Sometimes we talk, you know, of remission of sins; that is just the same, is used in the same sense.

The Son of Man has power on earth, power over our spirits to remit or send away the sins which have made us captive. That is what He did for the man sick of the palsy. That is why we call Him a Redeemer.

5. Once more; He has power on earth to forgive *sins*. What sins? I can give but one answer—mine and yours. You do not know what evil habits I am most prone to, I do not know what you are most prone to. But whatever they are, the Son of Man has power on earth to break these habits in pieces—to send these sins away.

And, therefore, when it comes into the heart of any one of us to say, 'Well, I daresay I am bad, but I do not lie as that man, or cheat as that man does,' let us answer the devil who puts us upon that thought in this way: 'This evil of mine is my enemy, my tyrant; so I will ask the Son of Man, who is near me at all times and all places, to set me free from that; then I will go and say to my neighbour, "Thou, too, hast a great Friend and Deliverer, who is able to send away thy sins from thee." For He is the Son of Man, the common Lord and Saviour of us all; and He is also with each one of us, and can say to each one of us as He said to the sick of the palsy, " Son, thy sins be sent away from thee." '

Perhaps you think, ' But it came all at once to him, and for me to get rid of my bad habits is very slow work indeed.' No, brethren, it did not come all at once to him in the way you fancy. The discovery that he had a Friend who cared for him, who wished to do him good, in whom he might trust, *that* did come to him with a wonderful joy, that was the greatest deliverance he had ever known, that took the palsy from his heart. But all the time he lived afterwards he will have had a battle to fight with his sins; much more of a battle than he had ever fought before, and oftentimes I daresay he lost the recollection of his Friend—it seemed as if the Son of Man were gone. Then his old sins would become his masters again; he would feel that they were always at hand to overawe him. Nevertheless, the thing was true and certain; the Son of Man had been with him before he knew Him, and was with him when he forgot Him. And so it is with us. We are members of Christ's body. He is with every one of us. To believe that He is; to believe that we have Him as our Helper and Deliverer; to believe that He is stronger than all the enemies that are mightiest within us, this is infinite comfort and joy; this assures us that the sin which seems so near us is really divided from us; that it is not our master; that we shall be able to trample it under foot. But, with us as with the palsied man, it must be a daily, hourly fight, to remember that Christ, the Son of Man, is our Master, and that the world, and the flesh, and the devil, are not our masters.

You will say, perhaps, 'But we have no tokens such as our Lord gave when He was on earth, that He forgives our sins.' Yes, brethren, we have all these tokens and very many besides. We have all these tokens; for when you read to-day how Christ healed the sick of the palsy eighteen hundred years ago, you may say boldly, 'That is a token to me of what He was, and is, and is to be always.' If that showed that He had power to send away sins from the Galileans, it shows the same just as much for the people of Shropshire. But you have other tokens. Every one that gets rid of any disease in your parish is raised out of it by the Son of Man. Every such recovery is a token that He has the power to put away sins as well as to put away diseases. And remember the sins which each of us commits affect our parish and our whole nation. We speak of national sins because sins destroy the nation. Now does not Christ give us tokens that He has power to put them away? I have asked you to

come and meet me here to-morrow to give thanks for
the harvest. Do not you think that is such a token?
Does it not say to us, 'The Son of Man who makes the
seed to grow, and bring forth, and bud, can make all
good seed spring up and grow, and bring forth fruit in
our hearts—can destroy the weeds that choke and
stifle them.' Again, I have asked you to come next
Sunday to receive the bread and the wine which Christ
blesses and feeds us with. Is not that a token that the
Son of Man is with us; each of us and all of us? What
is that but the feast of Forgiveness; the feast when we
come confessing our sins against each other and against
God, asking Him that we may forgive each other as
He in Christ forgives us? Does not the Son of Man say
to each of us there, 'These are the signs that I have
power on earth to forgive sins. Go, therefore, in the
strength of my body and blood which I have given for
you, to serve with pure and humble hearts your Father
and your brethren.'

SERMON VII.

THE MARRIAGE FEAST OF THE KING'S SON.

Preached at Welsh Hampton, 20th Sunday after Trinity, October 5, 1856.

"The Kingdom of Heaven is like unto a certain king which made a marriage for his son."—St. Matthew xxii. 2.

IF I searched ever so far, I could find nothing fitter than the Gospel for to-day to tell us what the sacrament of the Lord's Supper means, and why you should receive it.

It is a marriage feast; it is the feast which the great King of earth and heaven makes to celebrate the marriage of His Son.

It is a feast to which most of those who were first bidden would not come. It is a feast to which God bids all from the highways and the hedges, ignorant people, sinful people.

It is a feast at which some present themselves without a marriage garment, who therefore are cast out.

Let us think of each of these things for a few minutes, brethren, and may God Himself enable us to understand His words.

First, then, it is a *marriage* feast. Men were scattered up and down this world. They spoke different languages; they had different customs; they had rivalries and enmities with each other; it seemed as if they had come upon the earth to fight with each other. Yet they felt a continual drawing to each other, they could not live without each other, they must sell and buy from each other; some of them yearned to be friends. Men and women bound themselves to each other in wedlock. All found that they were sons and daughters, if they were not brothers and sisters. Men must have been made to be one. How comes it that they are so divided? Their consciences said there would not be this separation unless there were a deeper separation besides. We should not be quarrelling among ourselves, if we had not quarrelled with One who rules over us. I say men's consciences told them this, or rather God told it them through their consciences. And therefore they worked hard to bring about a reconciliation, a union, between themselves and the Being whom they felt they were at war with. They offered sacrifices; they were ready to give up their goods and their offspring too, if they could but make peace with Him. But they did not know with whom they were to make peace. They thought He was like themselves, and was to be won over as they won over those whom they had made their enemies. They did not know that it was a God of perfect love from whom they had separated themselves. They did not know that He was their Father. They did not know that He was seeking after them to bring them into reconciliation. They did not know that all their yearning after Him was awakened by Himself. They did not know that He had kept them in fellowship with each other, that He had made them into families and nations. They did not know that all their discords came from resistance to Him. They did not know that He meant to gather them all into one.

This was the message which Jesus brought into the world. He said, 'He who rules over you is my Father. He has formed you in me. He has made you one in me. And now I am come to unite you all to myself. I have married your flesh and blood to myself; and that is that I may marry the spirits of you who have this flesh and blood to myself. For I tell you, you cannot live apart from me; your life flows into you from me.' And when He was going away, He gave bread to His disciples and said, "Take, eat, this is my flesh." He gave wine and said, "Drink, this is my blood. Do this in remembrance of me." That is to say, 'Do this in remembrance that I have married myself to your flesh and blood. Do this in remembrance that your spirits are united to me. Do this in remembrance that all your life flows into you from me. Do this because ye are married to me, and are one in me.'

2. Therefore you see that it is the feast of a marriage which God has made for His Son. When each of us said just now, "I believe in Jesus Christ, His only Son, our Lord;" each of us said, I believe that the Son of God is our husband; that God hath united Him to us. Thus I affirm that what He told the disciples about

themselves, is true about us. It must needs be so; for He did not take the flesh of St. Peter and St. John more than He took the flesh of you and me. He took the flesh and blood of man. He gave up that flesh and that blood upon the Cross. Therefore there is the same bond between Him and us, the same marriage between Him and us, that there was between Him and the disciples who sat with Him the night before He suffered. They were the witnesses whom He sent to tell us of it. And we have not more life in our spirits than they had; our life flows out of His life just as much as theirs did.

That is the reason we go on keeping the Lord's Supper in every parish of England. We know that none of us can live, that we cannot live for one hour apart from Christ, the Son of God. We know that He it is, and He only, who unites us to God, and unites us to each other. We know that if we forget Him, we forget that we are united to God, and are united to our brethren. We know that we are liable now, as much as we ever were, to be at strife. We know that when we have been at strife with each other, and have been doing wrong, there comes into our minds a sense of God's being our enemy, and that we act as if He were. We know that we shall then try, by all superstitious and wicked acts, to bring Him over to us just as the heathen did. We know that the only way to escape from doing that, is to remember the words He said, that He has reconciled us to Himself, that He may make a marriage for us with His Son; that He has made peace with us in the flesh and blood which He took of the Virgin, which He offered on the cross. And how shall we own that message to be true? This, He says, is the simple way: Receive these tokens that the marriage is not to be made, but that it *is* made. Claim to be united to Me and to each other in Christ, as I declare that you are.

But those who were first called would not come. Why was that? Because they felt it was their glory to be separate from other men; because they had no real wish to be at one with God. The Jews had been called out by God, that in them all the families of the earth might be blessed; that by them God might testify to all of His goodness and truth. They thought that He had called them out to be a curse to all the families of the earth; they thought they were to tell all the families of the earth, God cares for us and not for you: the only chance for you is to adopt our customs, and become like us. Therefore their minds were wholly alienated from God; they did not enter into His purpose; they were doing all they could to defeat it. And when the Apostles of Christ testified to them, saying, 'What God said to your fathers by the prophets He would do, He has actually done. He has made a marriage with men in His Son. Come and rejoice with us that He has made peace with all. Come and bear this message with us unto all tribes and kindreds'—some of them said, 'Nonsense, what have we to do with that; we have our farms and merchandise to look after; what do we want to be told of a Father of our spirits, and of our being reconciled to Him?' Others did not take it so easily; they did not laugh, but were furiously angry. They said, 'This is robbing us of our privileges; this is putting us on a level with other men.' So they brought the Apostles who bare these tidings before kings and rulers; they imprisoned them, stoned them, crucified them.

What came of it? These Jews had decried Him who bound them together. They had set at nought their king. Nothing could keep them at one. They became more and more divided. They tore each other in pieces. At last the day which had been foretold arrived. The Romans, so the Lord of all had appointed, destroyed them and their city. They became vagabonds on the face of the earth. So it was proved that the message was a true message. The King of Kings had made a marriage for His Son. It was a real feast which they had refused to partake of.

It is a feast to which God bids all sorts of people. That was the chief reason, as I told you, why the Jews spurned the invitation. They did not like it to be thought that all were the better for this marriage. They did not like to keep a feast at which publicans and sinners, yes, and heathen, were asked to sit down. In other words, they did not believe in the marriage at all. For if the Son of God has taken man's flesh and blood; if he is the Lord of men's spirits, there is not a single human creature of any tribe or kindred who has not a share in the blessings of it. There is not one to whom we may not say, 'Your Lord and ours calls upon you to remember that He has taken your flesh and died for you. Come and give Him thanks that He has done so. Come and have fellowship with His Father and your Father.' If you say, 'But was not this marriage then made for the sake of righteous and holy people? Was it not with them that Christ united Himself?' I say, no, brethren. It is by claiming to be united with Christ that a man becomes righteous. Whilst he tries to be righteous in himself, whilst he wishes to be separate from his true Lord, he cannot be righteous.

If a son goes away from his father's house, and says he will have nothing more to do with his father or his mother, or with any of his brothers and sisters, and if his father or one of his brothers went to persuade him to come back, do you think the man ought to say, 'By-and-by, when I am very righteous and good, I will come back and make it up with you and live with you again.' How could he do that? How could he become right while he denied his birthright and his parents? Do you not see that the proof of his being better would be, to do what he was urged to do, to confess that he had a father, and that he was altogether wrong ever to have broken away from him? Well, the case is exactly the same here. No one can make himself right while he stands apart from his

Father in Heaven and his Elder Brother. The way to be right is to turn round to his Father and say, 'I have forgotten Thee, my heart has been far from Thee. And I should never have remembered Thee, or have wished to find Thee, or to be at peace with Thee at all, if Thou hadst not sent me word by Thy Son that I am Thy child, and that Thou wouldst have me call Thee my Father in Him. But as Thou hast sent me this word, as Thou hast said that He has come down and taken my flesh, and died on the cross in it, on purpose that He might bring me to Thee, I yield myself; I will fight with Thee no more; I will not be the fool I have been in setting up my bad will against Thy good will. I desire that Thou shouldest rule me henceforth, and shouldest take away all my ignorance and wilfulness from me.' That is what a person says who heeds this message, 'Come to the wedding-feast.' He does not the least pretend that he has any goodness of his own. It is because he feels that he has not, and that he cannot have, that he wants to be thoroughly joined to Him, in whom all goodness dwells. And since he cannot, poor creature and beggar as he is, join himself to the Great Prince of the whole earth; he is greatly astonished and rejoiced to hear that this great Prince has joined Himself to him; that He has stooped to the state of the very lowest of us, on purpose that the very lowest of us might receive forgiveness, and strength, and life, and all that he wants from Him.

So you see why our Lord speaks of sending out into the highways and hedges, and getting in all manner of guests. You see He could not say otherwise. For all these people are human beings, and Christ has not been ashamed to call them brethren, and he has proved that He is their Brother by dying their death; and it is a sin for anyone to cut himself off from God's great family in heaven and earth, and to remain at strife with those who belong to the same race with him; so surely all may be told that they need not and must not commit this sin, but may come and join with all the rest of their family in keeping the Marriage Supper of their Lord.

But, lastly, we hear of some coming there without a marriage garment, and being, therefore, thrust out. I have told you already what this wedding garment is not. It is not a man's own goodness, *that* God does not expect him to bring. What is it then? It is the goodness, and mercy, and love of God Himself. When He made that great marriage for His Son, when He united Him to our flesh and blood, He showed forth in Him all His own goodness, and love, and truth; as St. John wrote, *we* saw His glory as of the only begotten Son of God, full of grace and truth. He showed it forth in Him, that we might say, This is what we want; this is what we have not in ourselves. When we say this in our hearts we begin to believe in God's love and righteousness, or, as the Scripture says, to *put our trust in Him.* So we become partakers of all these good things of

God, just as we take in the meres and the distant hills with our eyes, though they are so much greater than we are. But if a man will not trust in God's love and righteousness; if he does not think that God is loving and righteous; if he does not wish to be like God in His love and righteousness; if he had rather be just what he is in himself, then he will not put on the wedding garment which God has provided him, and God, who sees all of us that come to that feast, and reads the heart of each one of us, sees that we do not come there to seek Him; that we come there for some other end than that; for some low miserable end of our own; and so His light does not shine in on us; He leaves us in the darkness we have chosen; and we grow worse and worse, darker and darker, for having mocked Him and trifled with Him.

You say, 'That is very dreadful.' Surely it is. It is dreadful to distrust God who is all good, and to trust in ourselves in whom apart from God there is no good at all. It is dreadful to think highly of ourselves. If you think that, come to this feast that you may confess God's infinite goodness, which is manifested in His Son, His goodness in marrying that Son to our nature, that we might be clothed with His spotless garment of Justice and Love, come and own how empty you are that He may feed you with the food of eternal life. Depend upon it, He will send none away who desire that food. He will cast none into outer darkness who seek for His light.

SERMON VIII.

THE REDEMPTION OF THE BODY.

Preached at Welsh Hampton, 23rd Sunday after Trinity, October 26, 1856.

"For our conversation is in heaven, from whence also we look for the Saviour Jesus Christ. Who shall change our vile body that it may be fashioned like unto His glorious body, according to the working whereby He is able even to subdue all things unto Himself."—PHILIPPIANS iii. 20, 21.

ONCE upon a time St. Paul was imprisoned in the city of Philippi. He was thrown into prison because he had spoilt the gains of some enchanters by his preaching. They complained to the magistrates that he was exceedingly troubling their city, and teaching them customs which were not lawful for them to observe being Romans.

For Philippi was a Roman colony, and these people liked to be thought Romans. Now it so happened that St. Paul, too, was born in a Roman colony, and that his father, or some ancestor of his, had been made a citizen of Rome, and he succeeded to the honours. The magistrates of Philippi did not know this, or they would not have dared to seize him and put him into an inner dungeon, and set his feet in the stocks, as they did.

In the night, while St. Paul and his companions were singing praises to God, there was an earthquake, and the prison doors were burst open, and the jailer cried out in fear, "What shall I do to be saved?" The next morning the magistrates were affrighted. They sent word to St. Paul that he might go out of the city quietly. But he refused to go. "They have beaten us openly," he said, "uncondemned, being Romans; and now do they thrust us out privily? Nay, verily, but let them come themselves and fetch us out." And the magistrates did come. They became suitors to their own prisoners. When they knew that St. Paul was a Roman citizen, they were most anxious that he should not stand upon his rights and accuse them.

You see that the Apostle valued his privilege of being a citizen of the greatest city upon earth. The Philippians had reason to know that he valued it. He had made them understand by his conduct that citizenship is a great and honourable thing. Men are bound together as citizens of a city, as members of a nation, by God himself.

The heathens believed that every city had a God, who watched over it and saved it from going to ruin. They believed rightly; only they did not know that it is the same God of righteousness who watches over every city, and prevents its inhabitants from tearing each other to pieces by their selfishness and their enmities.

To be a citizen of Rome was a good thing, as it is a good thing to be a citizen of any English town or city, and a still better to be an Englishman.

But St. Paul tells the Philippians, in the words I have just read you, that he was the citizen of another country too. "Our conversation," he says—that is the same thing as our citizenship—"is in heaven." What did he mean by that? He did not mean as I have showed you, that he was not a citizen on earth; he did not mean that he set little store by that citizenship; but he meant, 'Just as I belong to a very great society, consisting of all who have a right to call themselves citizens of Rome now, and of all who have called themselves citizens of Rome since it was built, just so do I belong to a still larger society than that, consisting of members which no man can number, out of every kindred, and tribe, and nation.' He described this society in another epistle as the family in heaven and earth of which God is the Father. He speaks of it as being all named with His name. Sometimes he calls this society "the body of Christ;" and he speaks of himself and his brethren as members of this body, as each having a separate work to do, just as our hands and feet have separate works to do; as all suffering together, just as we feel through our whole body a pain or wound in any part of it.

But you will say, he does not speak of heaven and earth; he only speaks of heaven. You are right, and this is the reason. He had been complaining of some persons in the Philippian Church, whose God was their belly, whose glory was their shame, who minded earthly things. Now, though these persons were members of that great society of which St. Paul speaks, they were not behaving as if they were members of it. They were not thinking of others, they were thinking only of themselves. They were not looking up to God their Father, who had called them to be His children, or to Christ their elder brother, who had come to deliver them from their slavery to those things they saw and handled, and to give them His free spirit. They were bowing down to the things which they were meant to use and rule. They were becoming the slaves of those things; they were making gods of them; they were forgetting who had redeemed them to be true men; they were becoming like animals. 'Wherefore,' cries St. Paul, 'our citizenship, or conversation, is in heaven. We have friends and fellow-sufferers upon earth, our work is on earth; we live to do good to the earth. But our home is with God. He has bought us at a great price that we might be freemen of His kingdom, and might always fly to Him, and plead our cause before Him. He has made for us a new and living way into His presence through the flesh and blood of His Son, and we have a right to walk in that way, and not to be taking the downward way—the way of death.'

You will see what he says of the upward way in the other part of these verses.

What were these men who made gods of their bellies looking for? Perhaps on the next day for some rich food or some choice wines. But the day after? For the same, with less appetite to enjoy it. But the year following? For sickness and surfeiting; and then—for the grave! All this time they had been preparing food for the worms. They had been fattening themselves for their nourishment. A hopeless kind of existence this, surely! No thought of anything bright, or good, or free, to come hereafter; no power of lifting themselves above the pleasures of the beasts—even the power of enjoying those pleasures growing less and less, and bitter pains always mixing with them and following them.

Meantime, what was St. Paul, the citizen of heaven, looking for? "We look," he says, "for the Saviour, Jesus Christ."

I spoke to you of this expectation last Sunday. I told you that just as St. Paul expected the sun to come out after each dark night, and to scatter the darkness, and to shine out clear and bright upon himself and upon the world, and to show everything as it is, so he expected the Saviour Jesus Christ to come forth in the glory of His Father and the holy angels. He believed that he should stand in the open presence of his Lord, and that every man on the earth would stand in the same presence.

This he looked for and waited for; this was the salvation he desired; for he was certain that there could be no other salvation for men but in the appearing of their true king and deliverer.

And St. Paul desired nothing for himself which he did not desire for all human beings; he did not think there could be a blessing for him which was not a blessing for them. The sight and knowledge of Jesus Christ is the blessedness of all men, and no man is able to be satisfied with any blessedness which is lower than that. You will say, perhaps, 'All this is very well if we were angels, or if we had only got souls; but we have bodies; these men who made gods of their bellies might go too far in their respect for their bodies; but they did need something for them too; else why did God create bodies at all?' Now hearken, brethren. These men did not pay too much respect to their bodies; they paid too little. They did not know what mighty, glorious gifts these bodies were; if they had, they would not have destroyed their bodies by indulging them.

St. Paul had the greatest reverence for his own body, and for the bodies of his fellow-creatures, that any man could have. For he believed that the Lord Jesus Christ, the Saviour, had taken a body such as ours, and had eaten earthly food, and had drunk of earthly water and wine; and had given that body to die upon the cross, and had raised it out of the grave, and had ascended with it to the right hand of His Father. Therefore when St. Paul recollected his citizenship in Heaven, when he claimed to be a member of Christ's body, and prayed in His name to His Father and our Father, he could not but think how this body, which is so curiously and wonderfully made, has a hidden glory in it, which, when Christ appears in His glory, shall be fully made manifest. Yes, he said to himself, this poor, vile body of mine, which is subjected to aches and pains of all kinds, which is liable to accidents of weather, which may be set ajar by want of food, or by overmuch of it, this body which may be racked with fever or rheumatism, or palsy or consumption; this body upon the dust and corruption of which the worms must feed, shall be made like to that glorious body which my Lord has redeemed from the grave, and has gone up with into Heaven. Everything seems to be threatening it with death, but Christ, in whom is the fulness of life, has overcome death, and is stronger than death. He has raised up my spirit that was sinking lower and lower, to trust in Him and hope in Him. He will raise up this body too. Nothing shall be lost of all that God has given us, for Christ has redeemed it. Only death and corruption shall perish; for they have assaulted God's glorious handy works. What God has created, God will preserve.

Fathers and mothers, could you bear to look upon the children whom you have brought into this world, who will be exposed to such innumerable accidents and sicknesses, if you did not believe this? Do you not know that when you bring them to Holy Baptism, when you put them into Christ's hands, you ask Him to take care of their bodies as well as their spirits, to raise up both, to make both after His image? And do you think He is deceiving you? Do you think He will ever betray His trust? No. Commit them and commit yourselves to Him. In the darkest hours that come to you or to them, still look up to Him; still ask Him to strengthen you to wait for Him, to long for His appearing. If you do long for it, you who are poor

THE REDEMPTION OF THE BODY.

will be able to bear your poverty; you who have enough to eat and to enjoy will not make Gods of your bellies, or mind earthly things. You will be sure that there are better things than these which God has for us. In the assurance that there are, you will resist the temptation to make your bodies the slaves of lust. In the assurance that there are, you will not destroy bodies and souls both with drunkenness. You will remember that your bodies as well as your spirits have been bought with Christ's blood. You will remember that your bodies as well as your spirits are intended to be like His.

Are you determined that they shall not be like His? Are you determined to give them up to everything that is vile, and low, and accursed? Are you determined to give away to the devil what Christ, at such a price, has taken from him? Oh! do not so! Swear upon God's altar that you will not! Ask His strength hour by hour that you may not!

And then, whatever slow disease or sudden shock may show you that your bodies were made out of the earth, and must return to the earth, you may say boldly He is able to subdue all things to Himself.

As He raised His body out of the grave, He will raise mine. As He ascended with his body to Heaven, He will give mine power to use all the energies which He has given it, with no hindrance from earth or from death. As He will appear in the glory of His Father, He will enable me to shine forth with all His redeemed children in His Father's kingdom.

SERMON IX.

THE SPIRIT THE HELP TO PRAYER.

Preached at Ockham, 9th Sunday after Trinity, August 21, 1859.

"Likewise the Spirit also helpeth our infirmities; for we know not what we should pray for as we ought: but the Spirit itself maketh intercession for us with groanings that cannot be uttered."—ROMANS viii. 26.

You have been praying this prayer to-day: "Grant to us, Lord, we beseech thee, the spirit to think and to do always such things as be rightful; that we who cannot do anything that is good without thee, may by thee be enabled to live according to thy will; through Jesus Christ our Lord."

Did you consider what you were asking for when you said these words? You were not asking for sunshine or rain, for food or raiment, to be stronger in body, or to have more money. You were asking the God of Heaven and Earth to give you His own Spirit; to give you the Spirit which dwelt in our Lord Jesus Christ; the Spirit which urged Him to go about doing good when He was upon earth; the Spirit by which He offered Himself to God upon the cross; the Spirit who raised Him from the dead; the Spirit in whom He and the Father have been united before the worlds were, and will be united for ever.

It was a mighty petition. How did we dare to offer it? God Himself can give us no greater gift. What have we done to deserve it? Look at the Collect again and see: "We who cannot do anything that is good without Thee." We confess that we cannot stand before God and say we have done any good things which can entitle us to this blessing, or to any blessing at Thy Hands. We say plainly, if we are to be good, Thou must make us good; if we are to do any right thing, Thou must enable us to do that right thing. Without Thee we shall do wrong things. Nay, without Thee we cannot even think right things. These thoughts of ours will all go awry. They will be vain and silly; they will be full of mischief. We shall have bad devices in our hearts, and the bad devices will turn into bad deeds. And because we have had so many of these bad thoughts, and because we have done so many bad deeds—because we are helpless and sinful—because we feel that we are, and every day makes us feel it more, therefore we ask this of Thee, which is more than food and raiment, than sun and rain, than health and wealth; therefore we ask Thee to grant us this Divine Spirit—Thine own Spirit.

The more we look into this prayer, the more wonderful it seems. What could an angel in Heaven wish for more than that he should be like God—that he should have the very heart and mind of God in Heaven? And yet here we are asking it because we are so little like angels—because we are continually tempted to break God's commandments—because we have broken them—because all sorts of vile desires come into our minds—because we find it so very hard to get any better desires into them.

Yes! that is the way we are taught and trained to say this prayer. We find out how inclined we are to be unkind, unclean, unjust, untrue; we look hither and thither for help. We try if no one can tell us what we ought to do, and how we are to do it.

Many are ready with their advice, and often we would give the world to follow it. But they cannot make us follow it; they cannot get down into the heart of us and mould and fashion that. Our thoughts go on taking their own course; whatever good words we hear, the words seem as if they could not catch these thoughts —they run so fast, and in all strange zigzag ways. We want some one who can overlook them—who knows them all, yours and mine; and the man's who is at the other side of the globe. And He who is able to do that—who can enter into all the thoughts of men everywhere, who knows them, who can guide them, who can turn them from bad to good, from darkness to light, from false to true, He must be the Spirit of the living God. For that Spirit we dare to ask, because we are sure that God does not wish us to be disorderly, miserable, evil creatures, and yet we are sure it will come to that if He does not take the government over us and enable us to live according to His will.

But though we find out how much we need this Spirit, and how little any other can help us in our straits, we might still think it was only a few people here and there who could ever hope to win such a blessing. People have had that belief, and they have it still. They have said to themselves, 'These ministers, who preach to us and give us God's sacraments, they may receive this Spirit of God, or men who have got some new and rare wisdom or can tell us about some better way of being religious than our fathers have told us, they may have it; all we poor, common people can do, is to listen to what these ministers or these wise people say, and to get some crumbs that fall from their tables.' It would be very natural for you to say these words, and I am afraid that we should be wicked enough to be pleased with you for saying them, and to boast that we were greater favourites with the Father of all than you are. But mark how the last words of the prayer mock this insolence and vanity of ours; how they teach us that the Spirit is for you as much as for us, "through Jesus Christ our Lord"—through Him, who took upon Him the nature of us all—through Him, who was called the carpenter's son—through Him, who ate and drank with publicans and sinners—through Him, who preached the Gospel to the poor—through Him, who died for all men—through Him who rose again for all men—through Him, who ascended on high, to be the Advocate of all before His Father—through Him who sent His Apostles to tell all that they are the children of God in Him—through Him, who came into the world that He might baptize men with His Spirit. Do you not see that this language would be a mockery and a lie if we dared to set up any pretension for ourselves which would separate us from any one of you? What we are sent to testify is, that the highest gift of God is that which is for all alike. We need the Spirit of God for the works we have to do. We can speak no true, honest, sound word, unless we ask Him to teach us what we shall say, and how we shall say it. But, most of all, we need His help to take the conceit and self-sufficiency out of us—to make us understand that we can of ourselves make you do no right deed, and think no right thought; that we cannot of ourselves do any right deed, or think any right thought; that we are all on a level—all feeble, and paltry, and sinful, without God; all redeemed and purchased by Him; all able to live according to His will, if His own Spirit, as He promises, worketh in us to will and to do of His good pleasure.

I have been speaking to you so far about the Collect because I wished you to use it as if its words were true, mighty, blessed words, such as I take them to be, and that you should not merely repeat them as if they meant nothing. But I should not have spoken to you of anything in the Prayer Book, if I did not think its lessons were in the Bible, and if they did not send you back to the Bible, where you will find them more bright, clear, and full. The passage I have taken out of the Epistle to the Romans tells us something more even than the Collect. We need to *know* it, if this Collect, or any of the Collects, is to do us real lasting good. We often say in our hearts—I have said it to myself a thousand times—yes! we might have this Spirit of God, if we could pray for such a gift. But I do not feel that I can. My tongue seems tied, or what is worse, I speak readily enough; but there is nothing in my heart that answers to the speech, as a poor miserable king, who had murdered his brother, said, after he had tried to say a prayer:

"My words fly up, my thoughts remain below,
Words, without thoughts, never to heaven go."

Now, brethren, what is the way out of this perplexity for you, and me, and all of us? What are we to do when we feel as if we could not pray? as if that were the greatest difficulty of all. Hear what St. Paul says, for he had suffered in this way, as in most other ways—that was his training to be an Apostle:—"Likewise the Spirit also helpeth our infirmities, for we know not what we should pray for as we ought, but the Spirit itself maketh intercession for us, with groanings that cannot be uttered." So you see it is the Spirit who helps us not only to think and to do, but also to pray—who draws out our desires towards God, who speaks more for us and in us than we know. It is very wonderful, but yet it must be so. We could not pray if God Himself were not stirring up prayer in us. It is not we who seek first for fellowship with Him, He seeks to have fellowship with us. The children begin to ask for their Father, because the Father has been first seeking for His children. That is what our Lord is teaching us in such a number of passages. It was, as I may say, the ground of all His teaching. The Pharisees complained of His keeping company with sinners. Nay, He said, but what does a shepherd do who has lost a sheep out of his fold? What does a woman do who has lost a piece of money? What does a father do whose child has wandered away from him? Whatever these do, He said, *that* your Father in Heaven is doing for His sheep that are running into the pits and falling over precipices—for the hearts that He has lost—for the children that are forgetting themselves and Him. And He said that He was come to do His Father's will, which was, that all should come to the knowledge of their true state and should live. Be sure, then, brethren, that when we are able to ask for God's Spirit to help us, it is because He is seeking after us, and prompting that wish of ours, and stirring us up that it may not be a lazy half-wish, but a real, strong, earnest cry. Be sure that when we feel as if we needed to pray, but cannot, God's Spirit is teaching us our weakness, and His strength; how much more He cares for us than we care for Him; how impossible it is for us to be right, or to be at peace, till we believe in Him and yield to Him. Be sure that these deep longings, which there are in all of us, even in those who are going most wrong, are the groanings of that Spirit whom we have grieved and resisted. Be sure that He speaks to our true, better mind; that the other mind, which is contrary to His, is a false, accursed, devilish one, which we may ask Him to cast out. And oh! is it not a blessed thought that this Spirit is uttering His groans for the deliverance of this world of ours from all its sin and slavery and wretchedness? Should not we rejoice that God knows what is the mind of this Spirit; for it is His own mind? Should not we confess that all the evil that there is in us, and in all men, comes from our fighting against that gracious mind of the Father and of the Son? Should not we trust, with all our hearts, that His will should at last be done on earth as it is in Heaven? And do not think that those who have prayed that prayer here on earth, pray it less fervently when they leave the earth. Then their tongues are loosed; then they can pray for us and all their friends fighting here below, as God's Spirit would have them pray; then they begin to know that no prayer, or groan, that has been uttered in the lowliest chamber, or in the darkest dungeon, shall be in vain. God's Spirit inspired those prayers and groans, and His new Heaven and new Earth will be the answer to them.

SERMON X.

THE LAW OF INHERITANCE.

Preached at Ockham, 10th Sunday after Trinity, August 28, 1859.

"Honour thy father and thy mother, that thy days may be long upon the land which the Lord thy God giveth thee."—EXODUS xx. 12.

I AM going to speak to you this afternoon of one of the Commandments. Some people tell us that the Commandments generally do not concern us, they belonged to the Old Dispensation. Some say that it is a great bondage to impose them upon Englishmen who live under the Gospel. Some say that this Commandment, especially, is not meant for us, however good it may be in itself, because it speaks of a land which the Lord gave the Jews, and we are not dwellers in that land. I shall not argue against these opinions. I wish to try what they are worth in one instance.

The Israelites were travelling from the land of Egypt, in which they had been bondsmen, to a land which had been promised them. They were told that the Canaanites who occupied that land had become filthy and brutal—the cup of their iniquity was full. They had fancied that the land was their own, to do what they liked with it. They did not acknowledge that they were set in it to till it and dress it. They did not acknowledge that there was any one who would call them to account if they misused it, and became plagues to each other and to mankind. The Israelites were taught that men were only tenants of the soil on which they dwell. It was bestowed on them for certain uses. If they forget these uses they will be turned out of it. The Canaanites were to be cast out of this land because the true owner of it had found them mischievous and corrupt. The Israelites were to succeed them. These Israelites were never to fancy, as the Canaanites had done, that it was their land. They were always to recollect that they were only husbandmen, set by the Great Landlord to watch over it for Him. They were to count it as a great blessing to have this stewardship entrusted to them. And they were to ask very earnestly, What was it that caused these people not to live longer in the land? The same wrong doings would lead to the same result. There was no favouritism. They were there to be witnesses of a truth—to do a work. If they were not witnesses of this truth, if they failed to do this work, they would perish off the land; others would dispossess them. What was it, then, this people had done which had taken the land from them? The great answer to the question is given in the first and second Commandments. "Thou shalt worship the Lord thy God who brought thee out of the house of bondage. Thou shalt not worship the likeness of anything in heaven or earth or under the earth." The Canaanites had not worshipped a God who makes free. They had worshipped gods who are tyrants, who make slaves. They had worshipped gods whom they dreaded and hated. They had supposed these gods to bear the likenesses of things in heaven and earth and under the earth. They had stooped and crouched to these things. Some of the objects were noble and glorious; but worship had degraded them. For men thought of them only as they ministered to their wants, or awakened their fears; so they became different in each land. It was impossible to think of them as blessings common to the whole earth. And if they were thought of only as ministering to men's wants, men would glorify all things whatever which ministered to their wants. The lowest animal might be as much an object of reverence as the sun or moon.

And here was the mighty contradiction. The men felt they were greater than the greatest of these things, whilst they were bowing down to them. They could not help thinking so. They wanted a God to govern them; to tell them what they should be and what they should do; to hold them in fellowship with each other. The sun and moon could not do this, nor the animals. They could not teach them to keep their oaths; they could not teach them to work or to rest; they could not tell them when they should make their children or their servants work and rest. Here were some of the causes why these Canaanites were living in slavery, and why they were to be driven from the land.

The fifth Commandment gives another reason. When Ham exposed his father's nakedness, it was said, "Servants of servants shall his children be." That is to say, Ham's own sin of not honouring his father will be the curse not only of him, but of future generations. Wherever there is a race of people who do not honour their parents, there will be a race of slavish people; this cannot be otherwise. And this, I have no doubt, was a main cause of the brutality and slavery of these Canaanites, inseparable from that of which I have just spoken. They did not revere the father who had begotten them, or the mother who had brought them forth. The child had no thought of its parents; perhaps scarcely knew who they were. The parents had no thought of their children. When it came to this in that or any country of the old world, the inhabitants of that country were becoming curses to themselves and to all about them. The land was taken from them. If we believe the Bible, we shall believe that God took it from them.

You see, then, why it is said here, " Honour thy father and thy mother, that thy days may be long in the land which the Lord thy God giveth thee." That is as much as to say, ' You Israelites must not fancy that your days in that land which I am about to give you will be longer than those of the Canaanites, if you do not honour your fathers and mothers ; for it cannot be so. By my everlasting law it cannot. I have placed you in families. I have given you fathers and mothers. And I have created you sons and daughters to look up to them and pay them reverence. And if that reverence departs from you, if you do not care for the family to which you belong, then you will not care for the land to which you belong. You will not love it and fight for it. You will not think it a sacred place because it has the tombs of those who went before you in it. You will not call it your home, and wish to come back to it whenever you wander. You will not believe that you have anything to do with the generations that lived here of old, and with those that shall be born when you are in your graves. You will be mere miserable creatures, thinking only of the present hour, how much you can get to eat and to drink, or how much you can scrape together. And then, be sure, there will creep over you idleness and cowardice, and any invader that comes upon you will be too mighty for you and will eat you up.'

And this, which was said to the whole people, was, you see, said to each one of them. Each man there had his own father and mother. Each was to honour his father and his mother; otherwise he would become a poor vagabond. Either he would run away from his land, just because he was tired of it, or, if he stayed in it, he would be a useless sot or gambler, caring for no one but himself; always trying to please himself—his own enemy and his country's enemy.

And yet how many temptations did the Israelite find when he came into the land which the Lord God gave him, not to honour his father and mother! How often the evil spirit will have whispered to him, 'How they grudge you this or that thing, how unfair they are to you! How much wiser you are than they are! How can you be such a feeble creature as to care for what they say to you? Surely you know best what you have need of?' All these things they heard, and some of them were partly true. The fathers and mothers might be often unfair and foolish; they might neglect their children; very likely they might, in their youth, have not reverenced *their* parents. So that the young man would frequently persuade himself that he had the right on his side. And except he believed that the Lord his God had said amongst thunders and lightnings to his fathers, and was saying then to him, "Honour thy father and thy mother," and unless he believed that the Lord who spoke these words was indeed his God as well as his father's God, and unless He believed that this God knew what was good for him and for all men, and was commanding the thing that was right and true; and unless he believed that this God would give him strength to obey that which He commanded, he would yield continually to his evil nature; no fear of what was coming upon him would keep him from doing so, his anger and his self-will would be too strong for that. But the words would be fulfilled to him. His days would not be long in the land which the Lord his God gave him. And if there were a great multitude like him, they would hasten the time when the whole land should be desolate.

My friends! do these things belong to the history

of the old world, to what people call a former dispensation? I hold that they belong to us, I hold it to be just as true of England as it was of Judæa, that it is a land which the Lord our God has given us. It is not ours, any more than the land of Canaan was the Israelites'. We are tenants of it, just as they were. Our forefathers understood that they were to till it and subdue it for God, and to drive wild beasts out of it, and to root out the thorns and thistles, and to hand it down better than they found it, to their children and their children's children.

Whilst we remember this, every one of us, if he has not a foot of land that he calls his own, may yet say, 'I hold this land of God; I have a share of it; yes, and in all the good things that have been done, and in all the brave and good men that have dwelt upon it.' It is not more the rich man's than the poor man's. All who walk upon it, and breathe the air, and look up to the sun may say, 'It is my inheritance.' And this is the tie by which the Lord our God has bound us to it, and given us a property in it. Our fathers and mothers belonged to it, as their fathers and mothers did, and while we reverence them, while we count it a great and wonderful thing to have had them to watch over us, and a great and wonderful thing that we should be allowed to care for them, then every one of us may feel that his days are indeed very long in this country. Yes, for they are not bounded by our birth nor by our death either. The country had people in it who belonged to us before we came into it; it will have those belonging to us when we have gone out of it. And that is a pledge and assurance that our ancestors are concerned in all its blessings and sorrows wherever they are, and that we shall be concerned in its blessings and sorrows wherever we go. For it is the Lord God who is, and was, and is to come; who has watched over our family, and will watch over those who shall come hereafter.

But then, dear friends, we, too, have the very same temptations which the Jews had. Some are tempted not to honour their fathers on one ground, some on another; some have tolerable excuses for their sin; some have very poor excuses. Some honour their fathers and not their mothers, or their mothers and not their fathers. Some scarcely know what honouring means; they can only think of themselves and their own importance. And oh! brethren, how bitter is the anguish of recollecting that the honour has not been rendered, and that the time for it is gone; their gray hairs are in the dust; they want no more the services that were withheld, the reverence and the love which were refused them. It is an awful thought, and yet God may use it for bringing us to deep repentance before Him, for leading us to arise and go to that Father whose Spirit we have grieved whenever we have grieved our parents upon earth. And that is what Christ bids us remember. It is this Father, the Lord our God, the Father who gave up His only begotten

Son for us all; the Father who loves and honours that Son, and is loved and honoured by Him, world without end, for one Spirit of love binds them for ever and ever; it is He who says to us, in that still small voice which made the prophet tremble more than the thunder, and the earthquake, and the fire, "Honour thy father and thy mother." He has set over thee a father to remind thee of His justice and truth, a mother to remind thee of His mercy and gentleness. Oh, ask for His Spirit, that thou mayest honour thy father and mother as He would have thee honour Him. Do not let their waywardness, their weakness, or even their sins towards thee, check this, which He who has no waywardness, or weakness, or sin, asks of thee, and would put within thee. Receive it and cherish it as His own gift, which it is the highest good to have, and the greatest calamity to want! Count the commandment which He gives thee to be thy life. So out of the earthly honour there will spring one that is eternal. The vision of the perfect Father, and the joy and blessedness of being His child, will dawn upon thee more and more. And with the higher blessing will come a greater enjoyment and appreciation of the lower. Thou wilt know more of the mystery and wonder of belonging to a family, more of the mystery and wonder of belonging to a nation. Thou wilt see how the prosperity of England is linked to the prosperity of every English hearth and home, how one will be sound and safe as long as the other is sound and safe.

My friends! this may be obsolete teaching in the opinion of wise people. The writers of our Catechism did not think it so. Those who wrote the Communion Service did not think so. They believed that the God of Abraham and Isaac and Jacob is our God; that the God who delivered the Israelites and gave them their land is our God. They believed that He has promised in His new covenant to write His laws in our hearts by His Spirit. And I believe that thunders and lightnings as terrible as those which confirmed the commandment on Sinai, will show us that they were not mistaken. We may talk of refinement and civilisation as much as we will, but if these old words do not stand as the words of a living God, we shall sink back into barbarism. We may talk of national prosperity as we will, but if children do not honour their parents, no contrivances of statesmen, no commercial successes, no religious profession, will keep us on the land which God has given us. We may talk of free institutions as we will, but if the ground of freedom be cut from under our feet, the oldest of all curses will be fulfilled in us, "Servants of servants shall they be."

SERMON XI.

THE DELIVERER FROM CRIME.

Preached at Ockham, 11*th Sunday after Trinity, September* 4, 1859.

"Thou shalt not kill. Thou shalt not commit adultery."
EXODUS xx. 13, 14.

LET me remind you once more how these commandments begin. "I am the Lord thy God which brought thee out of the house of bondage." The Israelite was to hear those words spoken in his ears before each of these sentences:—I, the Lord thy God, thy Deliverer, say to thee, thou shalt not kill; I, the Lord thy God, thy Deliverer, say to thee, thou shalt not commit adultery.

And let me remind you also once again, that the self-same God, who is, and was, and is to come—He who is our God, and has chosen us to be His people—He who has redeemed us from the service of evil and cruel gods—He who is our Father, and has made us His children—is speaking to us just what He spoke to the Israelites.

The commandments are written in a book, but He is saying them to the heart and soul of every man and woman and child, who cannot even read the letters of the book.

Consider that. Every Englishman knows that it is against the laws of his country to commit murder. He knows that if he does commit it and is found out, he shall be put to death, or be shut up in prison and set to hard labour. And yet murders are committed—dark, foul murders—in our land, by men born and brought up like ourselves, breathing this air, nursed upon the knees of mothers who have had good thoughts in them, who perhaps have done kind deeds. The fear of the law is not enough to stop them; for they say, we shall not be found out. The deed can be done in some out-of-the-way field or wood. The body can be hidden in the ground, or we may choose a secret way of murder, we can use slow poison that even wise people may not understand the working of. Being punished hereafter may sometimes come into their minds; but that hereafter seems a long way off, and who can tell what may happen in the mean time? And so the man broods over this thought of a murder, and at last it gets ripe in his mind, and he does it, and the papers are filled with the news of it. And people read of it, and talk of it, and are not generally much the better for what they read and what they talk. But now, supposing that murderer had believed what the Bible says to us. Suppose he had understood that the Lord his God was saying to him then—just when the deed was going to be done, just when he was purposing it and plotting, just when he was trying the knife or the poison—'Thou shalt not do it! No one else knows what thou art after, but I know it. No one else may follow thee in all thy contrivances, but I shall follow thee. No one else may be able to tell where the body has been buried, or how the drugs have been mixed, but I shall see it all.' Would that have made no difference? Would it have been nothing to him that he was going to part from a friend, to separate from one who had been with him, and watching over him in all his doings? I ask you, if the man had believed this, would it not have stopped him; though the fear of being hanged would not stop him; though the fear of what should happen to him after death could not stop him? Yes, brethren, that was just what he wanted; that was just what he did not believe, what very likely he never believed. He comes to know afterwards that it is so. There is a blankness and dreariness and dread in his heart, as if he had lost something; not an enemy—not the man he had taken so much pains to get rid of—but a well-wisher, One who cared for him, One who had kept him from a thousand wrong deeds before. He is at war, and he sometimes feels that he is at war with the Lord his God. He wishes that he could kill that thought, ay, that he could kill God. It is that he has been trying to do, and a man may come to the state when he shall think that he has done it; and this state is more miserable and horrible than any other.

But what is the use of troubling ourselves about what unhappy murderers might have believed, and did not believe? This is the use of it, brethren, you and I may believe it. You and I may think this commandment is true and not a lie. The Lord our God, our Father, is always with us; knowing our acts, knowing our thoughts and wishes, knowing all the secret influences that may be working in us to do any evil deed. And He has the will to keep us from it. And He has the will to take away the dark, horrible imaginations that lead to it. He has the will to drive them clean and clear out of us, and to put right and blessed and loving thoughts and purposes in the place of them. As our Lord was telling us in the lesson we read this morning, in the Sermon He preached on the Mount, He is calling us to account for the first rising of anger in our heart; He calls us into judgment for the bitter curse that goes out of our lips. He makes us feel what a hell-fire we have kindled in our hearts, when we begin to scorn our brother and call him fool! Yes, all that is verily so. Christ is Himself speaking in our consciences, and accusing us of bad thoughts and words, long before they start into bad deeds. He begins at the beginning. Is not that good for us to remember, for us who have the same nature with the murderer, for us who may be tempted sometimes as he is tempted; for us who may be cherishing a cruel and savage hatred of some fellow-creature, even if we are kept from hurting his body?

And what I have said of this commandment, is just as true of the next. In the Sermon on the Mount, our Lord speaks of that as well as of the words, "Thou shalt not kill." He speaks of the secret lusts which work in a man's heart before he dares to defy the law, and defile his neighbour's wife. He says to every one of us: thou canst not hide from me the deed of darkness, though no mortal may be acquainted with it—thou canst not hide from me all the secret desires that are leading thee to ruin another and thyself—thou canst not make excuses with me. I know thy temptations, but I can give thee the victory over them. I can save thee from destroying the soul of one thou pretendest to love, the peace of a family, thy own truth. The dread of being detected and exposed may not hold thee back in thy evil way; but I can. Here, again, I say, the adulterer and adulteress sin, because they do not believe this. It seems to them an idle tale. But they know afterwards that it is not an idle tale. There comes to them, as there does to the murderer, the certainty that they have lost something that was infinitely precious. They have set themselves at war, not with the world and with men, but with the living and true and loving God. The misery that awaits them is not when people are looking on and scorning them; they might bear that; they might comfort themselves with the thought, 'perhaps if they had been in our circumstances they would not have been better.'

But it is in lonely hours, when no one is condemning them, when they are trying to find comfort in each other, or to look back upon the days of their childhood, or to hope for better hours—it is then that some voice speaks to them, and says: you have sold your birthright; you would not have a Father. You did not let His Spirit govern you; you have given yourselves to an evil spirit.

Brethren, there are very sad and fearful thoughts connected with these commandments. But there are also very blessed thoughts connected with them. Is it nothing to remember that the Lord God Himself watches over the life of every one of us, poor creatures as we are? that He has declared and does declare how precious it is in his eyes? 'I say to thee, poor man and rich man, beggar and king, "Thou shalt not kill." I say to the man with the strongest arm, with the greatest dominion over his fellow-creatures — that strength is mine; that dominion is lent thee by me, to defend life not to take it away. And if thou usest it for the wrong purpose instead of the right one; if thy strength become a plague and a destruction to thy fellow-men, though none of them may call thee to account for it, I shall call thee to account for it. Thou wilt answer to me for every drop of this sacred life which thou spillest; of every man's brother will I require the life of man.' And thus, too, we come to understand better what God's promises are concerning this life of ours. It is subject to a thousand accidents. All things seem to conspire against it. Death seems to get the mastery over it at last. But no, He has said, 'Death, I will be thy plague.' As every plant and tree seems to die in winter and to revive in spring, so He says to this more wonderful life in our bodies: 'It shall go on, and this is the pledge and witness that it shall. The head of you all, the Son of Man, the only-begotten heavenly Son of God, died Himself and rose again. God's conflict with death is accomplished. The grave shall not kill.'

And so again, the Lord thy God is the God over thy household. He watches over the marriage bond. He does not, in his care for the whole universe, forget thee and thy wife. He has uttered His decree that you shall live together in holy wedlock, and that no man shall break that covenant betwixt you made, and that you shall not break it to each other. His curse goes forth against that sin.

Yes, against sin. For, recollect, that there is no more precious life than this of wife, of husband. The life of trust and affection; the life of friendship and wedded love; the life of doing good to men; the life of reverence and worship. This is the true life of a man; not the life that is sustained by eating and drinking. And, therefore, God who cares much for that bodily life, cares more for this better life which He has bestowed upon His human creatures. And He encourages and wishes them to give up one for the sake of the other. Brave men have been ready—are ready—to give up the life of their bodies, that their households may be safe from pollution, that their country may be governed by righteous laws; that they may save it from falling under wicked tyrants; that they may worship the true God in spirit and in truth. He who says thou shalt not kill, bids us understand that it is well to pour out blood as if it were water, rather than to become base and foul creatures—beasts, instead of His servants and children. That was the reason he sent the Israelites to drive out the Canaanites. They were corrupting and defiling the earth with their murders and adulteries and abominations. It was time that the earth should be cleared of them. It was time that a God of righteousness, who watches over life and marriage, and does not leave men to follow their own lusts, should be proclaimed among them. And as I said to you last Sunday about the commandment, "Honour thy father and thy mother that thy days may be long in the land which the Lord thy God giveth thee," that a nation in which the reverence for parents is gone, will not stay long on the land which the Lord its God has given it; so, I say, now, about the crimes of which I have spoken to-day. A land is defiled with blood, whether we think it or not; a land is defiled by breaches of the marriage vow in the high or the low. And when these crimes spread far and wide, when they are spoken lightly of, when they are thought only to concern those who commit them, and not to concern us at all; when we are amused by reading about them, instead of being ashamed for the sake of our people; then let us look well that that does not come upon us which has come upon other people before us. Let us recollect that the God who gave these commandments is King now, as He was when they were heard on Sinai, and that there is no respect of persons with Him, and that He has sworn that He will set righteousness and truth on His earth, whoever shall prefer unrighteousness and falsehood.

But there is a question which you may very well ask me about this matter, which I will try to answer.

I have spoken as if murder and adultery were crimes which would certainly bring down God's righteous punishments upon the men who commit them, and upon the land which suffers them. But am I not sent to preach forgiveness to those who have sinned? ought I then to have spoken as if these judgments were sure; as if there were no escaping them? Brethren, I am sent to preach the largest and freest forgiveness that God can give, or man can receive. I am sent to tell you that God gave His Son to reconcile the world to Himself, and that Christ is the Lamb of God who took away the sin of the world. And this message we are to proclaim without stint or measure to all manner of people; and those who proclaim it in hulks, and prisons, and penitentiaries, and convict settlements, to the worst and most guilty people, are true servants and handmaids of God, and are blessings to their country. But they are so if they give this message as God gives it, not as man changes it. Christ died to take away the sin of men; He died to unite men to the righteous and sinless God. The Lord our God who has redeemed us out of the house of bondage will always deliver us from sin; will always give us a new and right and clean heart. He did that for David, the Jewish king, who had committed adultery and murder. He will do it for the poorest Englishman who has been guilty of the same sins. But He did not free David from punishment; He punished him all his life long. He made him feel all his life long that to seduce the wife of a poor soldier, and to get him slain, was a horrible offence in the eyes of the King of Kings, which He would visit not with some pretty little punishment, such as David might have invented for himself, but with sore and tremendous punishment, with the ingratitude of his children, and the rebellion of his people. It would have been very bad for this king if it had been otherwise. He would then never have known what God's righteousness is. He would never have sought for himself righteousness, or a deliverance from his own folly and sin. He would never have been righteous in his execution of God's laws, and yet tender to sinners who were not so bad as he had been. And so it is still. He who says, "Thou shalt not kill; thou shalt not commit adultery"—because He is the Lord our God, our Redeemer, our Father—will take away the murderous spirit out of the murderer, and give him a loving and gentle spirit, even His own; will drive the foul spirit out of the adulterer's heart, and give him a holy and pure spirit, even His own. But He will not suffer either the one or the other to escape punishment. And I am well convinced that the murderer and adulterer to whom He has given repentance would be very sorry if they did escape it. They would feel that He was not the great God such as they believe Him to be. They would feel that He was not the Saviour such as they believe Him to be, seeing that He did not keep them in mind of the evil which had separated them from Him, and did not compel them to turn away from themselves and seek Him. Whenever the thought gets into the mind of any people that God can be persuaded by any prayers or intercessions of one sort or another, in earth or heaven, to release particular people from the punishment that He has thought good for them, that people will go further and further from righteousness; adulterers and assassins will both abound amongst them. And as they go further into evil they will become more superstitious, and will practise more arts to keep God at a distance from them. Therefore, brethren, drive all such thoughts from you. Understand that a man cannot have any curse so terrible as to be left in his sin, or to be allowed to go on without punishment; and that he cannot have any such great blessing as to be raised out of his sin, and to have it treated as his blackest and bitterest enemy. For this end Christ died and revived—not that He might save us from our Father in heaven, but that He might bring us nigh to Him, and make us sharers of His goodness and truth, which are the everlasting foes of all that is not good and true in us, and in the whole universe.

I beseech you to recollect this, you who are bringing your children to be baptized, promising in their name that they should keep God's will and commandments, and walk in the same. I beseech you to think of it who are learning these commandments at school, and you who are old and who have learned what it is to break them. To all of you God speaks words of mercy and deliverance. He loves you all too much to leave you easy when you are disobeying and forgetting Him. And especially I beseech you who have eaten the bread and drunk the wine to-day at our Lord's table, to remember that these were the witness and assurance that He is with us everywhere, wherever we are, and whatever we are doing, and that He can make us obey what St. Paul calls the royal law—what St. James calls the law of liberty—thou shalt love thy neighbour as thyself—and if this is written in our hearts, there is no fear that we shall do any wrong to our neighbour or to our country.

SERMON XII.

ST. JOHN BAPTIST'S DAY.

Preached at Lilleshall, Sunday after St. John Baptist's Day, 1860.

"In those days came John the Baptist preaching in the Wilderness, and saying, Repent ye, for the kingdom of Heaven is at hand."—
St. Matthew iii. 1, 2.

The 24th of June (the day before yesterday), we call, you know, Midsummer Day; we call it also St. John the Baptist's day. You can easily find out why it is Midsummer Day, but what is St. John the Baptist to us? why should we care to remember him?

I am going to speak of him—what he was, to whom he spoke, what he spoke, why he was called the Baptist, what he told of One greater than himself. You have heard it all before, but it may not be bad for any of us to hear it again; for the seasons come round again—the summer comes each year, bringing its flowers and fruits; they are new, though we seem to have seen the like every June. And we ourselves, though we change very much, yet we are the same.

We miss many faces that we used to see; young faces that we have not seen come to cheer us; but there are the old sorrows and trials which we cannot leave behind us, and which stand up in different shapes; there are old thoughts that appear again in our minds, though new ones may be with them. We are tempted to do wrong now as we used to be, and we do not forget the old temptations, they come back; old deeds that we did years ago return and look us in the face. The friends that we knew are there also, and that is the reason why I believe John the Baptist has something to tell us still—why his day may be as good for us as it was for our forefathers.

First, what was he? A very plain man, with a leathern girdle about his loins, caring little for what he ate, getting his food anywhere that he could—and his chance of getting anything was not great, for he was not seen in cities, he was chiefly in a desert.

Then this strange rough man was preaching, and the people came to him from all quarters, from the city of Jerusalem, we are told, and from all the country places round about; men who dwelt near the sea and far from it, men and women, rich and poor, people of all trades, and people without any trade, all came to hear what this man had to say. What could it mean? What did they want of him? What message could he bring them which could be meant for them all?

These people were all looking out for a King. They had heard that God one day would send them a King, a righteous King. Their country was subject to foreigners; these foreigners had set up princes over them; these princes had been tyrants, and had not cared for them. They wanted One who did care for them; they wanted One who would set their country free; they wanted One who would set *them* free. For each one had a burden and a slavery of his own; each one said in his heart, ' When the true King comes He will be able to take away my burden; He will break the yoke that is on my neck! '

Well, this preacher said, "The Kingdom of Heaven is at hand!" That was a message that concerned all. If the news were true, it was just the news they needed to hear. The King you are looking for is coming. He is not far from you. He is going to establish His Kingdom amongst you.

But what did this mean? The kingdom of "*Heaven*" is at hand! Was it not to be a kingdom on earth, then? How could it reach them if it were not? How could it be governed by a native prince, one of themselves, if it were not? Such thoughts were in the minds of the people, you may be sure. And yet there were other thoughts in their minds too. If this kingdom was not from Heaven, could it be what they were seeking after? Did they not wish for one that should be all just? And could there be a kingdom that was quite just if it was not from Heaven, if it was not God's kingdom? Did not they want one in which poor and rich should be cared for equally? Would that be, if it was only a kingdom set up by men? Even if the king was one of themselves, might he not lord it over them all the more for that? Might he not be the prouder because he had risen to such a height above them? But if it were the King of Heaven that was coming among them, would they like to meet Him? Another king might not know what they had been doing, but He would; another might speak to the crowd of people and not notice this man or that man in the crowd. The King of Heaven would look straight into each man's heart; He would understand what he had done, and what he had wished or purposed. Supposing each man knew that he had been doing wrong things, and wishing and purposing wrong things, would he like to stand before this King?

Each man in those crowds of people who went to hear John the Baptist preaching, did know this; and yet that did not keep them from going; it was that which urged them to go; it was that which convinced them that the rough man with his camel's hair was no deceiver, but a true prophet. He spoke of a Kingdom of Heaven being near; and the heart of a man or a woman said, 'Yes, He must be near me, or how should I have remembered how I cheated my neighbour years ago, or plotted to cheat him? Who told me of it? I did not tell myself. John the Baptist could not tell me; it must be this King of Heaven who has told me. He cannot be far off. How shall I prepare for Him?'

Now John said that this was his business; he was

sent to prepare the way of the Lord! he was sent to tell men how they might meet their King! and, therefore, he joined the message, "The Kingdom of Heaven is at hand," with 'Repent; your King is near you! Turn round to Him; He has found out your secrets! Confess them to Him; you cannot see Him; but if you do this, there will be a way between your heart and Him. Your bad doings and bad thoughts have stopped up that way; He wishes to get rid of the rubbish, and to open the way again.'

And that brings me to the next part—what John's baptism had to do with his preaching. He preached, it is said, the baptism of repentance for the remission of sins. Remission means sending away. Their sins had choked their hearts. Their sins had been the rubbish which closed the way between them and God. Could they clear away the rubbish? Could John? I think not. Could He who created their minds and hearts? Surely He could. Surely He could turn their minds to Himself, if they found it ever so hard to do so. Well, this baptism was the simplest token which could be given them that God did this for them. Just as the water cleanses your bodies, so does He cleanse you—you, your own selves. He sends away that which you have been confessing to Him; that which is oppressing you, that which you cannot rid yourselves of. So the baptism was part of the preaching, it was as good as saying, 'It is not I who am preaching to you, it is God who is preaching to you!

He is preaching to you, one and all. It is He who is giving you, one and all, what you need, if you will have it.'

And, therefore, John joined other words to these, which were to show more clearly still that it was not he who was doing them any good, or who could do them good, except as he was God's minister, and that the water could do them no good except as it told them what God's mind to them was, and what He would work for them.

"I, indeed," he said, "baptize you with water, but there cometh One after me who is mightier than I; He shall baptize you with the Holy Ghost and with fire." 'He shall give you of God's own good Spirit to call out your spirits; He shall burn up all that is foul and false in you.'

But before you can fully enter into the next words, I must speak to you of those who came to John to be baptized. There came the crowds of which I spoke, each with his own weight upon his own heart. Each told what was in him; and each found that the remission was not less for him because it was also for his neighbours. Each had sinned; each might turn and say, I have sinned; each might go away with this assurance, 'God hath given thee this pledge that He puts away thy sins.' But there came some, we are told, whom John rebuked, whom he called by a very hard name. He said to some Pharisees and Sadducees who came to him, "O generation of vipers, who hath warned you to flee from the wrath to come? Bring forth therefore fruits meet for repentance; and think not to say within yourselves we have Abraham to our father; for I say unto you that God is able of these stones to raise up children unto Abraham." Why did he speak thus? Might not these men repent as well as the others? Would not God put away their sins, and make a way for them to draw nigh to Him? Surely He would; John had come to say so to one and all. But these men thought themselves better and wiser than others; they supposed the way was quite open between them and God. Why then did they come to have their sins put away? If they were better and wiser than others, how could they want a blessing which put them on a level with all others? They thought they were the best of all the descendants of Abraham. 'You must find out,' said John, 'that you are not better than those who are not descendants of Abraham at all. God cares for all. If you do not wish to be like the rest of men, it will go badly with you. When the King comes, He will burn up all that is mere chaff, all that is foul and worthless in one man or another. He will gather in all that is wheat, all that is good and true, all that trust Him who is good, whether in one man or another.'

And so we are prepared for the next tidings. There came one to John the Baptist who was humbler than all who had come there yet. John did not see why He should come. "I have need," he said, "to be baptized of Thee!" But Jesus answered, "Thus it becometh us to fulfil all righteousness." And as He went up out of the water, the heavens were opened, and the Spirit descended upon Him like a dove; and lo! a voice which said, "This is my beloved Son, in whom I am well pleased."

Thus the word of John the Baptist was fulfilled—the kingdom of heaven had appeared. *He* had received the Holy Spirit, who was to baptize with the Holy Spirit and with fire; *He* was come who was to gather all nations into one; *He* was come who was to bring remission of sins to all; *He* was come who was to give repentance to each.

All this happened in the country of Palestine, far away from us, eighteen hundred years ago. But about twelve hundred years ago, people came into the towns and villages of England and said, 'This kingdom of heaven of which John the Baptist spoke is fairly set up in the world. The King who was baptized in that River Jordan, is the only true King over men. He has said that His Father is our Father. He has said that He will give us, the people who dwell in the villages and towns of England, His Spirit, that we may be right and true men, and that we may turn from bad ways to good ways. Come, therefore,' they said, 'and be baptized into the name of the Father, and of the Son, and of the Holy Ghost. Come and claim this King as your king and your elder brother. Come and claim His Father as your Father; claim Him as your children's as well as your own. Ask that you and they may not merely be baptized in water, for the sending away of your sins, and the witness of God's forgiveness, but that you may have His Spirit of truth and love to guide you every day and hour, and to teach you what His kingdom is, and to prepare you for dwelling in it when you leave this earth, and when your place here knows you no more.'

These were strange tidings for our forefathers to hear, for they were worshipping all kinds of gods. They fancied their gods were their enemies, who wanted to be pacified and brought to forgive them by all kinds of offerings which they made. And now to be told this news—the God who made the heavens and earth is your Father and your friend; He seeks to turn your hearts to Him; He desires to put away all the wrong that is in you, and to make you right; He has sent His Son to bind you all together—men of all different callings, men of all different countries, men of all different languages—into one. He would have no one think himself better than another. He would have all feel that they are His children, and members one of another. To hear this news, I say, was very strange to these men, who had fancied it was all so different in this world, and in the world they could not see; but somehow or other they did accept these tidings; they were baptized into this Name, and their children were, and their children's children. And England became a Christian land—that is, it confessed the Christ of whom John spoke, to be its King. And boys and girls were brought up in schools to believe that it was even so, and that His Spirit was given them that they might understand the things on earth and the things in heaven, that they might do their work as fathers and husbands, and brothers and sisters, as squires and farmers and labourers here, and might know the truth and righteousness and love, that are to last for ever and ever.

But now my friends, if all this is true, we need to be reminded of it year by year, and day by day, for it cannot be a thing written of in a book merely; it must be about our bed and our board; it must concern us in all our common business. For you see the message of John the Baptist concerns the God who liveth for ever, what He is, whether He is altogether good and righteous and true, one who hates all evil and pride, or whether He is what men often take Him to be—unmerciful and cruel, and like themselves. And it concerns us men, whatever we are, whether we are bound together in one dear Lord, who took the nature of all and died the death of all, or whether we are, as we often take ourselves to be, each with a separate interest from the other, sent into the world to trip one another up and destroy one another. And it concerns the question whether we have a good and loving Spirit to bring us right and to keep us from wrong, or whether we are left to ourselves and all the bad influences that are about us, and all the wild thoughts that spring up in us. It concerns the question whether, when we have gone out of the good way, there is anyone who cares to bring us back into the good way. It concerns the question whether we are separated from the friends that have gone away out of our sight, or whether we are part of the same kingdom with them, and whether we may all come to serve our King better and more truly through ages upon ages. So, then, you will not wonder that we keep John the Baptist's day. And you will not think it out of place in the bright summer days; for surely if we heed the message which it brings, every summer day may be more beautiful to us, and no winter day need be dark. Midsummer and Christmas may rejoice together, for the first says, "Repent, for the kingdom of heaven is at hand;" and the second says, "Unto us a child is born, unto us a son is given, and the government shall be upon His shoulder, and His name shall be called Wonderful, Counsellor, the mighty God, the everlasting Father, the Prince of Peace."

SERMON XIII.

THE TRANSFIGURATION.

Preached at Lilleshall, 1860.

" And after six days, Jesus taketh Peter, James, and John, his brother, and bringeth them up into an high mountain apart, and was transfigured before them."—St. Matthew xvii. 1, 2.

WE have heard strange things in the second lesson. Let me try to recall them to you, and let us then think what they have to do with us, who are met in this church to-day.

Three fishermen, who are called here Peter, James, and John, had left their father's ship and their nets. A Person had said to them, " Follow me, and I will make you fishers of men." They had felt that they must follow Him. He had a right to call them. Their business was to obey. They had gone with Him wherever He went. He had explained to them the world in which they were dwelling. It seemed as if they had never known the commonest thing before. Yet He spoke of very common things—of sowers sowing corn; of husbandmen hiring themselves out for the day; of fishermen getting good and bad fish into their nets. These old things became new to them, when He spoke of them. And what was more, through these things He enabled them to understand what was passing in themselves. He showed them what a wonderful world was within them. And He spoke to them of a Father who had created the world which they saw with their eyes, and who ruled over that inner world which they could not see. He called *that* especially God's kingdom. His Father watched over the ravens and the lilies; but their hearts were His own dearest treasure.

These poor men had listened to these discourses of Jesus, and they had seen His acts. They had been with Him when He healed the sick, and raised the dead, and cast out devils. They had these proofs that He was a King; and moreover He had given them power to do as He did. They were sent to preach the Kingdom of God, and to heal the sick. So their countrymen were to find out what kind of kingdom that was; so they were to see that their King was their friend and deliverer.

But there was nothing in the appearance of their teacher which marked Him out from other men. He was not clothed more gorgeously. He stood aloof from none, even the poorest. They were not the wise nor the great who were His chosen companions. He hungered and was weary, as they were. He seemed to feel the sicknesses which He took away. He had told them that He should die, and die by a shocking death, the death of slaves and criminals.

On a certain day, St. Matthew says, He led these fishermen to a lonely place in a high mountain; and then a sudden change came over Him. His garments became white. His face became bright and glorious, like no face they had ever looked upon; and presently there were companions with Him, who had not come up the mountain. They were men who had dwelt on the earth ages before. One was the old lawgiver and deliverer of the Israelites, that Moses who had brought them out of Egypt, and had died before they entered the promised land. The other was Elijah the prophet, who bore witness for the Lord God, when the king and the people had forsaken Him. The fishermen were not left in doubt who they were. They talked with Jesus. They spoke not of the law, nor of the wandering of the Israelites, nor of Elijah's chariot of fire; they spoke of the death that Jesus should die in Jerusalem—*that* they seemed to care for more, and account more wonderful than all that they had known while they walked the earth, and all they had known since they left the earth.

It was a marvellous vision; the eyes of the Apostles were dazzled. Peter wanted to stay always on the mountain, and to build tabernacles for his Master, and for Moses, and for Elijah. But he knew not what he said. While he was speaking, a cloud overshadowed them; a voice was heard, saying to them, "This is my

Beloved Son, in whom I am well pleased: hear ye Him." They fell on their faces, and were sore afraid, till another voice said to them, "Arise, and be not afraid." It was their Master. He was with them still. But the strangers were gone. The brightness had passed away.

We find them next coming down from the Mount. They are wondering as you may suppose. He, with whom they spoke so freely, so familiarly, is then a very awful Being. Moses and Elijah do Him homage. The voice spoke of Him as a Son. Are they to proclaim Him by that name? Not yet! the time will come. But He must first die and rise again; till then they are to tell the vision to no man. Must they not now ask questions of their Master, as they did before? They cannot help asking Him questions; the sight they have seen obliges them to ask Him. Who else can give them an answer? They had been always told that some divine Person was to come. But their teachers had said that Elijah would come first to prepare His way. They had seen Elijah on the Mount. Was he coming into the world again? Their Master tells them that one had come in the spirit and power of Elijah, to prepare His way. In John the Baptist, clad in camel's hair and with a leathern girdle, they had seen God's prophet. But he had been beheaded; and the Son of God would not have better, but worse treatment.

So they converse as they come down the slope of the

hill. At the bottom of it they find a great crowd; some of their companions are in it. There is loud disputing. In the midst of it is a boy, tossed about in a fit, foaming at the mouth, not to be held; his father has been begging Christ's Apostles to cure him. They have tried and failed. Here is a change from that still mountain, with the white garments, and the glorious face, and the holy men of the old world. Nothing but clamour and anguish and helplessness; at first it seems as if the boy's case were indeed hopeless. The voice of Christ only increases his raving, but at last he becomes quiet; the spirit that tormented him departs; he is cured from that hour.

All this history is contained in a few verses. You can read it over in two or three minutes. But for eighteen centuries it has had hold of people's hearts. It has been written of, spoken of, turned into beautiful pictures. Every man who has thought about it seriously has felt that it was a message for him and for all men, and not only for Peter, James, and John, for the disciples below the mountain, for the boy, and his father. Why have they thought so? What message has it for us?

I have told you that Jesus called these poor fishermen, and that He walked with them, and opened their minds to truths that had been hidden from them. Was not that a special privilege of theirs? No, brethren; Jesus called Himself the Son of Man. He selected these disciples from the humblest class of men, that they might be specimens to all men of what He is doing for them. It was not because the disciples saw Christ with their eyes, that they were able to receive His instruction. He spoke to something within them which could not see it. He spoke to their hearts; they understood Him better after they had ceased to see Him than when they could look into His face, and when His lips moved to answer their questions. And therefore do not doubt me when I say He is teaching you and me, even as He taught them. He is walking with us as He walked with them. Every one of us may believe that. As you sow, or reap, or go leasing, you may be sure there is an eye upon you, and that eye is the eye of the Son of Man; you may be sure that a teacher is with you, and that teacher is the Son of Man; you may be sure that there are parables in your fields, as there were in the fields of Galilee through which He walked, parables in all your doings as servants or masters, which He can draw out of them, as He drew them out of the common tasks which His disciples were engaged in.

Whatever we are busy about, God has set us that business. And there is a way of doing it which is the right way, which is His way; and the Son of Man would open our hearts to understand that right way, and to shun the wrong way; and when we learn the right way from Him, then He shows us more. He enables us to see that God governs us, and governs the world according to that right and true way which He has marked for us in our little pursuits and toils.

My friends, if we did think that we have this secret friend and teacher with us at all times, and that He is the secret friend and teacher of our neighbours too, it would be a mighty help to us. And then we should understand that, if we ourselves or our friends fall sick and we recover, it is Christ who raises up, as He raised up the palsied man and the lepers in the cities of Galilee; that when a man who was possessed with all bad thoughts and was running on in a bad way, a drunkard and a fornicator, a man full of spite and malice, comes to his right mind, it is because Christ drives the devil out of him. And then we begin to believe that when men go out of the world, He does not leave them, but raises them again, as truly as He raised Lazarus in this world. We are dull in our faith just as the disciples were. But Christ can kindle it in us all by His Spirit, and we should ask that He will.

And sometimes it comes to pass that he makes men now-a-days, as He made Peter and James and John, feel that He who has been speaking to them in their private walks, and teaching them things they would never have learned but for Him, and curing their sicknesses, is indeed the King of glory, the Prince of all the earth. Sometimes men have felt, perhaps when they were kneeling at the Lord's Supper, eating the bread and drinking the wine—perhaps when they were in lonely chambers, or in prisons for righteousness' sake—that they were not with Him only, but with His saints, with those who had left the world, with the noble men of other days, with the friends whom they had lost out of their sight. All these have been drawn together by His cross; all have owned Him as their common Lord, who has died, and who lives.

Only three of the disciples were on the Mount. And only two or three, just at rare times, may feel as if they were carried into a brighter world, and as if they beheld things as they are, not hidden by the mists of our earth. I do not know to whom God grants such manifestations; but I have no doubt from what I have read that there are some, probably those who have some special work or suffering to go through—humble people, I dare to say, of whom the world takes no note. But this also we should remember, these bright visions soon pass away. A cloud comes over those who have enjoyed them; and to them, too, there comes a voice out of the cloud, 'This is my Son, hear Him.' That is to say, what you are to learn from the vision is to be more meek and gentle, as the Son of Man is; to observe more what He is saying to you in all common things; to be more thoughtful about other people, because He is thoughtful about them. Hear His commandment to be true and faithful in all your transactions with your fellow-men; hear Him warning you, when you are tempted to be vain and greedy; hear His voice checking you when you are exalted, and bidding you arise and be not afraid when you are downcast. You know it is the voice of the Son of God. And He tells you not to speak much of anything that merely concerns yourself, if you have ever so much reason to be thankful for it. Speak of His resurrection from the dead, which concerns all persons living as well as you.

And now you see how the remaining part of the story also belongs to us. Men who have had hours of quietness and peace and bright visions, do not like the noise and clatter of the crowd. They find it very distracting. They would rather forget that people are disputing, and that ministers of God are proving their weakness, and that men are tormented with all kinds of plagues and sorrows. But God does not let them forget it. In this world they are to live and work. If they are Christ's disciples, these are the sights they must witness continually, not those on the Mount. They must be continually taught, which is harder still, their own folly, and ignorance, and incapacity; and if they will get these lessons by heart, there are others and more cheering ones for them. Christ is in the crowd, as He was in the Mount. He is showing His power in the midst of noisy, disputatious men. He is doing what His disciples cannot do. He is at work to help fathers and children to whom no mortal can bring help. The disciples got at least a diviner teaching, they knew more of Christ, from what they saw below the mountain, than from what they saw upon it. They learnt more fully that Christ was the Son of Man, and

K

that He cares for all men; they learnt more that He was the Son of God, and that He had come into the world to do His Father's work. And so may all of us learn more of the Son of Man and the Son of God from our own sufferings and from the sufferings of others, than we could learn if we were carried out of the world and saw His countenance shining like the light, and Moses and Elias talking with Him.

But that vision was not granted to the disciples for nothing; and it is not for nothing that we are permitted to read of it in this distant land, so long after it has departed. It was to tell the disciples, and to tell us, that one day He who appeared on earth as a poor man, walking with poor men, and dying the death of a slave, would appear in the glory of His Father and of His holy angels; that Moses and Elijah, and every one of those who had done His work on earth, would be with Him. It was to tell them, and to tell us, that every human creature shall see Him when He is manifested in His glory; that all the mists which have hidden Him from us shall be scattered; that the quick and the dead shall alike hear His voice. It was to tell them and us that this glory will only confound us and overwhelm us if we are not listening to Him now, living for Him now; that if we are, if we are asking Him to purge us from our sins and make us true men, we shall long for His appearing to end the conflict and anguish of the world, and to set all things right.

SERMON XIV.

THE PUBLICAN.

Preached at Redmarley, 11th Sunday after Trinity, August 11, 1861.

"I tell you, this man went down to his house justified rather than the other: for every one that exalteth himself shall be abased, and every one that humbleth himself shall be exalted."—St. Luke xviii. 14.

Two men, it is said in the Gospel we have just read, went up into the temple to pray. They went to the same place: they went for the same end. They were both Jews and they went to the place in which the Lord God had told the Jews that He would meet with them and hear them. They went to ask that He would do what He had promised.

Our Lord says one of these men went back to his house justified rather than the other. He returned with a lighter, freer heart. He had got the thing he sought for; our Lord tells us this; and he knows it. The hearts of these men are open to Him. He understands what they desire. He understands why one obtains what he desires and the other misses it.

And He wishes us to understand the secret also; for

we are all interested in it. This story of the publican and the Pharisee is called a parable. That is to say, it is an example of what is going on in a thousand different places, in times thousands of years apart. It happened in the temple of Jerusalem. It happens in every English church. It happened when our Lord was upon earth; it happens in the year 1861.

What, then, was the difference between these two men—the Pharisee and the publican? Had the one who went down to his house justified, some great advantage over his neighbour? No; he had, to all appearances, great disadvantages. He was a man in bad repute. He belonged to a class of men who did many evil things. People charged him with sharing in them. You see what the Pharisee thought of him. He thanked God that he was not like that publican or tax-gatherer. He thought that the man who was praying a little way from him was very likely an unjust man or an extortioner; he knew that he had a bad name.

The Pharisee himself had a very good name. He was one of a class to whom the people looked up. He had a character to preserve. And he says—and for aught we know he says truly—that he had preserved it. He could not be accused of any crime against his fellow-creatures. He could not be accused of neglecting the service of his Creator.

So far all seems in his favour; all seems to go against the publican:. and what is more, the publican thinks so himself. He does not try to prove that he has done his duty to God or his duty to his neighbour. He does not believe that he has. Nay, he is sure that he has not. He does not venture to raise his eyes to heaven. He smites upon his breast. He says, "God be merciful to me a sinner."

And what comes of this? *That* comes of it which God had said should come. He had bidden men who had any load upon their hearts to come into His temple and lay it bare before Him. He had bidden those who had broken His law to own that they had broken it. He had invited those who were not serving Him as they wished to serve Him, frankly to tell Him that they were not. He had invited those who were not loving their neighbours as they wished to love them, not to keep that wrong to themselves, but to ask deliverance from it of Him. The publican had done this. He was not satisfied with himself; he said that he was not. He could not say much about his trouble or his need. Perhaps he did not know precisely what it was, just as we often feel a pain or a sickness without knowing where it is. But he had come into the presence of One who understood what he did not understand. His muttered words even would be interpreted rightly. He was seeking the God of mercy; he was seeking the Deliverer from sin. "Be merciful to me a sinner," was enough for him.

Therefore he went down to his house justified. He could not justify himself. God had justified him. He had given him a clean conscience and a right heart.

His sin did not cleave to him any longer, did not press him down, did not take the strength out of him. He could say, 'God counts it as His enemy even as I count it mine. He is my Lord; this sin is not my Lord, and shall not be. In His strength I will defy it.'

Now the Pharisee did not get this justification, for he did not desire it. He justified himself. He was content with his own thoughts and doings. He wanted nothing. He had prayed in the temple because he believed it was a proper and right thing to pray. He had not prayed because there was any divine blessing which he could not do without, any great curse from which he must be set free.

And so it will be, so it must be, our Lord says, always. Is it not reasonable? The God of grace and mercy gives to each that which he craves for; if we think all is well with us, He will leave us to try whether all is well. If we find that there is something not well, something that must be set right in us, He will set it right.

And yet, brethren, this is not all. God does not justify those who justify themselves, who trust in themselves that they are righteous, and despise others. But He does—like a merciful Father—show us that we cannot trust in ourselves, and that we are not righteous, and that we have no excuse for despising others. He lays bare the secret wrong that is in us. He make us see that we are just as likely to fall into sin, that we have just as little strength of our own to do what is right as any of our neighbours whom we have been looking down upon. He shows us that all our strength is in Him. He humbles us when we are exalted in our own conceit, just that He may exalt us when He has humbled us. That is the course of His wise and gracious government with every one of us. Let every one of us try to understand it, and then we shall profit by all the things that befall us. We shall profit by the foolish and wrong doings that we have committed in time past. We shall profit, above all, by the prayers that we offer when we are alone, and when we come to this house.

1. We shall profit by all that befalls us. If it is good and necessary for most of us to be humbled—if we cannot be anything or do anything right till we are humbled, then be sure God means all that He sends us for this purpose. Sometimes it may be a great trouble, sometimes it may be a little vexing trouble which overtakes us. One may do the work as well as the other. One may bring down our self-confidence as well as the other. God knows which will do it best for each of us. Or He may send us good and bright days. They may tend to our humiliation as much as the others. We may wonder what right we have to them; how such people as we should have blessings that we have done so little for. Anything may turn to the increase of our pride if we receive it without asking for God's Spirit to make it good. Anything may help to take the pride out of us if His Spirit comes with it.

2. Yes, and therefore I say a man's past transgres-

sions and his most easily-besetting sin may be used, if he will use them, for this end. Sometimes a person is inclined to forget all the things he has done amiss in past times, and would fain think they have nothing to do with him now. Then up starts the recollection of some one of them. It flashes across him as he lies on a sick bed: he cannot throw it off. Or it comes to him in another way. He thought he had got rid of some bad habit—of drinking perhaps. He supposes he is quite safe; but he meets an old companion. The old sin catches him and throttles him again. It was lying hid; but it was not gone. He said he had not that sin still; he deceived himself. Is that to make him despair? Is it to lead him to say, 'I must be the slave of this wicked power. I must confess the devil for my ruler.' No; it is to make him cry, 'God be merciful to me a sinner. I am worse and weaker than I knew. I find I cannot trust myself for an hour. The past evil comes back to me. It seems always present. But Thou, O God, canst raise me out of it. It drives me to Thee. Be merciful to me, not in sparing my sin, for that is my foe and my curse, but in separating me from it as far as the East is from the West. And I am separate from it as far as the East is from the West, when I am finding my refuge and my home in Thee.'

And so you will see what I meant when I said that our Lord is teaching us to-day what all our prayers at church are for, and what all our prayers at home are for.

The first words you hear in church are a call to confess your sins. The first act you join in with the minister is that of owning to the Almighty and most merciful Father that you have erred and strayed from His way like lost sheep. That is to say, we are all treated alike. No one is allowed to trust in himself that he is righteous, and to despise others. Each brings his own burden. Each says, "Be merciful to me a sinner." Each cries against his own wrong; each asks for help against his own guilt. And yet we all come together. There is a common salvation for us. We call upon God as the Father of us all. We call on Him in the name of Jesus Christ our Lord, who has redeemed us all; in whom there is no sin; in whom He loves all, and is satisfied with all. While each is trying to stand on his own ground, while each is pleased and satisfied with himself, there is nothing but discontent, envying, and backbiting. When each one gives up his own pretension to be good, and trusts in the good God, and believes that that God has given up His Son for his neighbours as well as for himself, and asks for the loving Spirit to dwell with us all and keep us one, then do we indeed become Christ's family on earth, part of that great family in heaven and earth, of which He is the head and elder brother. And we may be sure that as we kneel by our bedsides, or as we cry when we are out in the field or at our work, 'God be merciful to us sinners; keep us from doing this wrong thing; help us not to neglect this act of duty or of kindness,' He will present that prayer before God. It will be joined to the prayer of that publican in the temple, and to all the good prayers that have been offered since the world began. And the man who has poured it out will go to his home with a clean heart and right spirit, humbled in himself, exalted in God; waiting for the day when He who was humble, and lowly, and merciful, shall be revealed in the glory of His Father and the holy angels, and when all pride, and vanity, and sin shall be banished out of His universe.

SERMON XV.

THE SPIRIT AND THE FLESH.

Preached at Redmarley, Morning of the 14th Sunday after Trinity, September 1, 1861.

"I say then, Walk in the Spirit, and ye shall not fulfil the lust of the flesh."—GALATIANS v. 16.

THE Galatians, to whom St. Paul wrote these words, were a warm-hearted people, but they were very changeable. At one time they were exceedingly fond of St. Paul. They would have plucked out their own eyes, he says, to give them to him, if that would have done him any good. But within a short time they began to suspect him; they listened to people who said that he had deceived them, and that he was no true apostle. They counted him an enemy, and many of them became his enemies. How had this come to pass? It had come to pass thus: St. Paul had brought them a good message. He said that the Eternal God had sent His Son into the world to adopt them into His family, to make them His own sons and daughters. He said that through His Son God had sent His Spirit to dwell with them, that they might know Him and love Him, and that they might love one another. The Galatians had listened to these words; they had never heard any that were like them before. They had thought the powers above looked very enviously at them, and wanted a great many things of them; they thought they had done wrong, and offended these powers; they thought if there was one power greater than all, they must have offended Him most, and He must be the most angry with them. How wonderful it was to be told that the Lord of all— He who had created them—loved them; that He felt to them as a father feels to children who have forgotten him and gone away from his house; that He was Himself fetching them back; that they were not to turn away from Him because they had done bad things, but might turn to Him, and He would put the evil from them, and blot it out. And how wonderful to hear that they had the Spirit of the Father near them at all times to help them and strengthen them; how wonderful to have all this sealed and assured to them by this token, that they were baptized into the name of the Father, and of the Son, and of the Holy Ghost. And yet the hearts of these Galatians said this good news must be true; and they would have been glad to put out their own eyes for his sake who had brought them the news.

But as time went on, they began to feel bad thoughts rising in them; and they yielded to these bad thoughts, and bad acts came out of them; they were bitter and cruel to one another; they cheated each other; they fell into wantonness and drunkenness, just as they had done when they were heathens—just as the heathen people around them did. 'Well,' they began to say to themselves, 'but how can this be if St. Paul was right in what he said to us at first; did he not speak of our being cleansed from our sins? did he not speak of our being made new men? But our sins are with us still; we are just the same now that we were before.' Then came people who said to them, 'Yes, Paul has indeed led you wrong. This baptism into the name of Christ does not mean what he would persuade you that it means. You are not really taken to be children of God. If you would get any advantage from Christ's coming, you must become like us Jews. You must come under our law; then perhaps God may give you some blessings hereafter. But you must not begin with thinking that you are already delivered and brought into God's family.' The Galatians gave heed to what these men said, and so they counted St. Paul for their enemy.

St. Paul was very much grieved; but the pain they caused him was nothing. He knew that he had told them the truth, and that these people who had come among them and slandered him were not telling them the truth. He knew that they wanted the truth which he had told them; that they could not be right and good men without it. But how then could he account for their having fallen into these bad ways? How could he justify what he had said to them about their being children of God and members of Christ, and of their having the Spirit of God with them to help and teach them? Could he have meant that really? Must he not have meant it for some of them and not for others?

No! what St. Paul said to all, he intended all to receive. If it was true about one, it was true about another. If *any* who were baptized could say, 'God has given us the sign that we are His children,' *all* who were baptized could say, 'God has given us the sign that we are His children.' And if they believed that, they would soon find what enemies they had who were trying to hinder them from acting as if they were His children. They would soon find that they had a flesh in them that was leading them to think all manner of wrong things, and to do all manner of wrong things. And if they gave way to that flesh of theirs, it would be a very cruel master to them, and would drive them very hard. What then? Were they not to count themselves God's children because this was so? That would be just as if any son or daughter on earth were to say, 'I have no father or mother,' because he had been rebellious against his father and mother, and had not chosen to do the things they commanded. That would be to shrink from confessing how much they had offended, and what a gracious loving God they had grieved. That would be saying that He had changed because they had changed.

That would be cutting themselves off from the only way of being set free from the evil and being made right. And St. Paul told them plainly that if they tried to keep God's law when they had ceased to believe in this covenant that He had made with them as His sons and daughters, they would not be able to keep it; they would fight against it; they would do the things which it told them not to do.

But he says in the Epistle we have read to-day, "Walk in the Spirit, and ye shall not fulfil the lust of the flesh."

What does that mean, "Walk in the Spirit?" It means: Live as if this were true which I have told you, and as if you were God's children, and God were looking upon you as a Father, and as if He were wishing you to do right, and were helping you to do right, and were giving you His own good and right Spirit, that you might do right. And then you "shall not fulfil the lusts of the flesh." They will rise up in you; they will tell you that you must obey them. But you can say, 'No, we are God's children; we will not yield to them. They may be very strong, but His Spirit is stronger, we will yield to that.' For he goes on, "The flesh lusteth against the spirit, and the spirit against the flesh, and these two are contrary" to each other. He does not say that about other men more than about himself. He could tell other men that it was so with them, because he found out that it was so with him. It was a continued battle in him. He had something in him which was looking up, desiring what was good, and wanting to know what was good, and asking to be good. He had something in him which was looking down, and wishing for things that were not good, and not caring to find out what was good and what was evil; and choosing to have its own way, and not to ask to be guided into the right way. It was so with St. Paul; he could confidently say to each of the Galatians, 'It is so with you, and it is so with me.' "And, therefore," he says, "we do not the things that we would." The bad man does not do all the bad things that he thinks of; there is a right spirit checking him. The good man does not do all the good things that he thinks of, there is a flesh checking him. 'But yet,' he says, 'you may be led by the Spirit. The weakest of you may; those who feel yourselves weak, and desire to be led by such a gracious and loving Lord. And then you will not be under the law.' *That* he says in answer to those people who told the Galatians that they must not think that God was their Father; that they must come under the law which God gave men before He sent His Son to claim them as His children. He reminds them always that that is their state and their glory; they must not give that up if they wish to get the better of their bad inclinations. 'You are led by the Spirit,' he tells them, 'because you are God's children; you are not servants but sons, and, therefore, He sends His Spirit into your hearts, that you may say, Abba, Father!'

Then he goes on to tell them, in very plain language, what kind of things they would do if they were left to themselves and did just the things which their flesh stirred them up to do. "Now the works of the flesh are manifest, which are these—adultery, fornication, hatred, variance, emulations, wrath, strife, seditions, heresies, envyings, murders, drunkenness, revelling, and such like." As much as to say— If you look at the world and see what things are going on in it—how wives are separated from their husbands, how men and women live to ruin each other, how nations fight with each other, what strifes there are in neighbourhoods and families, how men quarrel about the least things and the greatest, even about the religion which should unite them together, how thousands and ten thousands become beasts instead of men through drunkenness, how they give themselves to revelling, and out of that comes hatred and often murder—if you look at all these things, you will understand what there is working in us all, and what we should become if we were our own masters. And he says of these things, "I tell you now, as I told you in times past, that they which do such things shall not inherit the kingdom of God." That is as much as to say, 'I have not changed my mind in the least. I always said to you that these things are the curse and damnation of all people who give way to them. It does not signify who they are, whether they call themselves Christians or heathens, they who do such things choose the devil for their king, and ask him to rule over them.' But then he goes on, 'there are other works doing on this earth, thanks be to God its King. There is love in this world, there is joy in the earth, there is peace on the earth; you see parents who are caring about their children; you see men and women who are doing kind, and gentle, and good acts; you see people in sickness and poverty who are full of faith and trust; you see people who are bearing injuries meekly; you see people who are restraining themselves when they are tempted to drunkenness.'

Where do all these good fruits come from? They come, as I told you before, from the Spirit of God. They are the things which God Himself is working in us to do. Well, if you believe that, you can take your choice. You may walk in the Spirit, and claim your place as God's children, as baptized men; or you may follow the flesh, and then you will always be ready for some of those dark and devilish works of which I spoke to you just now. If you take the first course, you will never find God's law against you; it will always be on your side. In you will be crucified, in Christ's name and in His strength, those things which God hates and which make men miserable.

Now, brethren, remember that all this is spoken to us. Just as St. Paul and the Galatians had this flesh and this Spirit fighting in them, so have you and I. Just as the flesh was drawing them down to low, vile things, to those things that ruin the body and soul and set us at war with each other, so it is with you and me. We are not different, so far, from other men. Christians have not a whit better natures than Jews or heathen. Oftentimes they seem to be much worse; oftentimes Jews and heathen do good things which should make us ashamed. And why is this? If we believed in baptism we should have obeyed its teaching. We should know that all the good which is in them would come from God's dear and loving Spirit; that whatever kindness, gentleness, truth, there is in any, comes from the goodness and gentleness and truth of God. And then we should say, 'Oh, God! Thou hast made us Thy children: Thou hast told us Thou art our Father in Christ Jesus our Lord. Hold us fast to Thee. Fulfil Thy promise of writing Thy law in our hearts by the Spirit. Never let us go out of this bond. Our godfathers and godmothers renounced for us the service of the world and the flesh and the devil. They said they were not our masters and should not be our masters. Help us to say the same every day and every hour. Help us to fight the good fight of faith. For it is only by faith in Thee that we can do anything that is right, or avoid anything that is wrong; only while we believe that Thou art altogether good, and that Thou art our Father, and that Thou hast delivered us from our sins, and that Thou art always on our side; it is only then we put to death our lusts and our hatred and our revelling, only then we can be meek and gentle and brave and true, as Thou hast made us to be.'

SERMON XVI.

MAN'S DOMINION.

Preached at Redmarley, Afternoon of the 14th Sunday after Trinity, September 1, 1861.

"Oh, Lord, our Governor, how excellent is Thy Name in all the earth."
PSALM viii.

WE have been reading this Psalm together this afternoon. Let us try if we cannot get some good out of it that will go through the week—that will make us rejoice more together in the bright skies, and the harvest, and in all other good things that we receive at God's hands.

I suppose the person who wrote it was out on some evening or night when the moon and the stars were shining very clearly. Perhaps he was out on the hills with his flock of sheep; for you know that a shepherd sang a great number of these psalms; one who, the Scriptures say, was taken from following the ewes great with young, that he might be a leader and shepherd of the people.

That shepherd must have seen many beautiful nights

and mornings whilst he was about his work. But I doubt if merely seeing them would have done much for him. Many of us have such sights often before us, and yet we do not mind them at all; they are not much more to us than they would be to a blind man. But David had believed that He who created the heavens, and stretched them out, was the Lord God of his fathers and of him; that He had cared for his fathers, and that He cared for him; that He had desired them to trust Him and know Him and worship Him. He sang songs to God because he believed in Him as a helper and as a friend; as One from whom every good thing, and every good thought and good work, must come.

Well, that was what was most in his mind on the evening that I spoke of. "Oh Lord," he says, "our Governor, how excellent is Thy name in all the earth; Thou that hast set Thy glory above the heavens." "Oh Lord, our Governor," that is, the governor of us— Thy people Israel, whom Thou hast watched over and brought out of the house of bondage, and to whom Thou hast given a good and righteous law; and whom Thou defendest against our enemies. Surely Thy great name is not confined to us. It is "excellent in all the earth." Thou rulest over all this wide world, however far it may spread, though there may be countries in it that I have never heard of, or dreamed of. Yea, Thou canst not be confined to this earth. These heavens over my head speak of a *glory* that goes further than I can think or dream of. This moon, and these stars, what are they?

Who can tell me? I only know they show forth Thy glory; Thou that art our King and our Deliverer.

Then a thought comes to him of his own littleness. He is venturing to think of God, and to pray to Him; he, a mere child! Yes, he says, Thou hast ordained me to do so: Thou hast put these thoughts and praises into my heart and my lips. Thou choosest babes and sucklings to praise Thee; Thou showest them what beauty and joy there is in Thy universe. When the enemy and the darkness say, I have spoiled it all; I have brought death and sin and misery into it; I am the lord of it—No, cry these babes and sucklings, Thou art not the lord of it. Evil and death have not conquered the Lord, our Governor. See how these glorious heavens, that last over from generation to generation, bear witness of Him; see how they tell of a living and unchangeable God.

Yes, he goes on—" I will consider the heavens the work of Thy hands, the moon and the stars which Thou hast ordained." It is a great strength and comfort and wonder to consider them, and to be sure that they are Thine, and that Thou art our God.

But then, when I consider them, I cannot help thinking again what poor beggarly creatures we are. Can it be that Thou who madest these heavens carest for such worms? "What is man that Thou art mindful of him; and the son of man that Thou visitest him?" he stops for a moment at that question; it staggers him. These glorious heavens, and then the little creature who lasts at the best but three-score years and ten, and who may be cut off in an instant; who is weaker than any of the animals about him; whom an insect may kill; who spends his time in such trifles—what is this man, that Thou the creator of the heavens and earth, should think about him, should even want him? But he recollects himself—He does not speak meanly of man, for all he looks so poor and contemptible. "Thou madest him lower than the angels, to crown him with glory and worship."

This poor creature—man—may be very weak, the weakest of Thy creatures; but there is a spirit in him. He is more like an angel than all these beautiful and glorious things which I look at. Yea, and though he is lower than the angels; though he suffers sorrow and death; I believe that Thou hast permitted these only that thou mayest crown him with glory and worship. I believe Thou hast made him to show forth Thy glory and worship more than angels even can show it forth. I may not be able to see how that should be, but I cannot doubt it. For I see that "Thou makest him to have dominion over the works of Thy hands. Thou hast put all things in subjection under his feet. All sheep and oxen, yea, and the beasts of the field, the fowls of the air, and the fishes of the sea, and whatsoever walketh through the paths of the sea." Very wonderful indeed that that should be so, and yet David knew that it was so. Flocks of sheep, droves of oxen, obeyed him, a feeble man; they did the things which he bade them do. He was able to direct them, not by the strength of his arms, but by the power of his words. He was able to direct them best when he was most gentle with them. With the wild beasts of the field—those that preyed upon other creatures—it was different; these he had power to kill if he could not tame them. David told King Saul how when a bear and a lion came out against his flock might was given him to slay them; *that* assured him that he should have might to slay the huge Philistine who was defying the armies of his country. In all these ways he was taught that it is the spirit that is in a creature—not its size or its fierceness—which makes it victorious, and that this spirit is what God put into man when He made Him after His own image. Therefore, He did not doubt that some day or other it would be shown him how glorious man is; how truly God had put all things under his feet. It was hard to expect that when he saw how mean human beings made themselves; how they stooped to all the animals and even worshipped them; how they seemed to prize the food which the fowls of the air, and the fishes of the sea, supplied them with, more than their own bodies and souls; how wicked they were, while the birds and beasts and fishes were innocent—it was hard to think that one day men should be shown to be indeed what God had made them to be, in spite of their own wilfulness. And yet he who wrote this psalm could not believe in God and not believe that what He had said must come to pass. It must be shown that neither the moon nor the stars were so great and divine as the lowest human being that they shine upon. He was sure of this, and therefore he could say again, " Oh Lord, our Governor, how excellent is Thy name in all the world." Thy purpose will prevail, however we may try to set it at nought. Thou wilt make Thy name glorious, and men shall be glorified in Thee.

Was the psalmist mistaken? We were reading a few Sundays ago the Epistle to the Hebrews. That letter was written to the Jews who heard the Psalms full a thousand years after David's death. It was written forty or fifty years after the death of Him whom we call the Son of David and the Son of God—Jesus Christ our Lord. And the writer says in it, We do not yet see all things put under now, as the psalmist says they are meant to be ; " but we see Jesus, who for the suffering of death was made a little lower than the angels, crowned with glory and honour." What has that to do with what we have been speaking of this afternoon ? Everything. " When we consider the heavens and the earth the work of God's hands, the moon and the stars which He hath ordained," we must needs begin to think, as the psalmist does, " What is man? "—this poor, wretched, sinful, dying creature—"that Thou art mindful of him." And then we who believe in God the Father Almighty, Maker of heaven and earth, and in Jesus Christ, His only Son our Lord, can make answer and say, 'Yea, verily, but the Son of God, by whom the world was made, and all the host of them, was born of a woman, became a poor man upon this earth of ours; and He, while He was upon earth, showed that the winds and the waves and all creatures were subject to Him. And then He suffered the death of the Cross, and was buried and went into hell, and rose again from the dead, and sitteth at the right hand of His Father. And, therefore, no people shall frighten us and crush us with talking about the heavens and all the host of them. We verily believe that a Man is above all these. We verily believe that One who is of our nature, and who bore our sins and died our death, is the King who was before all ages, and so He shall live on through ages upon ages. And, therefore, we are sure that God has not created all things in vain; and that it is a truth, and no lie, that He has created man in His own image; and that every little baby just born has a glory upon it which does not belong to all works of God's hands, let them be as great and glorious as they may. And we believe, moreover, that He who has exalted His own Son to be our King, has sent His Spirit to raise up our spirits, that we may not be poor crawling creatures, meaner than all the things we see and handle, but that we may look up to Him where He is, and may call His Father our Father, and may join with Angels and Archangels in blessing Him for all the works of His hands.'

And, my friends, this is what we have desired for that little infant whom we have just received into the congregation of Christ's flock, and signed with the sign of the cross. We said that that child was one of the race for which Christ died; we said that that child was one of that family of which He is the elder Brother and the Head; we said that this child is a spirit child, and is therefore greater and diviner, not only than the sheep and the oxen, the fowls of the air, and the fishes of the sea, but than the earth and the air and the sky about us. Do not forget that, you that are parents. Do not forget what treasures God has put into your hands. And since you know that you cannot take care of them yourselves, do not forget that you have committed them to God; that He has promised them greater blessings than you can ask for or dream of, and that that promise He for His part will most surely keep and perform.

Take every autumn as it comes round and brings you in the fruits of the tiny seeds that you sowed last autumn, or last spring, as a witness and pledge that He does not neglect any, the least things, and that He does not merely give you rain to nourish them, and sun to ripen them, but that He gives you what is much better—power to work, and wisdom to know how you should work in the right way. Thank Him for not scattering the fruits in your path without your labour; you would soon become miserable heartless creatures if He did. Thank Him for caring more to make you brave and true than to make you easy and weak and self-indulgent. Thank Him for having set you over the sheep and the oxen, and the fowls of the air, and the fishes of the sea. Thank Him for having given you the moon and stars, not only to direct you in your path, but to make you wonder and ask after Him. Thank Him that He has given you all these lesson-books for your children as well as you. Thank Him because He has said there will be a day in which He will gather up all things unto Christ, both things in heaven and things on earth, unto Him who is the Head over all His universe; and when every child, and every star, and every animal, and every flower, shall be seen to have been created by infinite love for His infinite glory.

SERMON XVII.

GOD AND MAMMON.

Preached at Redmarley, Morning of the 15th Sunday after Trinity, September 8, 1861.

" No man can serve two Masters, for either he will hate the one and love the other, or else he will hold to the one and despise the other—ye cannot serve God and Mammon."—ST. MATTHEW vi. 24.

OUR Lord Jesus Christ knew what was in man. He knew what the people in Judæa were thinking and were trying to do eighteen hundred and sixty years ago. He knew what the people in England would be thinking and trying to do in our day. The people of Judæa professed to worship one God—the Lord God of their fathers; the Lord God who had delivered their fathers out of bondage, who had given them bread and water as they came through the wilderness; who had promised them a good land in which they should dwell; who had been with them and with their seed after them. That was the God to whom the temple was built. That was the God to whom the priests offered sacrifices. But when they were not in the temple they were about their farms and their merchandise. It was their duty to be about their farms and their merchandise. They were set in the world to till the land. The sea was given them that they might send their ships across it, and might send their good things to other lands, and receive the good things of those lands in exchange. God had appointed the sea and the land; God had set them their work to do. How cheerfully they would have done these works if they had believed that! With what glad hearts they would have risen in the morning if they had been sure that the good God, their deliverer and their friend, was rousing them to their day's labour, and would be with them all through it! How pleasantly they would have laid themselves down at night if they had remembered that He who never slumbers nor sleeps was watching over them while they slept! How comfortable it would have been to remember all the day, 'He is our God and our neighbours' God. He helps them to work as He helps us; He cares for them as He cares for us.'

But it was not so. These Jews, when they were at their farms and their merchandise, did not remember the God whom they had worshipped in the temple. They thought chiefly of what they were to get by their labour; how much money would come of it. Each thought, 'How much more money can I get than my neighbour? How can I hinder him from having the profits that I want for myself?' What came of that? Were they without a God, while they were thinking and plotting this way? No, my friends; men cannot shake off the thought of *some* God, try as hard as they will. They may forget the good God, the true God, the

Maker of heaven and earth—their deliverer and friend. But then they will make to themselves a god; they will make him out of their own hard cruel fancies; they will make him like themselves. So it was with the Jews. They loved money, and money became their god. They did not know it; they would not have confessed it—but so it was. And a very hard savage god it was which they set up for themselves. Not a helper, not a deliverer at all—but a bitter tyrant; not one who cared for all, but one who set up this man and scorned that; not a god who made the people better that served him, but one who made them meaner and baser. This is the god whom our Lord calls mammon—a false god, a god that men had formed for themselves, but all the worse and more mischievous for that.

Now, what our Lord tells the Jews here is, that they could not have these two gods—the gracious loving God of their fathers; the God who sets captives free; who gives liberally to all; who seeks the good of all—and this selfish hard-hearted mammon-god—"Ye cannot serve God and mammon." If you will love mammon, you will hate the good God; if you hold to God, you will despise mammon. You cannot worship one god on the Sabbath days, and the other through the week; you must have the same on the Sabbath days and in the week. If you worship mammon in the week, it will be to him you bring your prayers and offerings on the Sabbaths. You will each come to get him to do something for you, not for your neighbours; you will each of you come to persuade him not to be your enemy. And again, if you worship the true living God on the Sabbath days, you will have Him with you on all other days.

So He goes on—"Therefore, I say unto you, take no thought for your life what ye shall eat, nor yet for your body what ye shall put on." How is that? Did He mean that His disciples were to be idlers; that they were to trust in God to give them food for their bodies, and clothing for their bodies, without working for it? No, my friends; His disciples were to be hard workers; they were to hate begging. St. Paul said to some of those who had got this notion into their heads of being idle and trusting God, "Those of you that will not work shall not eat." But our Lord knew that it does not make men work better to be anxious and miserable about what should come of their work. He knew that makes bad workers; He knew that turned workers into beggars. They despised getting food and clothing by the labour of their hands, so they ruined themselves and their children by telling stories and asking other people for food or money. So he says—'Do not you act so. Believe you have not a cruel hard mammon-god over you, but a gracious, loving, tender Father, the very same that you pray to in the temple. And, therefore, do not be anxious about what shall come of your labour; trust that to Him. Does He not give you life every day, and is not that more than the meat by which you support life? Did He not give you these curious wonderful bodies of yours?

And is not that more than the dress that you put on your bodies? Look,' He says, 'at these birds that are flying about in the air; does your Father in heaven let them starve? Does not He find food for them? And do not you think that you men whom He has made in His own likeness, whom He so loves that He has sent His Son to take your flesh upon Him, do not you think that you are better than the birds? Suppose you were ever so anxious to be tall men; could you become tall men by being anxious about it? Would that add one inch to your stature? So you see it must be God who is providing for you every minute, every hour. It must be He who is causing your babies to grow. It must be He who is giving you all that you want. Cannot you trust Him?'

And then about your dress. Look at the flowers that grow about the fields and the hedgerows. Do you think any king had ever such beautiful raiment as these have? Do not you know that all the kings of the earth can do is to imitate the beauty of these flowers; to get some robes that look a little like them? And yet these flowers in the fields will be soon mown down. You cast them away; you count them for nothing. Well, do you not think that the God who thinks of these will think of you? Oh, ye of little faith!

'Therefore,' He says, 'do not be anxious and miserable about what you shall eat and what you shall drink. It is all very well for the heathen to do so, for they do not know that they have a Father. They fancy their gods have a grudge against them, and want them to buy their favour with a great many gifts. But you are told that you have a Father who knows just what you want, just what strength you require for each day. Be remembering Him. Say to yourselves, " He is the King of all the earth, and we are His own children." He wants us to be right, good children. Let us ask Him to make us so; right in all our acts; right in all our thoughts; and then He will take care to send us whatever besides He knows is good for us.'

"Take, therefore," He says, "no thought for the morrow;" that is, do not be fidgety and restless about what shall come to-morrow. You have enough to do each day; enough of evil to bear each day. You need not make yourselves so many trials by fancying what you may have another day. Let that alone; only trust God, the good God who is the same yesterday, to-day, and for ever. And so you will have the true life, the life which will not pass away for ever and ever.

Now, my friends, I said when I began, that our Lord Jesus Christ knew what the Jews were tempted to think and to do at that time; and that He knew what we should be tempted to think and to do at this time. Our temptation is the same as theirs was, the very same. We come here to church on Sunday. We call God our Almighty and most merciful Father. We say that we believe He gave His only begotten Son for us all, to die for us, and that He ever lives for us at His Father's right hand. We say that we believe He so cared for us as to send His own Holy and Loving Spirit to dwell with us, that He might teach us the things we want to know, and help us to do the things we want to do. That is our Sunday doctrine. Then we go out to our different works during the week; and we forget that the God we have heard of in church is the God who rules over our houses and our fields; who gives us children; who enables us to work; who supports our lives. A man who has money, thinks, 'How can I get a little more of this, and a little more still, and a little more still?' A poor man thinks, 'How can I keep myself from starving? for surely all things are against me; the Ruler of the world is against me.' And so, brethren, all of us come by one way or other to get these thoughts into our hearts, that mammon, the money-god, is somehow our master; that he has the upper hand; that our main business is to serve him. I say we are all tempted to this faith. I know that I am. And I know that if I am tempted to it in the week, I must be tempted to it on Sundays. I cannot have two Gods—one for the world and one for the church. I shall have mammon in both if I have him in either. And I know not, brethren, how we should escape having him in both, if it were not for these dear words of our Lord Christ, and for the dear acts which He has done to make them good. I know we should set up a tyrant and worship him, even the cruel, brutal tyrant—this money-god—if He had not come down from heaven to show us what our Father is, and how He cares for us, and seeks after us, if He had not become a poor man, and had not died upon the cross and risen again and ascended on high. All this bears witness to every clergyman and to every one of his hearers, to every rich man and to every poor man, that there is a Father over all, upon whom they may all depend in all times of their tribulation, and in all times of their wealth, and in the hour of death and in the day of judgment; One to whom they may give up themselves and their children, their bodies and their souls, as to a faithful and loving Creator who has so loved them that He gave up His own Son for them all. Yes, verily, brethren, and it is not I only who preach to you of this Father. The birds of the air preach of Him, the flowers of the field preach of Him; all these say: 'The mammon-god did not create us; the Father of the Lord Jesus Christ created us. His love has called us into existence. His love watches over the life of every man and woman and child.'

Therefore, do you men and women and children trust in Him, and give your hearts to Him, and ask Him to make you right and true, and to make you love each other as He loves you.

And ask Him to deliver you from the worship of the mammon-god; for in very deed he is the false evil spirit, the devil who is seeking to destroy those bodies and souls in hell which the Son of God died to save, and to make heirs of Eternal Life.

SERMON XVIII.

THE GLORY OF THE CROSS.

Preached at Redmarley, Afternoon of the 15th Sunday after Trinity, September 8, 1861.

" But God forbid that I should glory save in the Cross of Christ Jesus my Lord, by Whom the world is crucified unto me, and I unto the world."—GALATIANS vi. 14.

I EXPLAINED to you last Sunday how the Galatians had been drawn away to think St. Paul their enemy, though they had once counted him their best friend. He had written them a letter with his own hand (commonly he employed some of his companions to write for him), to tell them how they had mistaken him, and how much they had injured themselves by listening to the people who slandered him. The words we read in the Epistle for this morning are the end of his letter. They are good for us to read and to think of, because they show us what bound St. Paul to these Galatians for all that they had used him so ill, and what binds him to us, for all that we were born into the world so many hundreds of years after he left it.

The Galatians had been persuaded that they must

become like the Jews, and must have the sign of the covenant if they would have God's favour. St. Paul was a Jew himself, a Hebrew of the Hebrews; he says he had once been very proud of his privileges as a Jew. He had once despised all other nations and thought that they were cut off from God; but he had cast away that pride; he had found that he was not in himself a whit better than other people, let him have been born where he might, let him have had ever so many advantages, ever such a good law, ever such a holy covenant. He could not, he would not, glory then on this ground any more. And he made the Galatians understand that if they tried to find this excuse for glorying, they would be sadly disappointed. They would not be able to keep God's law any better than they had kept it hitherto, if they made themselves like the Jews; they would not love one another or love God better. But he had not given over glorying because he did not glory in being unlike the rest of men. And he would not have the Galatians cease from glorying, though that was no good pretence for it. What could he glory in then? In that which did not separate him from his neighbours, but united him to his neighbours. In that which did not separate him from those who quarrelled with him, but was as great a blessing to them as to him. In that which did not belong to one people or to one time, but to all people and all time.

"God forbid," he says, "that I should glory save in the Cross of Christ Jesus my Lord."

Now just think what that means. The Romans had many ways of putting men to death, but there was one way which was the most shameful of all, one way which they kept for slaves and for people who had committed the greatest crimes, that was the death of crucifixion, a death of hanging on a cross. When St. Paul came preaching of Jesus as the Son of God; people listened to him for a while. They said, 'Yes; it is just possible that some great ruler may have come upon earth, or some very wise man who deserves that name.' But when he said, 'He whom I say is the Son of God, is Jesus of Nazareth, who was called a carpenter's son, and who was crucified by Pontius Pilate, the Roman governor'—then they cried out, 'How monstrous! Can you expect us to believe that? To think of the God of Heaven making himself known to us in a man who underwent such a death as this!' But St. Paul said, 'I can proclaim to you no other. That is the King to whom I bow. That is the Son of God in whom I believe.' Yes, and that is the King, the Son of God, whom you need, one and all of you. You want a King who can stoop to the state of the lowest and most wretched of His subjects. You want a Son of God who shows that the love of God is stronger than the wickedness of man, and than the ingratitude of man. You want a Son of God who can show that love is stronger than death. Any other will not avail you. Any other is not a King and a Saviour and a Son of God for sinful men. Any other is not a King and a

Saviour, and a Son of God for dying men. Any other is not a King, and a Saviour, and a Son of God for all men,—for men of every kindred and tribe; for all times; for the rich and poor; the wise and the unwise; for the man that is highest in the world's esteem, and for the outcast that is most trodden under foot. A crucified Lord is for all of these and for each of them. If He is the Son of God, the Image of His Father, then I can know what God is; what His character is; what His will to all human creatures is. If he is King of men, then I can know what sort of government men are under; what hope there is that they may overcome their enemies. And so he says, 'Since I cannot glory in myself, or in my descent, or in my difference from other people, any longer, I will glory in this, I will think of this, the cross of Christ, and I will boast of that, and be proud of that; I will say, He who hung there is my Lord. He who hung there is the Christ with whom God is well pleased. I will exult in Him because I know that He has redeemed me who would have been a poor slave of my own lusts and my own vanity if I had been left to myself. I will exult in Him, because He has redeemed all mankind as well as me; because there is no creature in any corner of God's wide universe whom He has been ashamed to call His brother. That is my warrant for boasting in this Cross, and nothing can take that right from me. If it is said that I am good for nothing, I confess it, therefore I glory in this Cross. If it is said that death and the grave have set their mark upon me, I confess it, therefore I glory in this Cross. If it is said that I cannot make out any reason why God should care for me any more than for any vagabond on the earth, I confess it, therefore I glory in this Cross. If it is said that the Cross itself was humiliating and degrading, I confess it, therefore I glory in Him who submitted to the Cross.'

And so he goes on. " By whom the world is crucified unto me, and I unto the world." That is as if he had said, 'I know perfectly well that this seems to Jews and Gentiles both—to those who call themselves God's people, and to those who worship idols—very strange, and ridiculous, and contemptible. It seemed to me as strange, and ridiculous, and contemptible, as it could to any one. But since I hold this to be the sign of my deliverance and of the world's deliverance, since this is what fastens me to all men and makes me care for all men, I cannot much mind their opinion or even my own opinion. The nails of this Cross go through the world's opinions, and my own. I know very well how one man glories against another, and one nation against another, one religious society against another. I know how I have gloried against my fellow-men, but now I cannot do that any more.' The Son of God is lifted up above all the conceit and arrogance of me and of you, and of all the people in the earth, let them be who or what they may. That, I take it, is at

least a little part of the meaning of these words—
"By whom the world is crucified unto me, and I unto
the world." It may be a very little part indeed, you
may find a great deal more of what it means hereafter;
I hope you, and I hope I, shall. If we hold fast to
the first part of the sentence and determine we will live
upon that, we shall be sure to find out something more
of the length and depth and breadth of the latter part
every day. Yes; each of you may do that; for consider, my friends, what is all·I have been saying, all
that St. Paul has been saying, good for, if it does not
declare what every creature upon earth may delight in,
what may lift every creature upon earth above the
earth, yes, may lift them out of a deep beneath the
earth. Why should St. Paul glory in the Cross of
Christ, if not because "Christ being in the form of
God, took upon Him the form of a servant, and was
made subject to death, even the death of the cross.
Wherefore God hath highly exalted Him, giving Him
a name which is above every name." And if it be so,
each one of us who is furthest from St. Paul's stature of
holiness may begin to do just what he did. We may
swear that we will glory in nothing save the Cross of
Christ, not because we are strong, but because we are
weak; not because we are great, but because we are
little; not because we have deserved anything of God,
but because we have erred and strayed from Him. We
may glory in the Cross of Christ because He bore it
that He might claim fellowship with all of us, and

might raise us out of all our sins, and might make of our crosses blessings, and love-tokens to us.

And if we do glory in the Cross of Christ, we may be sure that we are doing what the angels in heaven and the spirits of just men made perfect are doing. We shall be entering into the song of triumph; for it is this, "Worthy is the Lamb that was slain to receive glory, and dominion, and praise, and honour." And in that song, we are told, all that are on the earth, and all that are under the earth, will surely join.

SERMON XIX.

THE WIDOW OF NAIN'S SON.

Preached at Redmarley, 16th Sunday after Trinity, September 15th, 1861.

"And it came to pass the day after, that He went into a city called Nain; and many of His disciples went with Him and much people. Now when He came nigh to the gate of the city, behold, there was a dead man carried out, the only son of his mother, and she was a widow; and much people of the city was with her. And when the Lord saw her, He had compassion on her, and said unto her, Weep not. And He came and touched the bier, and they that bare him stood still."—ST. LUKE vii. 11—14.

THERE are not many instances of our Lord raising the dead told us in the Gospels. The daughter of Jairus, and Lazarus, and this one of the widow of Nain's son, are, I think, all: and I think it is good for us that there should be no more. We are all ready enough to fancy, as I said to you once before, that those who were upon earth when our Lord was here in the flesh, were treated better than we are. If widows who are weeping for their only sons in our day and our land were to think that all the widows in Galilee and Judæa at that time had their children given back to them, they might ask,

'Why were we not born there? Why are we so far from that blessed two years?' But if they only read of this one widow of Nain—they may begin to consider that that must have been intended as a sign to a multitude of people beside her; to them amongst the rest. And then they may ask, 'And what is it a sign of? How are we better for the sign? Will it give us any comfort in our trouble?' Let us look at the story and see.

It is a common story enough. Out of the gate of a city a body is carried to be buried. That is all that most would have said who saw the funeral passing. A few may have asked, 'Whose is it?' A few will have known that it was the widow's son. A few will have cared both for him and for her. But there is One who meets the bier; He is called in the Gospels the Son of Man. He, it is said, saw the widow, and had compassion upon her. He knew exactly what was passing in her mind, all the thoughts that she had about her son; all her recollections of him; all that she could not tell to any one else, or make any one else understand; all her anxiety about what he had been, and what he was then. Her friends might say a great many words in her ear— some good, some foolish. One or two of their words might go down into her heart. But He had compassion upon her—that is to say, He bore her pain with her; He felt it Himself in His own heart. He did not stand aloof from any one of her pains and perplexities. He went into them as she could not do. It is written, "Himself took our infirmities;" and that thought must mean more than I or any one can imagine—it must mean this, that He entered into the trials and infirmities of all human beings. Well, then, the compassion of Jesus the Son of Man, for this particular woman, is a sign of His compassion for all who are going through the trial which she went through. I say for *all*. We are not told that there was anything peculiar in this widow of Nain. She was a woman who had lost her husband and her son; that is all we know of her. No doubt she felt her loss as if no one had felt the same before, and as if no one could feel it after. Every one does; every one feels the whole burden of death pressing upon herself. And He bore that burden with her; and He bears it with all others who have the same laid upon them, in that country or this, eighteen hundred years ago or now. Remember that. And when you read the words, "Jesus had compassion on her," do not take them for light words; they are the mightiest words you can hear. It is the compassion of the Son of God and the Son of Man. It is compassion for all sorrowing people, and for each sorrowing man or woman, for He is the Brother of each, and He was Himself the great sorrower of all.

But next he said, "Young man, I say unto thee, arise." Here, you say, the likeness ends. The first words might be a sign to us; these cannot be. He does not meet the biers that we crowd into our churchyards. He does not say to those in them, "Arise." My friends, the Gospel calls these acts of our Lord *signs*, and I am sure the Gospel speaks truly. I am not, therefore, going to give up the belief that these words are a sign to widows, a sign to all of us, however at first we may be inclined to think that they are not so, and cannot be. I could not explain this to you, but Christ can. Let us hear His words, as they are written in the 25th verse of the 5th chapter of the Gospel of St. John—"Verily, verily, I say unto you, the hour is coming, and now is, when the dead shall hear the voice of the Son of God, and those that hear shall live." Well, perhaps that applied to Lazarus, whom the people to whom He was then speaking would afterwards see coming out of the grave in which he had been laid four days. But now hear how He proceeds in the 28th verse—"Marvel not at this, for the hour is coming in which all that are in the graves shall hear His voice and shall come forth." So that you see He tells them it was not wonderful that even men in their graves should hear the voice of the Son of God, because all that are in the graves shall hear His voice. Afterwards He gave them a sign in one case of what was true always. One man actually appeared before their eyes in answer to His voice; actually came back into this earth which he had left, that they might understand how it would be with all. And this was to show that, as He had told the Jews, He had life in Himself, and gives that life to men. As He told this to the Jews, so he told Martha—when she would not believe it, but spoke in a despairing way about the resurrection,—that He was the resurrection and the life, and that whosoever believed in Him, though he were dead, yet should he live. So then I have a right to tell you, that when He said to the widow's son, "Young man, arise!" He was as much giving a sign to other widows, as He was when He had compassion on her, and felt with her. He was saying to them all —'Your sons are all to arise.' You cannot see them again for a few years more, as the widow of Nain may have seen her son, and then had to part with him again when he died, or when she died. But you may be sure that they will hear the voice of the Son of Man; you may be sure that that will go through them, and will have power to quicken their mortal bodies. You may be sure that as He raised up His own body out of the grave, He will raise up theirs. For He died because He had taken our nature upon Him, and He rose again because He had redeemed us from death and the grave. Therefore, I say, we are to receive this sign—all of us—and to lay it to heart, and to assure ourselves that the Son of Man had not more power on earth than He has now; but that the power He used on earth was only a pledge and a witness of that which He has been putting forth ever since, and of that which He will put forth for all whom we know, and for every one of us.

And I would not have you forget the next words. "The young man sat up and began to speak." That was a sign that he was really the same person he had always been. He had the same power of speech as when his eyes closed, and he ceased to breathe. He was a human being still in all respects. He was able to know his mother, to care for her and comfort her again. It was by Christ's power that he had been able to speak, when he first called her by her name; and by Christ's power that that speech had been preserved to him up to that hour ; and Christ's power preserved it in him still. Do not think that it can be otherwise with any that depart out of sight. We may be quite unable to hear their voices. We need not to hear them, but we should not think that they have lost any power they had while they were on earth; we should not think they have less than when they lived on earth ; perhaps they may have more.

And there is one more sign still. He delivered the youth to his mother. Mothers ought to receive their children at first as delivered to them by Christ, as placed in their hands by Him. They should remember that He is entrusting their children to them from hour to hour, and then they may delight to receive them back from His hands when they have passed out of this world, and have gone where He is.

My friends, you must teach your children to know the voice of the Son of Man whilst they are on earth. You must teach them that that voice chose them in their baptism, when we sealed them at the font as His. You must teach them that that voice is speaking to them in their consciences every moment, and is bidding them turn from the wrong and do the right. You must teach them that the Son of God became a child and a boy, and grew to be man, that He might claim them as well as you for Himself. You must teach them that He will never leave them nor forsake them. You must show them by your acts that you know He is speaking to you, and guiding and governing you. You must show them that you may turn to Him in weakness and in sorrow; that you believe He died and rose again for us.

And then you may deliver up your children into His hands as to a merciful Saviour, to keep them His, and to use them for His purposes in His kingdom on earth, or in His kingdom in heaven; and then you shall find that He owns you and them as part of that great family which He has rescued from His enemies and presented to His Father.

SERMON XX.

JUSTIFICATION.

Preached at Charlcombe, 1st Sunday after Easter, April 27, 1862.

"It is God that justifieth. Who is he that condemneth? It is Christ that died, yea, rather, that is risen again."—ROMANS viii. 33, 34.

WE have been thanking the Almighty Father to-day that He has given His only Son to die for our sins, and to rise again for our justification. We have been asking Him to grant that we may put away the leaven of malice and wickedness, and serve Him in pureness of living and truth.

What did we mean by our thanksgiving? Is it true that God has justified us—you and me? How has He done that? What did we mean by our request? What is that leaven of malice and wickedness which we want to get rid of? Will God's justification of us help us to get rid of it?

My friends! these are great questions; the greatest that any one can ask. They concern every man and woman and child in this world. And there is an answer to them for every man and woman and child in this world. Let us listen to it, and try to take it in.

St. Paul, you see, has no doubt at all about this point. He says boldly, "It is God that justifieth; who is he that condemneth?" That is as much as to say, 'I know, verily, that God, the creator of heaven and earth, is on our side; that He takes our part. And, therefore, I do not care who takes the other side; there may be a host of enemies that seek to destroy us. But there is one Friend whose will is to save us, and I verily think He is stronger than they are.'

But of whom does the Apostle speak thus? He is telling us all through the Epistle of whom he speaks. The Jews had fancied that they were God's favoured people; that He hated all other people. It was a strange fancy; for God had said unto Abraham, "In thee and in thy seed shall all the families of the earth be blessed." He had chosen them out of all nations to do good to all the nations. He had chosen them out of all nations to tell all the nations, 'God is not the partial, changeable being you have taken Him to be; He is the righteous God. He is determined to set up righteousness in the earth, and to put down all unrighteousness.' But, in spite of this, the Jews had said, 'He justifies *us*; He counts us a good and true nation; all besides us are accursed and hateful to Him.'

Now St. Paul, who was a Jew, and who had been at one time as narrow and bitter as anyone of his countrymen, wrote this letter to answer this calumny against

Him who had made all men; he wrote to say that God had justified both Jews and Gentiles, one as much as the other. And how had He justified them?

It is Christ, he says, that has died. Whatever difference there was between Jews and the other people of the earth, there was one thing that was common to them —Death was common to them; they all died. And Death said to every man, 'I am coming to thee because thou hast done wrong; if all were right with thee, thou wouldst live and not die. I shall take thee away from thy neighbours, and thy family, and from all thy plans and purposes. Thou mayest have friends and helpers above and below, but who will help thee against me? Who will take thee out of my hands? And if I once get thee, dost thou think that I shall ever lose hold of thee?'

So Death spoke to each man; so Death claimed each man as his prize and his slave. Who could answer him? St. Paul says Christ has answered him. The Son of God became a man. He conquered Death for other men. He bade Death do his worst on Him. He did this not in obedience to Death, for He was not Death's servant; but in obedience to His Father, the everlasting God. He said, "Therefore doth my Father love me, because I lay down my life that I might take it again." He said on the cross, "Father, into Thy hands I commend my spirit."

Christ died then. The perfectly holy Lord—the Lord of Angels—the Head of every man—underwent death, the worst kind of death, the death that only slaves and criminals had to bear. Death had seemed to be God's curse upon men, cutting them off from the beautiful earth and all His mercies; Christ, who was perfectly one with God, suffered this curse. Death had seemed to be God's messenger, to tear men from each other. Christ went under death because He was the Head of all men; because He felt for all men.

If St. Paul had stopped there, he might have said to Jews and Gentiles, 'How can you dare to set yourselves up one against the other? Have you not a common enemy—Death, who hates you all? Have you not a common friend—Jesus Christ, who cares for you all?' But he could not stop there; He had said, "It is God that justifieth," and he must show that God had justified. So he goes on, "Yea, rather that is risen again."

Christ took our flesh upon Him. He died the death of men. He lay in such a grave as men's corpses are put into, but the grave could not hold Him. God raised Him out of the grave; so He declared that this was indeed His Son. But was that all He declared? Christ had been His Son before the worlds were. No! He said that men whose nature Christ had taken, whose death Christ had died, were His children. He came to claim them for God. He came to tell Death that he was not their master, not the master of any man whatsoever, because they were Christ's brothers, because they belonged to Him.

Thus you see what St. Paul means when he told his own countrymen the Jews, and the Gentiles who had been worshipping false gods, that Christ had died for their sins, and risen again for their justification. This was the belief that would raise them out of their sins; this was the belief that would lead them to trust in the true God, and to turn to Him, and fear Him, and love Him.

And this is what our collect this morning has been teaching us to do. It has put very bold language into our mouths. Almighty Father! What a name that is to address to Him who made the heaven and earth! Which of us can offer any reason why he should use it? Which of us has done anything or thought anything that can make him worthy of such an honour? But we, all of us, young men and maidens, old men and children, have a right to use that name; we have no right to shrink from using it. For God of His own free will has sent His own well-beloved Son to come into our death on purpose that we might not remain apart from Him, refusing to be a part of His family. And He has raised up His Son to justify us from all our accusers, who would keep us from Him. Therefore, do we believe that He is our Father; the Father of us who are here to-day, and of all those who are worshipping Him everywhere, and of all men who have not yet learnt to worship Him. For, as St. Paul shows, He has sent His Son for our nation, and every nation. He has not justified men of one age, but men of every age.

Wherever sin and death have reigned, there may we declare that Christ is a greater King than they; wherever men have chosen some god to worship who is not their Redeemer and their Father but their enemy, there we may declare that the God whom Christ has declared to us is the true God, and that there is none other but He.

But I said that we asked something of this Almighty Father. What is it? Do we ask Him to be more gracious to us than He has shown Himself to be? How can He be that if He has given His only Son to die for us; to rise again for us; to justify us? How can He be that if He has treated our enemies as His enemies; if He has himself declared war against death and the grave and hell; if He has redeemed us out of the power of the evil spirit?

What have we then to pray to Him for? It is for this, that He would enable us to put away the leaven of malice and wickedness.

We do not beg Him to change His mind, but we beg Him to change our minds. There are a number of false, mean, malicious thoughts in them, which make us suspicious of our neighbours; which make us untrue to ourselves; which keep us from worshipping God, as if He were our Father, and we were His children. We think ourselves better than our neighbours; we try to make out that we are better by hiding our own faults, and by making the most of theirs. So we never become humble as Christ would have us be; so we never really overcome our bad habits. And we suspect God of having some evil designs against us; we think He is malicious because we are. We do not heartily believe that it is His desire to bring us out of all bad ways into the good and blessed way. This is the leaven which defiles our prayers; this is the leaven which defiles all our actions. But how can we get rid of it? The more we try, the more we feel how it has worked itself into our very selves; how it is killing us like a slow poison. Men have been driven to despair sometimes by finding how insincere they were in all their best services, how pride ruined them all. But what a help is here! We may turn to our *Almighty* Father; we know what His mind is. We know that He has given His Son to die for our sins, that we might be united to Him who has cared for us all; we know that he gave His Son to be raised again for our justification, that we might draw nigh to Him as His holy and redeemed children in Christ; therefore we know that He is willing to cast the bad leaven out of us; all our malice and wickedness; therefore we know that He wishes us to serve Him in pureness of living and truth; therefore we know that His almighty power will be on our side if we turn to Him, and ask Him to do for us what we cannot do for ourselves.

Christ brought this great promise with Him into the world: That He would baptize men with His Holy Spirit. That is to say, He did not come to tell men to be good, but He came to make them good. He did not only say, 'Avoid this and that wrong thing;' but, 'I will give you strength to avoid it, yes and to hate it.' So when He had risen from the dead and ascended on high, He sent His Spirit to dwell among men. And those who believed in God's great love, and were baptized, received power to do good deeds, and to speak good words; and men that had been cowards became brave; and men that had been quarrelsome and hateful, loved one another; and men that had been given up to lust and filthiness became pure; for the Spirit of God led them to trust in Christ who had died for them and risen again, and to ask His Almighty Father to deliver them from the leaven of malice and wickedness. Now, brethren, that promise of Christ's has been fulfilled to us. We are baptized into the Name of the Almighty Father, and of His only Son, and of the Holy Ghost; our children are baptized into that same Name; and what was done in our infancy is confirmed or assured to us in our manhood. The bishop came into this neighbourhood the other day to confirm—that is, to assure those who had grown into young men and women, and were going out to their places as servants or to sell in shops, or to be prepared for being magistrates, and doctors, and lawyers, and members of parliament, that they should have God's Holy Spirit with them in all their temptations, to keep them from going wrong, and to make them true and righteous men and women in their different callings.

Think only what that means. The Almighty Father has given His Son to die for our sins and rise again for our justification, that we might be His own children in Christ. And because we are His children He has given us this Holy Spirit who knows our hearts, and all that is likely to corrupt and ruin them, and who desires to plant in us good thoughts and desires, and right counsels, and to make us do just works, that He may be with us wherever we are, and guide us and strengthen us in whatever we are doing. How shall we turn such blessings to account?

First of all, you are here in church to be assured that you have this Almighty Father, and that He has given His Son to die for your sins and to rise again for your justification. That has been done already. Christ said of this work, "It is finished." We are claimed as God's children. He has justified us.

Next, when you go out of church remember that this is ever so. It was not true just when you were on your knees or hearing a sermon. It is true always. And you want this truth for week-days just as much as for Sundays. You want it in the fields, you want it in the shops. Young men want it that they may be brave and true, and not poor and base and sneaking creatures. Girls want it in their places, that they may keep themselves from bad people who would lead them into sin, and that they may be faithful to their masters and mistresses when no eye but God's is on them. Masters and mistresses want it that they may be just and equal to their servants. Yes! we all want to remember the Almighty Father has justified us; He verily loves us and counts us His children. And, therefore, in all troubles, in all temptations, we may arise and go to Him, and He will certainly help us with His own mighty arm, and make us more than conquerors through Him who loved us.

And those want this belief who have fallen into bad and evil practices and find they cannot raise themselves out of them. A man who has become a sot finds the sight of liquor too much for him. He says he will not drink; but the next time the opportunity offers he gives way; his resolutions are gone, and no fear of what people will say to him, or of what will come to his family, or of his own health is enough. But if he will think thus, 'The Almighty Father who sent His own Son to die for me and for all men, and to be raised again for our justification, He does not wish me to be the slave of this accursed tyrant. He is stronger than my enemy; He can deliver me from this leaven of wickedness'—that will be a different kind of help altogether. He has God on his side, the Almighty Father, the Son, the Holy Spirit. And he may defy the world and the flesh and the devil to keep him down and drag him to hell when it is the will of God to raise him to Heaven, and to give him a place among His sons and daughters for ever.

Next remember, that whatever your place in the world, you are called by God, your Almighty Father, to that place. He calls you to be farmers, labourers, schoolmasters, magistrates, physicians, clergymen. They are all His servants. They may all serve Him in pureness of living and truth if they ask Him to be with them, and cast the bad leaven out of them. And He will keep them through their work here, and He will lead them to better and nobler work when He has kept them here as long as He sees fit. For Christ died and rose again, that He might not be separated from those who sleep in Him, but that we should all wait for the day when He shall put death and all His enemies under His feet, and when all shall be gathered together in Him.

SERMON XXI.

TRUTH.

Preached at Brampton Ash, 8th Sunday after Trinity, August 10, 1862.

"But lo! Thou requirest truth in the inward parts, and shalt make me to understand wisdom secretly."—PSALM li. 6.

WE have read the Psalm from which these words are taken to-day. It was written many thousands of years ago; it was written in a land thousands of miles away; it was written most likely by a king. Yet you and I have joined in singing it; we have taken it as ours. And that is not all; the man—or the king, if he was a king—who wrote it, had committed a great crime; there was the guilt of blood on his soul; he had broken the commandment, "Thou shalt not kill;" to all appearance, also, the commandment "Thou shalt not commit adultery."

Now what brings us and this man who lived in other days and so far away, together? How can a king speak for us humble people? How can a man who had done such horrible acts confess for us who cannot charge ourselves with them?

My friends, here is the reason. This king found he had something upon the heart within him which he could not get rid of; which all his friends and kinsfolk and subjects could not help him to get rid of. He tried to forget it; he tried what pleasure would do; he tried what business would do; he tried what making prayers could do; but it was no use. There the burden was still. He felt as if a hand was heavily laid upon him. The moisture seemed to be dried up in him like the fields in a drought. What was this? The man that he had killed could not speak and accuse him, his lips were silent for ever; the woman he had tempted did not accuse him, he had made her a queen. But some one accused him; who was it? He tried to escape from the thought, but at last it came full and clear upon him. God is accusing thee! God knew what thou wast doing, if no one else knew it. God has found thee out. The Judge of all the earth has taken account of thy deeds. It is he whose hand is upon thee. It is He who is making the time that has been, and that is, and that is coming, all very terrible to thee.

Now at first this discovery must have added very much to his pain and horror. 'What, God Himself is fighting with me! He who is just and pure has seen that I am not just and pure. How can I escape from Him? If I go up to heaven He will be there. If I go down to hell He will be there. And wherever I am He will feel to me as He feels to me now. He will not change. He will not be less just and pure a thousand years hence. And I, what shall I be?'

Then this thought came to him, 'Is he so just and pure? Why, then, He would have me just and pure. What He would have me be, He can cause me to be. He can take this foulness out of my heart; He can turn me into a right man again. Yes! that is the thing I want; the only thing I want! I have done wrong, and I must suffer for the wrong. But God can give me a right heart and a clean conscience. He can purify me; he can restore me. Therefore, instead of seeking to escape from Him, I will arise and go to Him. I will tell Him how the case stands with me; I will tell him how this sin is corrupting me, and tormenting me, and destroying all the life in me. I will ask him thoroughly to purge my heart and soul of it. I believe He can do that. I believe He will do it.' Well, that is what this Psalm is about from beginning to end. If you read it over to yourselves again, you will see that it is the cry of a man who knows that he has been wrong, utterly wrong; he knows that his wrong has been discovered, not by some mortal, but by the God that never slumbers nor sleeps. The man knows that he may ask Him, the God of all right, to deliver him from his wrong and set him right.

And, therefore, my friends, this Psalm is for all people whatsoever, in all countries, in all times, for kings and for beggars; for those who have committed great sins, and for those who have committed little sins; for those who feel a burden upon them too heavy to bear; for him who only hears some slight whisper in his heart, saying, 'All is not with thee as it should be. Thou oughtest to be a better man than thou art.' Each of us may take this Psalm to himself; each of us may pray it for himself. And I say boldly, we who are here to-day can understand it better, and turn it to better account, and join in it more thoroughly than those could who lived in King David's days, or than all the people could for whom the book of Psalms was chiefly written; for we can call Him to whom David prayed, our Father. We can use that word, because Jesus Christ, His Son, who took our nature on Him, and died for our sins, and rose again for our justification, has said, "I ascend to my Father and your Father, to my God and your God." We can do it, because He has sent forth His Spirit into our hearts, that we may call Him "Abba Father," and may arise and go to him, and may confess all our evil to Him, and may receive a right heart and a new spirit from Him. Therefore, let us try to get the Psalm well into our hearts. I think we shall do so best, if we consider that one verse which I read to you as my text. If we take that in thoroughly, all the rest will come home to us, and will be clear to us.

There are two parts you see in the text. The first is this, "Thou requirest truth in the inward parts;" the second is this, "Thou shalt make me to understand

o

wisdom secretly." I will speak to you a little of each.

"Thou requirest truth in the inward parts." That is to say, 'Thou, O God! who knowest me altogether, who knowest my downsitting and my uprising, who are about my bed and about my path, Thou wantest me to be a true man; Thou wantest me to be true in my dealings, true in my speech, true to those that are above me and below me and my equals; and that I may be so, Thou requirest me to be true in my own self, true in all that I plan and purpose. Thou requirest that I should not deceive myself or persuade myself that I am better than I am, or that I know what I do not know. Thou requirest that I should be true when I come to kneel before thee, that I should not mock thee with idle vain words.' 'What,' you say, 'does God require all that of me, a poor ignorant creature who have so little strength?' Yes, verily, God requires this of thee and of me, because we are His children, and because He is true, and because He would have us like Him. God requires this of thee, because He would not have thee be miserable and a cause of misery to other people; for all misery comes out of falsehood: there would be no misery in the world if there was nothing but truth in the world. Nevertheless this does sound like a very great thing to ask of creatures who have so much falsehood in them as we have; who have done so many untrue acts; who catch ourselves continually in untruths of word and deed. It does sound like a great thing to ask in a world where so many cheats are going on, and where they grow into customs before we are aware of it.

And, therefore, hear the sentence. "Thou shalt make me to understand wisdom secretly." That is to say, 'As I go about in the world and mix with other men, I am very likely to get into false ways. They may flatter me, and that may tempt me to be vain and conceited. They may treat me hardly, and that may tempt me to be cunning and treacherous. And I cannot keep myself from yielding to these temptations. I cannot hinder a number of false and evil thoughts coming to me when I am alone. But Thou, O God, who requirest me to be true in the inward parts, Thou canst give me the wisdom which I want. Yes! for I can tell Thee of all my folly and weakness. I can ask Thee to clear away my folly, and support my weakness; I can lay bare all that I have done and all that I am before Thee; I can ask Thee to reform me, because I cannot reform myself.'

Oh! my friends, in how many thousand circumstances may we turn these words to our use and blessing. Only let us remember these three things: 1st. What God is; that He is the all just and true. 2nd. What we are without Him, all unjust and untrue. 3rd. What He would have us be, and can enable us to be, just and true, after the likeness of His dear Son. For our Lord Jesus Christ showed us what God's truth is. He came from the God of Truth that He might deliver us from our lies, and might enable us to walk in His truth. And the Spirit who shows us our sins, and awakens us to repentance is the Spirit of Truth of whom Christ has said, "He will guide us into all truth." So, every time you say, 'Almighty and most merciful Father, we have erred and strayed from Thy ways like lost sheep,' you confess that God requires truth in your inward parts, and that you have not been true. And every time the minister says, 'He pardoneth and absolveth,' he means, God would set you free from your falsehood; God would make you know wisdom secretly. And when you say the Lord's Prayer, you ask that God's name, which is truth, may be 'hallowed,' and that God's kingdom of truth may come, and that God's will, which is the will of truth, may be done on earth as it is in heaven. Only be sure that what God requires is just what you require to make you blessed, and then you will ask for that, and He will give you more than you can ask or think.

SERMON XXII.

MINISTERS OF CHRIST.

Preached at Brampton Ash, Morning of St. Bartholomew's Day, August 24, 1862.

"And there was also a strife among them which of them should be accounted the greatest."—St. Luke xxii. 24.

This is St. Bartholomew's Day. We do not know much about St. Bartholomew. Some have thought that he was the same with that Nathanael of whom our Lord said, " Behold an Israelite indeed, in whom is no guile ! " If he was that Nathanael, we ought indeed to remember him. For if He who knows the heart testifies of a man that he is without guile, he is clear and honest, he hates his own falsehood, and cleaves to the God of Truth ; that is one to be reverenced above almost any. But we cannot be sure that Bartholomew was the same as Nathanael. All we can tell certainly about him is that he was one of the twelve apostles. So the passage I have read you from the Gospel does not mean Nathanael, or anyone more especially, but it has to do with all the apostles ; and because it has to do with them, it has to do with us.

You might fancy that on a day like this, which is called after one of these apostles, we should hear something very good of them. It is not so; we hear something that is bad of them. They were met at the last Supper they were ever to have with their Lord upon earth; that very night He was to be betrayed and seized and taken from them. They did not know what was coming upon them, but they knew that something was coming. He had said that He had a great desire to eat that passover with them before He suffered. What then were they doing at this time? Were they listening quietly to all the words that fell from His lips? Were they asking Him to tell them what was at hand, and to prepare them for it? No! "There was a strife among them which should be accounted the greatest." They had had such strifes before. Jesus had rebuked them once by setting a little child among them, and saying that he who was most like that child would be greatest in His kingdom. But the wish in each of them to be higher than the others was so strong that it burst out again. Just when it seemed most utterly out of place it burst out. They were eating of the same bread, and drinking the same wine; and they had one Master among them who had guided them all, taught them all, and to whom they all looked up; yet there was this strife among them, which of them should be greatest.

Perhaps it was not so strange as it might seem that they should be thinking of their own greatness, for our

Lord had spoken to them of a kingdom which He had come to establish; He had chosen them out of all their countrymen to be with Him. He had lately entered into the city of Jerusalem, the chief city of the land, and the people had brought branches of palm trees, and had strewed them before Him, and had hailed Him as the heir of the throne of David, the great King of the Jews. So, in spite of the sorrow that seemed to be oppressing Him, and in spite of what He told them about His sufferings, they thought He must be going to reign gloriously; and if He did, then was it wonderful that they should[1] be thinking, 'And which of us shall be nearest to Him; which of us shall have the highest honour in that kingdom of His'?

Our Lord knew this was what they were thinking of, and therefore He said to them, "The kings of the Gentiles exercise lordship over them, and they that exercise authority upon them are called benefactors." That is as if He had said, 'It is very true that in the kingdoms of the different nations of the earth people try to get the highest places; often they do it with a right purpose. When they are exalted above their neighbours they fancy they can do them good. And so the name which these rulers go by is benefactors, or doers of good.'

"But ye," He goes on, "But ye shall not be so." What! not doers of good? not benefactors? Can He mean that? No; but he is going to tell them how they may do good. It would not be by being raised above other men, by being in high places; "but he that is greatest among you let him be as the younger, and he that is chief as he that doth serve."

Now you see our Lord does not tell the apostles that they were mistaken in supposing that He had come to set up a kingdom over men. If He had, He would have contradicted all that He had been preaching, and all that He had sent them to preach up to that time, for He had preached saying, "Repent, for the kingdom of heaven is at hand;" very near you; and He had sent them with the same message; and He did not tell them that they were wrong in supposing that His kingdom was about to be proclaimed very soon indeed, in spite of all the suffering He had to go through; and He did not tell them that they were wrong in supposing that they were to be sharers in His kingdom, and that they were to help in making men subjects of it. But this is what He said. 'If you would be what you wish to be, high men, chief men in this kingdom of mine, then you must be servants—servants not only of Me, but servants of all people among whom you go. So, instead of quarrelling and disputing which of you shall be most above his fellows, let this be your desire, "Lord, teach me how I may be most a servant; tell me what persons Thou wouldst have me wait upon."'

"For whether is greater," He goes on, "he that sitteth at meat, or he that serveth? But I have been among you as He that serveth." 'You reckon that the master who sits at the table is more than the servant who hands him his food, but I, who am the Lord of all, have waited upon you; I have washed your feet; I have been in all ways working for you, doing the things for you that you could not do for yourselves. All my life has been a service. Remember that, and then consider whether you wish to be like Me or unlike Me; whether you wish to exercise the kind of power I have exercised, or some other kind of power. Because, if you wish to be like Me, you must be ministers or servants; if you wish to exercise the kind of power I have exercised, you must stoop and not rise; you must be more lowly, and not more lifted up.'

Then He went on, "Ye are they which have continued with Me in my temptations." 'You say I have called you and chosen you out of the rest of your countrymen, though you were but poor fishermen. Yes, truly, that is so. I have allowed you to be with me in the trials and temptations I have been passing through. They have been very sore. All manner of people—my own subjects—have been contending with me, priests and rulers and lawyers. Nay, even one of you is to betray me; and the devil has been contending with me, trying to separate Me from my Father. Yet you have seen that my Father has enabled me to heal sicknesses and cast out devils. I have been ruling in the midst of my temptations; I have been delivering other men from their troubles, whilst I have had harder troubles to go through than any of them.'

"And I appoint unto you a kingdom as my Father

hath appointed unto me." 'I am not going to cheat you or disappoint you; you are to have places in my kingdom; you are to sit with Me on my throne. But then see what a kingdom it is! See what the King of it has had to bear, and has still to bear! See to what depths He has sunk and will sink! Remember, if I appoint you a kingdom as my Father has appointed Me, I appoint you suffering as my Father hath appointed me. If I appoint you to rule over men, and to set them free from their bondage to death and the evil spirit, as my Father hath appointed me, I appoint you to be tried and tempted as my Father hath appointed me.'

And so it will come to pass that you "shall eat and drink at my table in my kingdom, and you shall sit on thrones judging the twelve tribes of Israel."

What does this mean, "You shall eat and drink at my table"? They were eating and drinking then with Him at the Passover, the Jewish feast. And whilst they were eating He took bread and blessed it, and said, "Take, eat, this is my body;" and then after supper He took the cup and drank, and gave it to them, and said, "This is my blood of the New Testament which is shed for you and for many for the remission of sins." Now as often as the apostles ate that bread and drank that cup, according to the Lord's commandment in remembrance of Him, they sat at His table and ate and drank with him. That was the sign and pledge that they were one with Him, though He was gone out of their sight! that was the sign that they were one with all His saints in heaven and earth. And they were never to forget that they were one with Him and one with all His saints in heaven and earth; one with Him in his sorrow and in His temptation, and His death; one with Him in the glory that He had with His Father; one with all suffering people on earth; one with all that have passed out of the earth, and are with Him where He is. This was to eat of His table in His kingdom.

And what was it to "sit on thrones judging the twelve tribes of Israel"? The tribes of Israel were called out of all the families of the earth, that they might be a blessing to the families of the earth; that they might tell all the families of the earth of God's truth and God's love.

Now these twelve Apostles, these poor fishermen, did go about as Christ's ministers, blessing all the families of the earth, telling them how God had sent His Son to redeem them, and His Spirit to bind them into one; so they judged the twelve tribes of Israel, who had failed to do their work, who had refused to bless men, who thought they were to live to please themselves. The twelve tribes of Israel lost their land and their city. But these Apostles who did their work still kept alive the remembrance of them; still bore witness of what they might have been; still showed that God would fulfil His purpose, however disobedient His servants might be. And now then, my friends, we have seen ourselves in these Apostles. They were men not richer or more learned than any who work in our towns or villages. They were men of like passions as we are, men who were easily puffed up with vanity, each of whom thought it would be very pleasant to exalt himself over the rest. But Christ, the Son of God, took them under His guidance. He said that they were to be ministers of His kingdom, and that in that kingdom He who was the chief of all was the servant of all. Let us understand then, my friends, that every one of us is a servant or minister in this kingdom. Some of us have the name of Ministers. That is not that we may be separate from our fellows, but that we may give them a sign what Christ would have them be. *All* of us are ministers. Every father is a minister of Christ to his children. Every mother is a minister of Christ to her children. Every brother and sister is a minister of Christ to his brothers and sisters. Wherever we are going, whatever we are doing, in a house or in a field, we are ministers of Christ. That is our calling. We may be faithful or unfaithful ministers; but He is our Master, and He has sent us to wait upon some or other, upon more or fewer. And we must ask him to teach us how to wait on them. What a wonder it is to think that He, the Lord of heaven and earth, was the great Minister; that He came down from heaven, not to get the service of men, but to serve them. So He proved Himself to be the King. He stooped more than all, so they felt and knew that He was higher than all. And for you, brethren, as much as for them, He stooped. For you, as much as for them, He took on Him the form of a servant. You, as much as them, He would have to sit at His table in His kingdom. You, as much as them, He would have sharers of His throne by helping them whom now, as much as ever, He cares for.

You need not strive which of you shall be the greatest. Ask Him to make you lowly and meek, and ready to help others; that was *His* greatness, and you would not wish to be different from Him.

And one thing more I must say. The Apostles were to judge the twelve tribes of Israel; but the twelve tribes of Israel, those poor Jews who were cast out of their city because they did not care to serve their brethren, will judge us, if we, who call Jesus our Lord, do not like to be what He was and to do as He did. They refused Him and put Him to death, not knowing what they did. We know far better. And we refuse Him as our King; we act as if He had never come down to save us and bring us into His kingdom, if we are not willing to serve our brethren for His sake.

SERMON XXIII.

THE LIGHT OF THE WORLD.

Preached at Brampton Ash, Afternoon of the 10th Sunday after Trinity, August 24, 1862.

" If we say that we have no sin we deceive ourselves, and the truth is not in us. If we confess our sins, He is faithful and just to forgive us our sins, and to cleanse us from all unrighteousness."
1 ST. JOHN i. 8, 9.

You are used to these words. You hear them very often at the beginning of our morning or our evening prayers. This afternoon you heard them as they come in the course of St. John's letter to his flock—those whom he calls his little children—at Ephesus.

He had been telling them the message which he said he had heard from his Master, Christ, and which was meant for them as much as for him. It was this: "God is light, and in Him is no darkness at all." St. John had been at that passover supper, of which I spoke to you this morning; he had been next to his Master. He was called the beloved disciple. He had lived many years since then. He had had visions of Christ in His own glory. And this was the best thing he could say when he was near the end of his pilgrimage on earth; the best blessing he could bestow on those whom he had known and loved; the best legacy he could leave to us—" I tell you God is light, and in Him is no darkness at all."

What! did not he know that before? Some one may ask, 'Did he fancy there was some darkness in God?' I must answer yes to both questions, though it may seem as if they were just the contrary of each other. He did know that God was light—that He was all clear pure goodness, *that* and nothing else. He had been told so from his youth, and he believed it. But yet he did fancy there was darkness in God. When he grew up and saw how much darkness there was in the world, how much evil there was in the world, the temptation was very great to say Does not this come from God? Is not He the cause of it? But recollect what things St. John had been witness to. He had seen Jesus Christ his Lord put to death by the hands of wicked men; and his own brother James had been slain by the sword because he preached of Jesus Christ and of what He had done for men. St. Peter and most of the friends that were dearest to him had been cut off for the same reason. The city of Jerusalem, in which he had walked with his Master, was about to fall, if it had not already fallen, for the wickedness of those who dwelt in it. Bad men seemed to have the upper hand; good men seemed as if they had no chance of making themselves heard. Must not the thought have often come to St. John, 'Well, God allows all this to be. I do not know how it is, but must there not be some darkness in Him? Must He not have some hard thought towards us? Can He be altogether light, *that* and that only?'

Yes, my friends, such thoughts do come to all men, and you must see that St. John had as much excuse for them as most men. And now let us consider how he fought his way out of these thoughts; how he came verily and indeed to believe that there is no darkness at all in God, let things look as dark as ever they may.

First, then, he stood firm on this ground. 'Christ my Lord and Saviour has shown me what God is; He spoke of His Father; He showed us of His Father; we saw in Him the grace and glory of the only begotten Son. Now I know what sort of acts He did when He was upon earth; I know that he went about doing good—to men —to all manner of men, good and bad. And I know how it was with him when all looked very dark indeed to Him; when the chief priests and rulers hated Him; when Pilate and the Roman soldiers were mocking and condemning Him; when His disciples fled from Him; when it seemed as if God His Father had deserted Him. I know that through all these things He held on; that He trusted, altogether trusted, in His Father's goodness and truth; through all that darkness He trusted in Him because He knew Him, because He knew what His Will was, because He was sure it was the same Will always, even when He could not see it, even when it seemed to be crushing Him.'

The Apostle then could say boldly, 'I mean to get my thoughts of the Eternal God from this Jesus Christ who has made Him known to us; from Him and from no one else, and from nothing else. Things may look very dark and black, but I am sure the darkness and blackness are not from God. What were all Christ's acts, the works which He did in His Father's name, which His Father sent Him to do, but works to vanquish the powers of darkness? What was His death? Death is the great darkness; all light seemed to be put out by it. It never was so dark as when it closed over the Son of Man, but He went through it; He despised it. His Father brought Him from the grave and hell. Therefore death and hell shall not be my teachers about God. I will gather no thoughts of Him from them. Christ, the conqueror of death and hell and the prince of darkness, is the only teacher about Him to me and to all people.'

But now I come to the Second point. Is there then no darkness? Do not I really find evil and death in the world about me? Yes, I cannot deceive myself about that. It is true. I feel it, I know it, and, what is worse, it is in me. If I say that I have no sin, I deceive myself, and the truth is not in me. There is light about me—God's own pure and blessed light—and that light comes to me. It shows me everything that is worth seeing; all beautiful things, all kind and gracious and loving things. But it shows me also many ugly things; many ungracious and unbelieving things. It shows me the bad that is in me. It makes me know how far I have gone wrong; how little I have loved those that are nearest to me; how ungrateful I have been; how hardhearted I have been. And it shows me that this unlovingness and ingratitude and hardness of heart are always in me, always ready to spring out on me and get the better of me. I cannot deny that. The truth is not in me if I deny it; for the truth that is in me shows me the untruth that is in me; God's light shows me my darkness.

If He was not light, if He did not send His light in me, I should not perceive the darkness; it could not torment me as it does. Christ, who is the perfect image of God, the true light of the world, is making me understand, what a dark creature I am without Him, what I should become and what the world would become if He withdrew His light.

3. But though there is much in this, St. John would still have been very ill content if he had been obliged to stop there. He goes on: "If we confess our sins, He is faithful and just to forgive us our sins, and to cleanse us from all unrighteousness."

That is to say, no doubt the light is here, and the darkness is here, but which is stronger? Which can drive out the other? I will try that. I will arise, and go to Him who is light, and tell Him of my darkness. I will ask Him if He cannot raise me out of it; and I find that He can. I tell Him of the sin that is in me, and He forgives it; He lifts me out of it; He owns me as His child. He not only puts away the sins that I have committed, but He cleanses me from all unrighteousness. So I know for myself that He is light, and that there is no darkness in Him, and that He means to scatter all darkness.

For observe, though I have told you truly that what St. John says he says of himself, I should speak falsely if I said he spoke it of himself more than of any other man. He says we all deceive ourselves if we say that we have no sin. He says the truth is not in us if we will not own the testimony it bears to our sin. And so he says of us all, "If we confess our sins, He is faithful and just to forgive us our sins, and to cleanse us from all unrighteousness." I showed you this morning how the apostles were cured of setting themselves one above another or above any man. All our Lord's lessons were to bring them down, to show them that they were just like other people; that they had the same evil as all others, and that they were to proclaim to all the same deliverance from the evil which they had found. So we are not wrong in reading out these words in the morning and evening Service to all men and women, though we know nothing of what they have been thinking or doing. They must be true for everyone if they were true for St. John and the Ephesians.

And what words they are! Let me repeat them to you. "He is faithful and just to forgive us our sins, and to cleanse us from all unrighteousness." Now a man often says, 'Oh, I hope and trust God will be *merciful* to me and forgive me my sins.' But can he ask God because He is *just* to forgive him? That depends on the forgiveness which he is seeking. Suppose he desires God to overlook his sins; to let him go on in them, not to let him be punished for them, he certainly cannot expect that God in His justice and faithfulness will do that. This he would expect from a judge who is not just and faithful; but could that judge be merciful? I think not. There is no mercy in letting a man go on in a course of villany; there is no mercy in letting him get worse and worse, and therefore more and more miserable—*that* is cruelty. A father who does that to his children is a cruel father; a ruler who does that to his subjects is a cruel ruler. And, therefore, if we mean by forgiveness what God means by it; if we mean that he should put our sins as far from us as the east is from the west; that He should give us clean hearts and a right spirit; that He should bring us out of darkness into His blessed and wonderful light; He is not only merciful and just, He is faithful and just to do that for us. He loves righteousness and hates iniquity, therefore He is ready to deliver us from iniquity, and to make us partakers of His righteousness. It was infinite mercy of the Father to send His Son to save those who regarded Him as their enemy; it was infinite mercy of the Son to take our nature upon Him, and to die the death of those who slew Him. It is infinite mercy of the Holy Spirit to come to strive with us when we are most untrue and rebellious and ready to give ourselves to the evil spirit. But all this mercy is because it is the purpose of God the Father, the Son, and the Spirit, to set righteousness and truth upon the earth, and to drive all unrighteousness and untruth out of it. It is because God is light, and in Him is no darkness at all. Therefore, we may arise and say boldly, 'Oh God, I have walked in dark and evil ways; I confess to thee that I have. I shall go on walking in them if Thou dost not forgive me my sins, and cleanse me from all unrighteousness. But I trust and am sure Thou wilt because Thou art faithful and just; because Thou hast manifested Thy righteousness in Thy dear Son for the forgiveness of sins; because Thou hast promised us strength to confess them, and turn from them, and to walk in Thy own right way.'

SERMON XXIV.

THE LORD OF THE WINDS AND SEA.

Preached at Brampton Ash, 12th Sunday after Trinity, September 7, 1862.

"But the men marvelled, saying, What manner of man is this that even the winds and the sea obey Him!"—ST. MATTHEW viii. 27.

IN the lesson for this morning you heard of a number of the acts of our Lord Jesus Christ when He was upon earth. First, you heard of His healing a leper. That poor man had a disease, which kept him at a distance from everybody. He might not go into the Temple to pray; he was to give warning to his neighbours to avoid him, by crying 'I am unclean.' There was fear that he might give his sickness to any who approached him. But he had heard the voice of Jesus speaking to the people. He thought with himself, 'That is a great king; He has authority to command men. I believe He could heal me, and it seems to me that He cares for the sick and the outcast. I will try.' He said, "Lord, if Thou wilt, Thou canst make me clean." The Son of Man answered, "I will; be thou clean." And cleansed he was; he became well within, and now could go to the priest who had the care of such complaints, and could show that the outward signs of his disease—the marks on his body—were gone. Next we were told of the servant of an officer in the Roman army, who was sick. His master besought Jesus to cure him. Jesus went towards the house, but the officer said, "Lord, I am not worthy that thou shouldest come under my roof, but speak the word only, and my servant shall be healed." The centurion knew the power of words; for he had a great many soldiers under him, stout men, as strong as he was. He did not rule them by terror. They obeyed his word. They came and went when he told them to come and go. So he had no doubt that Jesus could do what he desired for his servant without touching him or seeing him, only by uttering His word. 'That,' said our Lord, 'is faith; such faith as I have not found among those Jews who have had so many more lessons about God's word than the Romans. Some of them suppose I can do something by my hands and eyes; he believes that it is God's word which works by me even when I am out of sight.' The third story we heard was of Peter's mother-in-law, who had a fever. Jesus took her by the hand, and the fever left her. Then next we heard that when the even was come, they brought unto Him many that were possessed with devils; poor madmen who had not the command of themselves, who spoke all foul words, and did all wild acts which some unclean and bad spirit put it into their hearts to speak and do. And Jesus set them free from this bondage; He brought them to be reasonable men again. Then we were told how he was out one day with His disciples on a lake in a great storm. They were much frightened, for their ship seemed to be going down. He was asleep. They woke Him, saying, "Lord, save us: we perish." And He said unto them, "Wherefore did ye doubt, oh ye of little faith? And He rebuked the winds and the waves, and there was a great calm." Before the end of the chapter you have another story of His delivering two madmen whom no man had been able to tame; who ran about the tombs crying and cutting themselves with stones, who were dangerous to all that came near. At first the evil spirits who had possession of them cried out, "What have we to do with Thee, Jesus, Thou Son of God?" But at His word the evil spirits departed, and the men became as quiet and obedient as the winds and waves had been.

The words I took for my text were those which the people in the ship spoke, when the storm ceased. "What manner of man is this, that even the winds and the sea obey him?"

That is the question I want you to ask yourselves to-day. What manner of man is this we have been reading of?

Now I am afraid some of you would like me to change the words a little, and to say, 'What manner of man *was* He?' For many of us have a fancy that He was there in Galilee and Judæa, but that He is not now in England and among us; or that if He lives still, He is not now what He was then. If it were so, I do not know why we should read these lessons Sunday after Sunday in every church throughout Queen Victoria's dominion, or what good they would do us. Why should you and I care to know what happened in a country thousands of miles away, 1800 years ago? But if He who did these acts there in that country is, as we say He is, our Lord now; if He is ruling over all of us just as much as He was over those people in Judæa and Galilee; if He is the same person in His heart and His purpose and His power now that He was then; if that be so, why, my friends, it does signify to us to be told what manner of person He showed Himself to be then.

That is the reason why I would not change even a letter of this question which the men in the ship asked, "What manner of man is this?"

Now consider the different parts of this morning's lesson, as I have repeated them to you; and you will get the answer to this question, or at least a part of the answer.

1. He is a giver of health. This Lord Jesus Christ, by curing the leper and the servant with the palsy and the woman with the fever, proved Himself to be that. Not, observe you, a giver of health to those particular persons; they were only specimens of what He is doing every day and hour. When you awake in a morning strong and fit to work, say 'It is this Lord from

whom my strength and power to work come.' When you have been lying sick of any kind of disorder, and have risen again and feel the power coming back to your limbs, and that you can breathe freely again and eat your food gladly, then say, 'That Lord who healed the paralytic man and the leper has sent me this restoration. It is not someone else. He who dwelt among men, and went about doing good among men at that time I have read of, He it is who has been doing me good; He it is who has made this or that medicine of the physician to work for my cure.' And do not forget this, my friends, it is written in the chapter we have read to-day, "Himself took our infirmities and bare our sicknesses." He did not merely regard them from a distance. He did not merely send forth some command from Heaven about them. He became a man. He suffered with them that were suffering. He came into the very midst of all the troubles of all the poor people who were tormented with different ailments. He felt with them as no one else had felt with them. *That* was the manner of man He was on earth. And I must say again, He is the same yesterday, to-day, and for ever. He does not change as we change. The mind and character which He had then He has now. He is not confined to one land or to one set of people. He is Lord of all lands and of all the people who dwell in them. But He does not the less understand each sick man, and care for each. He is a healer and giver of health now as always.

2. He is the protector of those who are out at sea, in such storms as His disciples were in, on the Lake of Genesareth. You who live in an inland county may not think so much of these troubles as men do upon the coast, where they see ships so often dismasted and so often wrecked. But you have many of you had some son or kinsman on the ocean, about whom you have thought at night, when the wind was blowing a gale. At such times people often send up a hurried prayer, not much thinking to whom they pray or whether He is likely to hear them. But if they thought, 'He who rose up so calmly, when His disciples waked Him out of His sleep, and bade the winds and the sea be calm, He is as much with those who are going to America or Australia or New Zealand now, as He was with those who were on the Lake of Galilee then; He cares for them now as much as He cared for them then;' would not that make an amazing difference? Might we not trust our friends to Him, as we never could trust them to anyone of whom we had only heard that he was very powerful, and that perhaps he might be kind? And supposing some calamity did befall our friends, supposing they were drowned in the ocean, or perished by any strange terrible accident, might we not trust them to Him still? Might we not say, 'Lord, Thou Who didst bear men's infirmities and carry their sicknesses, didst also go through their death. Thou didst rise out of death. Thou didst conquer it for us. We believe that Thou art the Lord of health

everywhere. We believe that Thou wilt cure the sicknesses and diseases to which all Thy poor brethren have been subject, and wilt raise up their bodies and make them glorious bodies like Thine own. We are sure Thy power is not less now than it was when Thou didst call Lazarus out of the tomb. Yea, we know that Thou hast power to subdue all things to Thyself.'

Once more: He delivers those who are under the dominion of evil spirits from their power.

What, is there any comfort in that thought? Do we ever see people nowadays under the dominion of evil spirits? Was not that something which belonged to the days when our Lord walked in Judæa?

My friends, these stories of our Lord's delivering men from evil spirits have been to me an unspeakable comfort; not for other days, but for this day. There are enemies outside of us: what St. Paul calls enemies of flesh and blood. Some have more of them, some have fewer. But besides, there are enemies of our spirits. These attack us all. A wicked desire springs out upon us, and catches hold of us. We seem to like it; we cherish it; and yet we know it is a very devil. It will work in us and put us upon all kinds of wickedness. Is it nothing to know Jesus Christ, my Lord, is stronger than this devil? I cannot see Him any more than I can see it. But He is near me as it is near to me; I can cry to Him against it. There is something in you that says, "What have I to do with Thee, Jesus, Thou Son of God?" But there is something in you which will call Him to help you and drive the devil back for you. Oh, my friends, that is your own true self. Christ knows it. Christ will hear your cry. Christ will do what He did for the possessed with the devils in the city of the Gadarenes.

For sometimes that is the only way we can describe it. A man becomes possessed with some furious passion. He becomes possessed by some dreadful habit; for instance, he makes himself a sot. His pride cannot keep him from it; the fear of losing all his money, and ruining his wife and children, will not keep him from it; the fear of the law is not a chain strong enough for him. But Christ is there; the Son of God is there! Yes, a man who is in this case finds out, indeed, what manner of *Man* that was who rebuked the winds and the waves. From His compassion and tenderness he might suppose He was only the greatest, the most loving of men. But in this battle with the evil spirits that have been ruling him, he finds that this loving Man is the Eternal Son of God! There is nothing in heaven or earth or hell but must at last bow to Him and obey Him. All, it is written, shall confess that Jesus Christ is Lord to the glory of God the Father. Oh, learn to confess Him now! You need Him in sickness and health, on the sea and the dry land; when you are crushed down by wicked enemies, and when He has restored you to your right mind.

SERMON XXV.

THE MAN OF SORROWS.

Preached at Brampton Ash, 13th Sunday after Trinity, September 14, 1862.

"For even Christ pleased not Himself, but as it is written, The reproaches of them that reproached Thee fell on Me."—ROMANS xv. 3.

OUR Lord Christ is called The Man of Sorrows, and yet His life, even here on earth, was a life of joy. How could that be? St. Paul tells us how it was in the verse I have just read to you.

1. Christ pleased not Himself. My friends, the secret of most of our misery is that we are trying to please ourselves. We are continually craving for something that we have not; we are discontented with what we have. If you find me a person, be he ever so poor, be he in ever so much pain of body, who is not restless, who is not impatient, I say that person has more joy in him than one who has millions to spend, who has health and ease and all comforts about him, and is always contriving new ways of pleasing himself. The poor suffering man is thinking about his wife or

child, how kind they are, how they watch him; how pretty the flowers which they place by his bedside, how nice the food is which they cook for him. The rich easy man is thinking what more things he can procure for himself, what a number of inconveniences there are in his house, how one and another is interfering with his plans. One is satisfied, the other never is.

Well, but our Lord Jesus was the one person who was never pleasing Himself. He was never thinking of Himself. He delighted to do His Father's will, and to finish His work. He delighted to think of His Father and of all His infinite love, and of all His purposes of good which He had devised for men, and which He would accomplish for men. Every tree which grew by the watercourse, every flower in the hedgerows told Him something of His Father's deep, wonderful, careful Love; how He had made everything, and lo, it was good; how He was watching over everything, to keep it good and beautiful, and bring out the good and beauty of it fully at last. He delighted to think that there was not a publican or sinner despised by man, whom His Father did not look after and care for, and seek to bring home to His family. He delighted to think that His Father loved that His children should be healthy, and free, and true. He delighted that His Father had sent Him into the world to give health to the sick, and freedom to those who were in bondage, and to make them good who had been under the power of the evil one. It was meat and drink to Him to work for this end, meat and drink to be sending lepers away well, to be restoring to palsied people the use of their limbs again, to be giving back the dead child alive to its father and mother, the dead man alive to his sisters. He was pleasing His Father in all that He did. He was not seeking His own pleasure in anything. That was joy. If that had been all, Christ's life on earth would have been only one of joy; we should have no right to call Him the Man of Sorrows. But we must call Him by that name, and the second part of the verse tells us why we must.

2. "The reproaches of them that reproached Thee fell on me." He delighted, I said, to do His Father's will. He delighted in His Father's love. But all around, men were reproaching His Father, were finding fault with Him. It seemed to them as if there were good reason for their reproaches. 'For how is it,' said they, 'that things are going on so badly on this earth of ours? How is it that there is so much sickness and pain? How is it that there is so much oppression and cruelty? How is it that poor men cry and there is no comforter? How is it that good men often have a bad time of it, and suffer much trouble, and go to prison, and are burnt with fire, while the evil men are prosperous and seem to have everything their own way? How can this be if there is really a good God over all?' Now all these reproaches fell on Christ. They were anguish to Him. The more intensely He loved His Father, the more intensely He believed in His Father's

goodness and grace and truth, the more anguish they caused Him. And it was not only that. He did not only feel as we might feel if anyone said hard words of someone that we reverenced very much, and whom we knew deserved our reverence. These sicknesses and troubles of men actually burnt into Christ's very soul. They grieved Him as they had never grieved anyone else. He bore them as if they were His own. It could not be otherwise; for He knew about his Father's beautiful order, and here was disorder and confusion. He loved men one and all as His Father loved men, and here were men hating each other. He was the Lord of life, and here was death working its way among all human beings and separating them from each other, and mocking all their plans and proclaiming himself to be the great king. This was enough to make Christ a Man of Sorrows, yea, *the* Man of Sorrows. These reproaches against His Father did really break His heart. He knew that they had come to men because they had contradicted His Father's will, because they had set up their wills against His. He knew that His Father's will was to banish sickness and restore life and put down injustice and wrong. But here they were, and it seemed as if they had gotten the day.

But there was another way, and perhaps a more terrible way still, in which all the reproaches that men cast upon God, fell upon Christ. He was the express image of His Father. All the brightness and goodness and loving-kindness of His Father came forth in Him. Every act of His showed forth something of this brightness and goodness and loving-kindness. He went about, as it is written, doing good. But it is written also— He Himself spake the terrible words—'They hated both Me and my Father.' His goodness brought out the evil and bitterness and cruelty of their hearts. He was a continual reproach to them, so they cast all reproaches upon Him. The worst of all was that they called Him a blasphemer because He said God was His Father, and that they blasphemed Him by saying, "He casteth out devils through Beelzebub, the chief of the devils." He who bore all this must have been indeed a Man of Sorrows. The joy did not kill the sorrow; it made the sorrow keener, for the more He rejoiced in His Father, the more it pained Him that men should misunderstand His Father's purposes; the more He did the works of His Father, the more horrible it was that they should take them for the acts of Satan. But it is also true that the sorrow did not kill the joy—nay, that it brought forth His joy. He set His face as a flint. He gave Himself to show that His Father was not the cause of the misery of the world, but that it was miserable because it was at war with Him. He worked to show that death and the grave and hell were His Father's enemies, and that His Father could and would vanquish them. So He went down into death and the grave and hell Himself. They did all that they could do to Him. And having endured all that unspeakable sorrow and agony, He rose again the Conqueror of them all; He rose, as it is written, in the glory of the Father. He had triumphed over them in the name of His Father, and through the power of His Father; He had triumphed over them for you and me, and for the whole universe. He had shown that He was Lord over them; He had shown that His Father's will was to give Life, Eternal Life, to those who had fancied that He was their tyrant, and that He had doomed them to death.

And so the Lord who pleased not Himself entered into His Father's joy—the joy of saving and redeeming men; and in that joy He has dwelt ever since, and dwells now. But still we are bound to think of Him as the Man of Sorrows, as the man who bore all the sorrows that men have borne and do bear. And His Spirit, the Spirit of the Father and of the Son, is with us now, that we may enter both into His joy and His sorrow. If we ask that Spirit to come and dwell with us, we shall find that He is indeed a Comforter. For He teaches us of God's infinite love, and Christ's infinite sacrifice; He shows how the troubles which men have are not proofs of God's hatred, seeing that they all fell upon His beloved Son, but may be means of drawing us to trust in Him, and give ourselves to Him. His Spirit, the Comforter, will teach us not to please ourselves as we are all trying to do, but to forget ourselves, and live in Christ and for each other. The Spirit will teach us to bear the reproaches in our own heart which men are putting upon our Father in heaven, and to do what we can to overcome them by proving that His will is to bless them, and deliver them, and do them good. His Spirit will teach us to enter into the sorrows of our fellow-men, which are the sorrows of Christ, and to look for a day when the darkness shall pass, and the earth shall be set free from its bondage, and the sons of God shall shout for joy because their Father's face is shining without a veil.

SERMON XXVI.

ST. MATTHEW'S DAY.

Preached at Brampton Ash, 14th Sunday after Trinity, September 21, 1862.

"And as Jesus passed forth from thence He saw a man named Matthew sitting at the receipt of custom, and He saith unto him, Follow Me."—ST. MATTHEW ix. 9.

ST. MATTHEW is telling us here the story of an event which happened to himself. That is not the business of his Gospel generally. He does not care that we should know him; he wished that we should know his Master. And this is his purpose in this passage as much as any other. He only speaks of his own life that he may lead us to Christ's life.

Matthew, or Levi as he is sometimes called, was a tax-gatherer. He was sitting, it is said, at the receipt of custom—that is to say, he was sitting at the place where the taxes or tributes were collected. I have told you before that men of his class were much disliked among the Jews. The taxes went to foreign kings. Every time that they saw a tax-gatherer they were reminded that they were not their own masters, but had fallen under the power of a stranger. Moreover, some of these people turned their occupation to a bad use. They made the most of it, and got much for themselves by charging men more than they owed. I do not know that Matthew had ever done that; but he had got money by his business; he was a rich man, therefore his countrymen were likely to suspect him.

Well, as he sat one day at his office, he heard a voice saying to him, "Follow me." I cannot tell whether he had ever seen the person who spoke these words before. Most likely he had, for Jesus was going about continually in that region. One may suppose He must have sometimes been near Matthew; at all events he must have heard of Him. But seeing His face, or getting reports of Him from other people, did not make much difference to the tax-gatherer, he sat at the receipt of custom still. Perhaps he had sometimes heard Christ deliver discourses to the multitude; he might even have wondered at them; but he went on with his work. The discourses might be good; they did not seem particularly to concern him. These words, "*Follow me*" are altogether different. Why were they spoken? Who spoke them? He was apparently much poorer than Matthew; He was called a carpenter's son. What right had He to command a man to rise from his place, to lose the chance of increasing his gains, to come after Him? Matthew felt that this man had a right. Poor as He looked, he felt 'That man is my king; I must do what He bids me; I must go wherever He would have me go.' So he rose up and followed Jesus; he became a disciple of Jesus. By-and-by Jesus called him to be an Apostle. He sent him forth to preach His Gospel. In due time he was called to write one of the Gospels which have lasted from that day to this; which have been read this morning in every parish church throughout England.

We may be thankful, you will say, that Matthew had this call. We may be glad that he did not always continue a tax-gatherer. We should have been poorer if he had gone on making himself richer in that way. We should have been without those lessons which he has left for poor men and rich men throughout the world. But still you might think the call itself was something altogether strange; one which can never come to any of us; one which could only have been addressed to a man who was in that part of the earth in which our Lord was born, at that time when He was walking there. You might fancy this, but this is not what the collect you have joined in to-day teaches us. "Almighty God," it says, "who by Thy blessed Son didst call Matthew from the receipt of custom to be an Apostle and Evangelist, give us grace to follow the same Thy Son Jesus Christ, who liveth and reigneth with Thee and the Holy Spirit, one God, world without end." Now there, you see, we are told that the same Lord—the very same who called Matthew—is calling us who have prayed this prayer, and that we may follow Him just as truly as Matthew did. This is the subject I want to talk to you about. I want to find out how it is that a Lord whom we do not see can be calling us; and if He is, how we can follow Him.

How can He be calling us, though we do not see Him? You will remember what I have told you already. Matthew might have seen Him a hundred or a thousand times, and yet not have altered his way of life, or any of his doings or thoughts the least. Multitudes of people saw Him who went their way, and were just what they had been before. Some who saw Him hated Him, and went about to kill Him. It was then something which Matthew did not see that had such mighty power.

You know what the Roman centurion said, of whom I spoke to you a Sunday or two ago. He wanted our Lord very much to heal his servant, but he said he was not worthy that so great a person should come under his roof, but if He spoke the word only his servant would be well, for he knew what the power of words was. He was an officer, and he found that his soldiers came and went when he bade them, though he put no force upon them. Well, then, there was a word speaking to St. Matthew when he heard the sound "Follow me," which he felt he must not fight against. He might not have dared to say so at the moment, but he knew in his heart that it was the Word of the living God. He knew that he must go where that Word bade him go; that he must come when that Word bade him come. There might be something in him which said, 'No, stay, you are in a prosperous way; do not forsake it.' That voice he heard, I have no doubt, sounding in him perhaps pretty loudly; but the other, though it might be only a whisper, was a royal whisper. He knew that that was the one he ought to heed; the other he must despise if he could not silence it.

Now, my friends, the writer of this collect for St. Matthew's Day felt himself, and wished you and me to feel, that it is just so with every one of us, whether we are tax-gatherers, or labourers, or preachers. Whatever we are, there is a righteous Lord who is saying to us in our hearts, "Follow me," as there is an evil spirit who is saying to us in our hearts, 'Follow me.' We cannot be our own masters; we must have some master, a good or a bad one. There is always something for us to do, and something for us not to do—a right way and a wrong way; and there is always One near us who would guide us into the right way, and out of the wrong way. It is well to remember that; we are all exceedingly ready to forget it. A man says to himself, 'Yes, I should like to keep out of that bad course into which I see other people running, but how am I to keep from it? these people tempt me; I am drawn along after them.' And again a man says, 'Yes, if I could get over that accursed habit of mine—if I could be a sober man, for instance—I should be so glad. But how can I? my inclinations are so strong; something in me always gets the better of me when I make even the best resolutions.' Now all this would be true if God had left us at the mercy of other people, or of our own inclinations. But He has not. The Word of God, the Lord Jesus Christ, is stronger than all the bad people who can ever come near us; stronger than our own fancies and lusts. He is our King, as He was Matthew's King; and He says to us as He said to St. Matthew, 'Do not follow these men; do not follow the thoughts that come into your own hearts; follow Me.'

But then comes the second question, how can we follow Christ? What is meant by following Him? Do you recollect the text I was preaching to you on last Sunday afternoon? It was this—"For even our Lord Jesus Christ pleased not Himself." I showed you that that was what made His life so wonderful. He was the King over men; He commanded them; He healed them; He fed them; He did them good in a thousand ways; but He "pleased not Himself." That was the thing He was not thinking about. He was thinking of His Father; He was bearing the reproaches that fell on His Father; He was in all ways seeking to do His will. Well, then, if I would follow Christ this is the way. I must not be thinking of what would please myself, I must be thinking of what I ought to do; of what my Father in heaven intends me to do. But is not that very hard? Is not the first thought that comes to me, 'How should I like this thing or that?' Yes, my friends, that thought does come to me, and it comes to you. And if I yield to my thoughts, I seek my pleasure, though it may very much interfere with yours, though it may cause you a great deal of sorrow; and you seek yours though it may interfere with mine, and cause me a great deal of misery. But now there is a Lord, your Saviour and every man's, who cares for all; who would not have one be striving against another; who would have us all be working together, and would have each be helping the other, each ready to make sacrifices for the other. He made the great sacrifice for us all; He gave Himself for us all. And now He says to us, 'Be my disciples. I will lead you in the way in which I have walked; I will teach you how to behave to each other; I will teach you what you should do in all the difficulties you will meet with on earth; I will guide you at last to the house of my Father and your Father, and of my God and your God.' That is what He did for Matthew the Publican; that is what He is willing to do for every one of us poor sinful creatures who are here this morning.

SERMON XXVII.

MICHAELMAS DAY.

Preached at Brampton Ash, 15th Sunday after Trinity, September 28, 1862.

"Take heed that ye despise not one of these little ones, for I say unto you that in Heaven their Angels do always behold the face of my Father which is in Heaven."—ST. MATTHEW xviii. 10.

To-morrow is the Festival of St. Michael and All Angels, what we call Michaelmas Day. The passage chosen for the epistle on that day speaks of a war in heaven. Michael and his angels, it is said, fought against the devil and his angels, and conquered them. I believe that war in heaven has very much to do with us on earth. More may be meant by it than I know, but this I am sure is meant by it, that the devil has done his utmost to overcome Christ, and has failed; that Christ has proved good to be stronger than evil, light than darkness. He has done this for His whole universe, for the spirits in every other world, and for us poor men in this. The powers that are for us are greater than the powers that are against us. God our Father is for us; Christ, His only begotten Son, the express image of His person, is for us. A multitude of good angels, who never disobeyed Him, but who have always delighted to do His commandments, are for us. The spirits of just men made perfect, who were once on earth tempted as we are tempted, by the world, the flesh, and the devil, who sinned as we have sinned, but have washed their robes and made them white in the blood of the Lamb, these are for us. And they are not idle; it is written they are ministers of those who are heirs of salvation. They are helping us in ways that we cannot think of or dream of. When you read a good book written by a good man, no longer among us, that man is helping you. He knows more now than he could put into his book. He can speak to us out of it, and tell us what he meant in his book, and where he blundered in trying to express his meaning. The words of our parents, of dear friends that are gone, how they start up sometimes in our minds! how they come back to us as if they were speaking these very words to us! And are they not speaking these words to us? Do not they care for us far more than they did when they were less good, less loving? Cannot they teach us better now than then?

Yes, my friends, that battle in heaven is the beginning of many battles on earth: that victory in heaven is the assurance that we shall have a multitude of unseen friends in our battles on earth, and that we need never be overcome by the powers of wickedness, if they be ever so fierce. But after we have read this passage about the heavenly war, we pass on to a gospel about little children. Is not that a great change? From Michael and his archangels to infants? From those who could subdue evil spirits, to the weakest of all creatures upon earth! What can have brought them together? Our Lord Jesus Christ brings them together. He had a little child beside Him, and He said to His disciples, "Whosoever of you shall humble himself as this little child, the same is greatest in the kingdom of heaven!" He spoke and He knew, for He is the King of Heaven; He is the Lord of Angels. All do Him homage. He spoke for He had humbled Himself to become a little child. He who was the Eternal Son of God had become the Son of the Virgin Mary. He had lain in a cradle. He had grown up to be a boy. He had risen to the stature of a man. And when He was using all the powers of the Son of Man, and of the Son of God: when He was healing the sick and casting out devils, He was still the humblest of all. "Come unto me," He said, "and take my yoke upon you, and learn of me, for I am meek and lowly of heart." That was the way to be like the Lord and King of Heaven; that was the way to have power over evil spirits; to become meek and lowly of heart. He who could do that could enter into the victory of Michael and the angels.

This is part of what our Lord tells us in that gospel for St. Michael's Day. I beseech you to lay it to heart and think well of it. We commonly suppose that our great difference from the angels is that they are strong and we are weak. No, brethren! the great difference between us and them is that they are obedient, and we are disobedient; that they are humble, and we are proud. All other differences lie in that. Their strength comes from their obedience. They have God's strength because they depend upon Him and not upon themselves. The victory in heaven was the victory over spirits who think themselves strong, and therefore will not be dependent upon God; who will not be children; who will not rely upon a Father and give themselves to Him.

But our Lord, when He had begun to discourse about the little children, went on to tell us more wonderful things about them; very wonderful and very beautiful things; but also very useful for you that are parents, and for all people whatsoever, to take note of and to remember. "Take heed," He says, "that ye despise not one of these little ones, for I say unto you, that in heaven their angels do always behold the face of my Father which is in heaven." Now these words were surely spoken by One who knew the temptations of men upon earth—their temptations to despise or think lightly of little children.

And they were spoken by One who knew the secrets of the kingdom of heaven. They were spoken by One who came to bind earth and heaven together. If we could in any degree enter into them we should find another reason why St. Michael's Day speaks first of angels and then of children. Let us try to understand them at least as far as it is needful for us, that we may not transgress our Lord's commandment.

I find a child very naughty, disagreeable, ill-behaved; well, I am tempted to dislike or despise the child; I must dislike or despise it if I think only of the child's naughtiness, disagreeableness, ill-behaviour. I cannot help it. But that is not the child. That is what disfigures the child; that is what makes it different from what it is meant to be. That child—every child on this earth—has a true life in it, as well as this bad nature which leads it to show forth bad tempers and do bad things. This true life is what our Lord calls the child's angel. His Father in heaven, He says, sees this angel in every child. This angel looks up to Him through the eye of every child. It beholds His face. These are good tidings. God sees the true child, loves the true child, when we are most finding fault with the false child. And our Lord would have us recollect this, that we may always see the true child underneath the false child, and speak to the true child, to the angel in the child which can hear us, instead of speaking to the false child which cannot hear us. If I say to a child which has been naughty, 'Now you know better than this; you have a better mind in you; you have yielded to the bad mind that is in you,' the child will understand why I punish it, will confess in its heart that I am right to punish it, will feel that I am showing my love to it by punishing it. But if I see nothing but what is wrong in the child, if I never do justice to the right that is in it, I may punish it for ever but I shall never make it the least better; I shall make it harder and worse, and I shall make myself harder and worse too. All parents and teachers that are wise and good learn this lesson by degrees; mothers especially find it out very soon, for God teaches it them in their inmost souls. But all ought to learn it; and none will learn it thoroughly, not even fathers and mothers, unless they believe the words of our Lord Jesus, and really think that their Heavenly Father does Himself what He bids them do; that there is not a single child on earth, however perverse it may be, in which He does not see a divine and glorious and blessed creature made after His image.

Our Lord spoke those mighty words, and He added other words to explain them that are mightier still. "For," He said, "the Son of Man is come to save that which was lost." As much as to say —'I have come from heaven, my Father's house, to bring back His children that have wandered from Him, to tell you that in Me He loves you, that in Me He is well pleased with you, that in Me He has restored you to your places in His family. Do not, therefore,' He says, ' despise one of these little ones, for I have taken their nature and become one of them to save them from all their enemies, and make them my brothers and sisters. Do not despise them, for in heaven they are not despised, but loved and cared for. Do not despise them, since I love and care for them. Do not despise them, since they belong to the great family of the Angels, and of those who have been redeemed out of every kindred and nation and tongue and clime by my blood.'

My friends, if St. Michael's Day teaches you to lay these things to heart it will be a festival indeed to you. It will tell you how to regard the little ones whom Christ has committed to your care below—the little ones of your parish and neighbourhood, as well as of your own households. It will tell you how to expect the day, when all the Angel-children who have been taken hence to the home of their Father in heaven, shall come to greet you, and to rejoice with you, and that He who became a little child, has fought the fight and won the day for you and for them, and for His whole Family of men and Angels.

SERMON XXVIII.

GOD'S VISITATIONS.

Preached at Brampton Ash, Morning of the 16th Sunday after Trinity, October 5, 1862.

"And there came a fear on all, and they glorified God, saying, That a great prophet is risen up among us, and that God hath visited His people."—St. LUKE vii. 16.

You remember, most of you, the cholera which came upon this land eight years ago. Many of you will remember another a few years before that, and another still further back. That brought a great fear on many neighbourhoods. They saw one and another who was well one Sunday, carried off before the next. This seat was empty and that. Whose seat might be empty the next week? This they called a visitation of God. 'It is very terrible,' they cried, 'He is indeed visiting us. We must ask Him to stay His hand.' They knew, indeed, that their own neglect had often much to do with the spread of the disease. Houses were not kept clean; from mere idleness, or from their own selfish plans, people put themselves and their neighbours in danger. Many drank too much, and that made them weak when the disorder caught hold of them. 'Still,' they said, 'this is God's doing. He is visiting us.'

Now, my friends, in one way it was quite right to use this language. God does remind us of His presence by these things. Men recollected that there was One over them who cared for their doings, One who commanded them to be clean and sober, and to think of their neighbours as well as themselves. They start up suddenly as if they had waked out of a long heavy sleep, and say, 'He is there and we knew it not. We have been taking our own way. We have fancied we were left to do as we liked. And lo! it is clear we cannot take our own ways. We cannot do as we like. There is One whom we see not that has fixed which is the right course. There is One who is pointing to us very clearly, 'That is the way, walk ye in it; there is terrible danger in going out of it.'

So far it is a right and useful thought that God visits us in any plague, in any railway accident, in any calamity of any kind that comes to one or another of us. In many places, after the cholera, there was much improvement. The houses and the streets were much better. Nuisances were removed. Rich men saw that they were deeply concerned in the state of the poor; the poor saw that they must bestir themselves and correct their bad habits. A blessing came out of the misery. It was clear that God had been working among us, because that blessing came out of the misery. That is the sure token that neither man nor the devil has the upper hand. The pain and anguish are compelled to serve a good end. They work for a Father, not for a tyrant.

That turns the fear which a cholera or any like sorrow produces into a good fear. The fear alone is not good. It makes men cowards. It makes them more likely to catch the plague. It makes them shrink from services to one another. As long as they think that the plague has been sent by some cruel enemy who has a spite against them and wants to take vengeance on them, they do not exert themselves manfully against it, they merely crouch under it. Their fear very often renders them more careless and mad. They think it is too late to set their houses right; they drink harder that they may forget themselves. And as soon as they suppose the danger is over this poor, miserable, beggarly fear is exchanged for indifference. They remember nothing. They take their chance till the next time.

The true fear—the only fear that is not bad, that is not accursed—is that sort of fear which you are told of in the Gospel of to-day. What caused that fear? A poor woman had lost her only son. She was going out to bury him. A crowd of people were with her. As they came near the gate of the city, the Lord Jesus Christ met them. He said to the woman, "Weep not." He touched the bier. Those who bare it stood still. He said, "Young man, I say unto thee arise." He that was dead sat up. Jesus delivered him to his mother.

Now it is said, a great fear came upon all, and they said, "A great prophet has risen among us, and God has visited His people." That was what made the fear! 'Why, there is a Deliverer among us! There is One who is stronger than Death among us. We have feared Death. We have thought Death is the master of us all. He must carry all before him. And now there is One who *can* take a man out of his hands; who *can* compel him to give up his prey.' A great fear came upon them of One who had such power.

But was it only His power which they thought of? See what the Gospel says. "When Jesus saw the woman He had compassion upon her." They had never found any compassion in death. He had seized hold of the youngest creatures, of the most beautiful creatures. He had torn them away from mothers, not heeding their cries in the least. But the Conqueror of death is full of compassion. He feels not only for people in general, but for this one woman. He understands her grief. He enters into it. Can there be such a Being? Can there be One who cares, actually cares, for each one—cares for the sorrow of each one? Who can He be?

They could not doubt it. This must be a great prophet of God. He must be speaking the words of God. He must be doing the work of God. Only such an one could have this might—only such an one could have this pity! Yes! He who can mock death must have come from the Living God. He who is all good, cannot have learnt His goodness from selfish people such as we are. God then must have visited His people. This must be in truth His visitation.

My dear friends! I long exceedingly that we should all feel as this people in Palestine felt at that moment about God's visitations. I am sure we have more right to the feeling than they had. For we not only think as they thought, that Jesus is a great prophet from God, One who speaks the words of God. We believe, and say every Sunday, that He is the only begotten Son of God; that He came down from Heaven to do His Father's will and to finish His work; and that He did His Father's will and finished His work, by saving us men. We do not only believe he raised up the son of the woman of Nain, or the daughter of Jairus, or the brother of Mary and Martha. We believe that He went down into death and the grave and hell, and that He triumphed over them once for all, showing that if they were strong, He was stronger. We believe that He did this for them who, through fear of death, had been in bondage all their lives long. We believe that He overcame him who had the power of death—that is the Devil. We believe that He ascended on high to the right hand of His Father, and that all His enemies will be made His footstool. We believe that Death, the last enemy, will be destroyed.

And, therefore, we have a right to say that this was God's great visitation, and that by it we are to judge of all His other visitations. He visited His people by sending His Son to redeem one and another out of the jaws of death, and then by giving up His Son to suffer death for all mankind. He visited His people by raising up His Son to be the King of the whole earth; the elder Brother of His whole family in Heaven and earth. He visited His people by sending His Holy Spirit to teach them to call Him Father, to comfort them in their sorrows, to unite them to each other, to bestow His Eternal Life on their spirits, at last to raise their bodies out of death and corruption. These are the great visitations which the Bible tells us of, and explains to us. And if we believe, we shall think that He visits us every morning, when He causes the light to break out of the darkness, and when He rouses us out of our sleep. We shall think that He visits us in the gift of daily bread. We shall think that He visits us in seed-time and harvest.

We shall think that He visits us in the lessons of our fathers and mothers, in the kind words of every friend. We shall think that He visits us when we come to Church and hear His Holy Word and receive the food of His Sacraments. We shall not think less than before that He visits us when He sends sickness into our families or our neighbourhoods, or when we hear of strange accidents and sudden deaths. But we shall remember that it is Christ, and not death, who is

God's prophet—Christ, and not death, who tells us what God is. Therefore we shall consider every such visitation as a sign that He is among us who stopped the bier at the gate of the city, who had compassion on the widow woman, who said to the young man 'Arise.' A great fear and awe will come upon us while we remember how near He is to us, though we see Him not. We shall ask him to strengthen us to bear whatever we have to bear, to do what we have to do. We shall ask that the Holy Spirit, the Comforter, may visit us and visit all the sorrowers of the earth, and may give them that peace which the world cannot give. We shall ask that at last every one we have loved and known may hear the voice which says 'Arise,' and that children may be given to their mothers, and mothers to their children, by His own loving hand who came upon earth, who lives in Heaven, to heal the breaches in His Father's family, and to gather all together in one.

SERMON XXIX.

THE ETERNAL WEIGHT OF GLORY.

Preached at Brampton Ash, Afternoon of the 16th Sunday after Trinity, October 5, 1862.

"For our light affliction, which is but for a moment, worketh for us a far more exceeding and eternal weight of glory. While we look not at the things which are seen, but at the things which are not seen: for the things which are seen are temporal, but the things which are not seen are eternal."—2 CORINTHIANS iv. 17, 18.

MANY of us have said to ourselves as we have read these verses, 'Yes, it is no wonder that St. Paul should say that he might well bear any afflictions, if he could reckon upon an eternal weight of glory to come after them in a few years. And he was so unlike us, so unlike most people who have been upon this earth, that he might fairly cheer himself with this hope. But which of us can? What afflictions of ours can ever work for us an eternal weight of glory? How dare we ever dream of such a reward for anything that we ever have suffered, or ever shall suffer here?'

My friends, I have had this thought in my mind, as some of you may have had it in your minds. But when

I read the chapter we have read this afternoon, the one out of which these words are taken, I see that the thought is not good for anything; I see that St. Paul was not separating himself from other men, or trying to prove that he had better claims on God's goodness and love than they had. I see that he was learning all his life through to give up any claims of his own, to put himself on the level of the most helpless and the most ignorant. I see that *that* was the great lesson which God was teaching him by his afflictions. He was better than we are, because he had learnt it, and we have not learnt it. If we would get it by heart, if we would profit by God's schooling, and give up boasting of ourselves as he did, we should share the hopes which made even very sore trials look so light to him.

You remember that he was once a very proud man. He thought God favoured his nation and hated all other nations. He thought God favoured his sect in that nation, the sect of the Pharisees, and hated Sadducees and all other sects. This pride led Saul of Tarsus to abhor the disciples of the Lord Jesus. Their Master had eaten and drunk with publicans and sinners. They said that He had taken the nature of all men, and died the death of all men, and risen again to be King of all men. Though they had not yet preached this Gospel to the heathen, Saul of Tarsus saw that they would soon break down the barrier between them and the Jews. So he wished to destroy them, and gave himself up heart and soul to the work of destroying them.

As he journeyed towards Damascus with this intent, there shone a light about him brighter than the light of the sun. He fell on his face. He heard a voice speaking to him. The Son of God made him understand that he was going upon an evil errand. The Son of God made him understand that He cared for those whom Saul persecuted. And now it became evident to Saul that this Lord was *his* Lord, that all which was good and right in him came from this Lord; that in himself apart from Him there was nothing good. And now he learnt that he must do the very things which he had cursed the Apostles of Jesus for designing to do. He must tell people who were not Jews, people who had been worshipping idols, that God cared for them, and had sent His only begotten Son to deliver them from the tyrants to whom they had sold themselves, and to adopt them into His family. "When," he says, "it pleased God to reveal His Son in me, that I might preach Him among the Gentiles, I conferred not with flesh and blood." That is to say, he felt that the Father had made known His Son to him as the only root of all good in him, as the only Saviour from evil, on purpose that he might proclaim to all people everywhere, 'He is the root of all good in you, He is the Saviour from all your evil.'

That became hereafter his work. In performing that work he had to endure those afflictions of which he spoke. His countrymen persecuted him for his faith in the Son of God, as he had persecuted the older disciples. They told him that he did not care for being a child of Abraham; though he had been showing forth the goodness of the covenant which God had made with Abraham, by preaching that the seed of Abraham was come, in Whom God had promised to bless all the families of the earth. The Jews told him that he did not care for the law of Moses; though he was certain that it had never been so dear to him as since he knew that Jesus his Lord had kept it all, and had sent His Spirit to write it on men's hearts. The rulers and the priests of the Gentiles to whom he preached, were as much inclined to persecute him as the Jews; for they found that he drove men away from the worship of their gods, far more than the other Jews, who said that none had any portion in the true God but themselves. St. Paul had much to bear, he says, from false brethren; from men who pretended to believe in Christ, and did not really regard Him as a deliverer from sin, but went on in sin as much as before they confessed Him. Sometimes it seems as if the Apostle suffered most from bodily torments. But I suspect his worst afflictions were from battles with the enemies of his spirit; from the tempter who would have persuaded him to shrink from his duty and to distrust God's love, and to fall back into the pride and bitterness out of which Christ had raised him. "We wrestle," he says in one place, "not against flesh and blood, but against principalities, against powers, against the rulers of the darkness of this world, against spiritual wickedness in high places."

All these together one would have thought were not light afflictions, and yet he calls them so; when he weighs them against the blessing to which they were leading him. And what was that? He had found out that the Eternal God, He who is, and was, and is to come, is not, as he had supposed, the enemy of the human race, but its Redeemer and Father. He had believed that the Father so loved the world, as to give His only begotten Son to die for it. He had believed that this Father was sending forth His own Holy Spirit, to bring men's spirits from darkness to light, from the power of Satan to Himself. He had believed, for the Spirit had taught him, of a righteousness, and truth, and love, which could not change, could not pass away; a righteousness, truth, and love which are in God Himself, but which He has shown to men in the life and death of our Lord.

'Now, these,' he said to himself, 'are eternal things; this truth and love and righteousness will be the same always. I know but a little, a very little of them yet; ages upon ages must unfold them to me, but I am sure they cannot grow less. The more glimpses I have had of God's goodness, the more wonderful it has seemed to me; the more high and deep and wide. I see that His love passes knowledge, and yet that we may every day grow to know something more of it; something more of what it can do in overcoming evil, and in raising those out of evil who have yielded to it. What a reward is that! My afflictions have taught me to enter into God; to feel that the greatest delight I can have is, to let His charity govern me and possess me, and draw me on. The opposition of my countrymen, the rage of the heathen mobs, my pains of body, the temptations of the devil—all have forced me to take refuge in God; in His wisdom which I cannot measure; in His love which I cannot sound. Nothing short of this love can suffice for me; any love which has bounds to it, which prohibits any sinner from approaching it, would not have raised me out of my evil, would not keep me out of it; I must sink and be lost if I have not that to rest upon.'

Here, then, was that eternal weight of glory which the Apostle tells us of, and which he says his light afflictions that were but for a moment were working out for him. It was not a glory that belonged to him, or which ever could belong to him. The sun rose in great glory this morning—you in this parish may have seen it—people in the furthest end of England, of France, of Germany, may have seen it; there was the same glory about all; all might behold it and rejoice in it. I have sometimes seen sunsets of which I could only say—what a weight of glory is there; one can scarcely bear it; one feels as if one should be crushed by it! so St. Paul felt about that eternal sun and glory of God. 'I cannot see it,' he says, 'it is not a thing for my eyes to take in, as they take in the glory of the sun. The eternal things are not seen. But it is all real. It compasses the universe more than the light or heat of the sun compasses the universe. It warms and lightens the universe more than ten thousand suns could. And this will one day burst upon us. There will be a complete unveiling of the Son of God, who gave Himself a sacrifice for all men. Every eye shall see Him, and those also—like me—who have pierced Him.'

And so you will not wonder how that all through this chapter, St. Paul is speaking to the Corinthians as if what he lived for was that they might share this weight of glory along with him. They had given him much trouble; he had great cause to complain of them, but his complaints are always that they are too much lifted up in themselves, that each is seeking some prize or glory for himself. He wants them to know that God who commanded the light to shine out of darkness, is now shining into their hearts to give them the light of the knowledge of God in the face of Jesus Christ. He wants them to feel that if any miss this light—if there is a veil over the Gospel to any—it is because the god of this world, the spirit of pride and vanity, blinds their eyes that they may not see how God's glory is the humiliation and passion and death of Jesus Christ. He would have them understand that sufferings and sorrows —all these afflictions which are but for a time—are God's ways of delivering men from this blindness, His way of teaching them to seek for that love, which is for all and for ever.

Dear friends, that love of God, that glory of God—which is for all and for ever—is for us English as much as it was for the Corinthians; for us in the year 1862 as much as it was for those to whom St. Paul preached. Oh! let us hear His voice speaking to each of us, and saying, 'Brother, it is for thee; for thee the Son of God poured out His blood! for thee He overcame death! for thee He lives and pleads at His Father's right hand! for thee He sent His Spirit that thou mightest claim thy place as one of God's beloved children; that thou mightest possess the inheritance which He has prepared for them that love Him. Take thy portion of afflictions, whatever it be, that God sends thee here. Receive them as a Father's love-tokens to thee. Remember that He laid all first upon that Son in whom He delights, the Son who was with Him before the worlds were. Remember that He would use them to bring thee out of death to His eternal life; out of darkness to His perfect light; out of the vain glory which we covet for ourselves to the weight of glory which will be manifested to all creatures in the great day of redemption, when He whose face was marred more than any man's shall be revealed in the glory of His Father and the holy angels.'

SERMON XXX.

THE GRACE OF GOD.

Preached at Budock, 1864.

"Simon Peter, a servant and an Apostle of Jesus Christ, to them that have obtained like precious faith with us through the righteousness of God and our Saviour Jesus Christ: Grace and peace be multiplied unto you through the knowledge of God and of Jesus our Lord."—2 St. Peter i. 1, 2.

This is all we know about the persons to whom St. Peter's Epistle was written. They might be Jews, like Simon Peter himself. Probably most of them were, for his work was chiefly among Jews. But they might be Gentiles, for he had been the first to tell the Gentiles that God was no respecter of persons, and that in every nation those who feared Him and wrought righteousness should be accepted of Him. Whatever they were, they had obtained that blessing which St. Peter thought the most precious that he or any man could obtain.

What was it? They certainly had not obtained ease or quietness. Neither they nor the Apostle were leading more tranquil prosperous lives than their fellow-men. They had many troubles which other men had not. They were not to escape the troubles which other men had. St. Peter writes this letter especially to prepare them for great calamities which were coming upon the world, and in which they would have their full share.

And they had not obtained freedom from the temptations to evil which beset their neighbours. If they fancied they had that freedom, they would soon find how terribly they had deluded themselves.

This Epistle will show you how carefully and earnestly the Apostle warned his fellow-disciples that they might have a deeper fall, and sink into worse crimes than those who had never been sealed with the name of Christ. St. Peter had thought that he could go to prison and death for his Master. He had denied Him thrice. He certainly had not obtained the privilege of trusting himself. What he had obtained was the privilege of distrusting himself; the privilege of believing in God. That faith he calls precious; that faith he, as an apostle and servant of Jesus Christ, had invited Jews and Gentiles to claim as their treasure, just as it was his. He writes to those who had heard His Gospel, who had confessed it to be true. He writes to remind them what their confession meant; to show them how every event which befell them, every experience of their lives, was a confirmation of it; how they might act upon it; how they might bear witness of it to their fellows.

The verses which I have read to you are the beginning of what we call a general Epistle. Very general it is, not limited by the circumstances and the character of those to whom it was addressed; very general it is, not limited to the first ages, but carrying a message to this age. And yet I think also it is very special. It speaks to each man according to his own circumstances, according to his own deepest necessities; it tells each of us what need he has and what right he has to claim the like precious faith with the Apostle. Let us think first of the need, then of the right; afterwards we may see how St. Peter binds them together in his benediction.

I. How the Apostle found his need of faith I have told you already. He had been full of self-conceit; he had been chosen by One whom he regarded as the Son of David and the Son of God to be a minister in His Kingdom. I do not know that he actually thought himself the greatest of those ministers, as some in later days have said for him that he was, but at least he wished to be the greatest. He disputed, as his brother-disciples disputed, whether when the kingdom was established he should not have the highest place in it. He had been often told by his Master that in that kingdom the chief of all was the servant of all. A little child had been set before Him. 'You must become,' Jesus said, 'like that child if you would be great in my Kingdom!' But such words did not at the time he heard them carry much meaning to his mind. Had he not been chosen

—poor fisherman as he was—to be near the King? Had it not been said that he should sit on a throne judging the twelve tribes of Israel? Had it not been said that he should open the doors of the Kingdom of Heaven? These words were remembered, the others were forgotten. Then came the explanation of them. The great man found how little he was, how contemptible he was. What then did his grand calling mean? How could he be a minister of the King? how could he reign or judge? how could he open the Kingdom of Heaven? He could be a minister of the King when he knew that he was good for nothing; he could judge the tribes of Israel for their unbelief in the righteous God and for their refusal to bless all the families of the earth with the knowledge of Him, when he had cast away his own unbelief and learned to trust Him altogether; he could open the Kingdom of Heaven to men by declaring Him to them, by saying to them, 'Behold your God; behold Him in whom you may trust.'

In this school St. Peter learnt his need of faith. When he once found that he was not better than his neighbours; when his conscience accused him of sins of which he could accuse no other, then he understood that he must have faith in One who cared for him more than he cared himself. And I say, my friends, we are every one of us in this school; we are all under a discipline which is to make us feel after some one who is looking after us when we are least able to look after ourselves, who is upholding us when we stumble, who is directing us when our own way would be most crooked. All accidents and diseases are threatening my body, yet life is preserved in it. My mind becomes bewildered, incapable of judging, thinking, remembering, yet some one does put thoughts and memories into it, does enable it to exercise judgment. Often we seem unable to bear the load we have to bear, the dread of what we may have to bear. Whence comes the renewal of the mind, of the courage? Who is it that is near us in those terrible moments when we are tempted, as St. Peter was, to lie; who in the more terrible moment when we have fallen as he fell? The faith that there is such a One as this—an actual person—a living friend—it is this which we have all need of; no other will do for us. A man says to himself sometimes, 'I blundered terribly, but luck stood my friend; I committed that crime, but I was not found out; I was a fool, but I had kinsmen or parents who stood by me and pardoned my folly.' They say these things, but they know all the while that there is no ground of trust in any of these things. The luck may save them once or twice; it will desert them some day. The crime will not always be hidden; the folly will wear out the patience of kinsmen and parents. Sad would it be if this were not so! As long as we confide in chances, what miserable beggarly creatures we are. Every hour makes us feebler and baser. We want something to trust in, in which there is no chance, no variableness, not the shadow of a turning. We want One to trust in who perfectly knows us, perfectly sympathises with us, understands how weak we are that He may give us exactly the strength which answers to that weakness, bear with our evil and so raise us out of it.

II. Have we a right to this kind of trust? Is there any one in whom we may place it, any one who demands it of us? St. Peter speaks to us of the righteousness of God and our Saviour Jesus Christ. He tells us of One who is absolutely utterly right, right always, right without change. He tells us that this righteousness has been manifested to men in One who had their nature, who entered into all their temptations, who died their death, who conquered their death. Men had dreamed of gods who had might; of gods who could do what they liked; but they could never find the might in such gods which they knew that they had need of: the might of one contended against the might of another. The might of this god seemed to be exerted in their favour; the might of that one seemed to be exerted against them. This prevailed in one place, over one set of persons; that prevailed in another place, over another set of persons. They could not trust such gods. They only could trust them when they supposed they were better than themselves; when they supposed that they inspired what was right and trustworthy in men, and fought against whatever was wrong and treacherous. Simon Peter said the God of our Fathers, the God who revealed Himself to Abraham and called forth his faith in the God of righteousness—He has been asking in all ages for our trust. He has been complaining in all ages of our want of trust. He has been waging war with all unrighteousness; He has been raising us out of our unrighteousness. He has been the God of salvation, because He has been the righteous God. He has been delivering us from evil, because He hates evil. And now He has shown Himself as the God of all the families of the earth in His Son. He is showing Himself mighty to save all the families of the earth by that Son. The God of righteousness is the Almighty God—the God who not only rules in the armies of heaven and among the inhabitants of earth, but who is able to convert the inhabitants of the earth from unrighteousness to righteousness, from darkness to light, from the ignorance of Him to the knowledge of Him. Here is the true might—the might of the Father who created man in His own image to show forth His righteousness and glory; the might of the only begotten Son—the might which came forth in the agony of the garden, in the death on the cross; the might which was shown forth in the uttermost weakness; the might which could conquer hatred and enmity, and therefore which could conquer death and hell; the might in which He ascended on high, leading captivity captive, glorifying our humanity at the right hand of God. Here is the might of that Spirit who triumphs over rebellious wills; who has come forth that God may dwell among men, and that they may testify of a day when He shall subdue all things to Himself.

Here, then, is our right to the faith which St. Peter claimed for himself and for his fellow-disciples. It stands on no ground of superiority in us to other men; the moment we set up such a pretence, the faith disappears. It stands on the name of God Himself; on His eternal righteousness; on the manifestation of that righteousness in Christ, on the purpose of God and the power of God to make righteousness victorious over evil, life over death. The name of the righteous God was proclaimed in this far island of the west, as it was proclaimed in the eastern lands in which St. Peter preached. Here, as there, it overcame the unrighteous gods to which men had bowed down. Here, as there, the atonement of God to mankind in Christ overcame the accursed and hateful sacrifices by which men had sought to make themselves acceptable to the tyrants whom they served. Here, as there, the Spirit of truth and love showed that He could overcome the spirit of falsehood and evil that contended with Him. God called us to the like precious faith with that which the Apostles had preached to hard exclusive Jews and Greek idolators. Our right to it is affirmed by every lesson we read, by every prayer in which we join, by every sacrament which declares our union to God and to each other. The blessing of these lessons, these prayers, these sacraments, is that they express our own utter nothingness; that they bring us all to a level; that they say to us, 'Trust not in your righteousness, in your traditions, in your personal faith; if you do, your righteousness will be found to be sinfulness, your traditions will contradict themselves, your personal faith will be changed to unbelief. But trust in God's righteousness; thank Him for having called your fathers to trust in it, and for having preserved the record of His Name to your own day; ask Him to restore your faith when it is feeblest and nearest to death; ask Him to make you witnesses to all men of His will, that they should believe in Him—and your youth and your Nation's youth will be renewed like the eagle's; all personal circumstances, all past history, will give hopes of the future, will be quickened by Him who is, and who was, and who is to come; you will find that He has known us in all our struggles, and that He will give us that knowledge of Him which is eternal life.'

III. And so we may feel in some little degree the force of that wonderful blessing which we have heard so often and felt so little. "Grace and peace be multiplied to you, through the knowledge of God and of Jesus our Lord." If we only heard of such words as having been spoken by an old and venerable man eighteen hundred years ago, to a set of men some of whom he had known, some of whom he had never seen, they would be very striking. An echo of a voice that must have been very sweet would reach us through all these centuries of vicissitude and sorrow. But now suppose the old man spoke truly; suppose he did not only utter a feeble wish of his ; suppose he had a warrant to say, 'There is One whose grace and peace are over you and about you; there is One whose grace and peace will be over all the generations to come; there is One who will be seeking to bless them, as He is seeking to bless you; bestowing grace and peace on them, as He bestows them on you'—would that be a mere echo of a mortal voice ? would not Simon Peter, the Apostle and servant of Jesus Christ, however good and venerable, be lost in Him of whom he testifies as the same yesterday, to-day, and for ever ?

And if the thought comes to us, 'Yes, but this grace and peace are expressly for those who have like precious faith with himself, *that* may indeed discourage and almost crush us.' But when we consider what his faith was, how it grew, who gave it him, in whom it rested— when above all we read the words, "through the knowledge of God and Jesus our Lord"—our spirits are carried into another region ; we shall cease to dwell on what we are ; we shall remember what He is who gave His Son for us; what that Son is who humbled Himself, became of no reputation, and took upon Him the form of a servant, and who is therefore exalted far above all principalities and powers, that all things may be put under His feet. We shall not doubt that there is a grace coming forth from Him which can make even us willing in the day of His power; we shall not doubt that there is a peace in Him which we are meant to inherit, and which no tribulations of the world, no confusion in our minds can disturb. While we trust in that grace of God, in that peace in Jesus our Lord, we shall have the like precious faith with the Apostle—that faith of which he spoke in his first epistle, when he says—" Who by Him do believe in God, which raised Him from the dead, and gave Him glory, that your faith and hope may be in God."

Here, then, my friends, let our faith and hope be. Then it will be a hope not of some happiness for ourselves, but of the revelation of God's glory which shall fill the whole earth—that glory for which Apostles and Martyrs in all ages have longed, and for which they counted not their lives dear. In the knowledge of God and of Jesus our Lord they sought their heaven; of the grace and peace of God and Jesus our Lord they spoke to their brethren on earth. If we desire what they desired, if we join in their testimony, we shall not be disappointed; every part of our discipline here will prepare us for that heaven, because it will reveal to us more of the righteousness and the forgiveness of God. And the baptism of every child, the marriage of those whose hearts are one, the grave of every friend who has been separated from us, will repeat the benediction, " Grace and peace be multiplied to you, from God our Father, and the Lord Jesus Christ."

SERMON XXXI.

THE NEW COVENANT.

Preached at Burnham, 10th Sunday after Trinity, August 5, 1866.

(Burned.)

"For this is the covenant that I will make with the House of Israel after those days, saith the Lord: I will put my laws into their mind and write them in their hearts: and I will be to them a God and they shall be to me a people."—HEBREWS viii. 10.

MY brethren, we have said to-day that we are under this new covenant. When the Commandments were read from the Altar, we prayed, "Lord have mercy upon us, and write all these Thy laws in our hearts, we beseech Thee." The laws are written in the twentieth chapter of Exodus; they are said there to have been written on tables of stone. We are not content that they should be written in that chapter or on those stones. We do not think they can help us much whilst they are at a distance from us—whilst we only read them out of a book. They were spoken to the people of Israel. We want that they should be spoken to us. We want that they should be spoken not only into our ears but into our minds and hearts. We ask Him from whom they came to put them into our minds—to fix them in our hearts. That is what we believe He promised to do for the people of Israel. That is what we believe He promises to do for the people of England. We are sure no one else can do it. No one else knows the heart and mind of an Israelite or an Englishman; no one else knows what is scrawled there which has need to be blotted out, or how any new and better thing can be written in place of it. He does know. He can blot out the scrawl. He can write the clear letters which He wishes to be there.

Yes, my friends, this is the new covenant—what we call the New Testament. It is the covenant of our Baptism. When you bring your children to be christened, you claim this new covenant for them. You believe that your Father has accepted them as His children in His only begotten Son; you present them to Him that He may give them the Spirit who will put His laws in their minds and write them in their hearts. You are to rear them in the faith that what He has promised on their behalf He will surely keep and perform. You cannot make them obey your commandments or His commandments. You will find them inclined to disobey both. For their inclinations are just like yours, and you are inclined to choose your own ways, to go out of what you know and confess to be the right way. Therefore you need a wisdom and a power above your own to order yourselves as well as your children. This covenant tells you that the wisdom and power are always with you. The

Father, the Son, and the Holy Ghost, the one God blessed for ever, has sealed you with that Name. We are all living, moving, having our being in Him who has put it upon us. We may all say assuredly, 'Thou art our God, we are Thy people, therefore write Thy laws in our hearts, we beseech Thee.'

My friends, these words become very familiar to us. We repeat them as if they meant nothing. But they do mean that which is more wonderful than all the strangest things that we hear or read of in other days or our own. That God Himself should be taking care of your mind and heart and mine; that He, and not some mortal, should be teaching us what we are and what we have to do; that He should be curbing us when we struggle to run wild; that He should be urging us on when we wish to stand still. Is not that wonderful? For rich and poor to be alike in such a covenant as this; for each one to be able to say, 'Yes, He was giving me my lesson then and there; I did not take it in; I needed the rod to make me heed it. And the stroke of the rod came. I felt it. That was His way of putting His law in my mind, of writing it in my heart!' Yet this is even so. We are all to say that and to think that. A sharp twinge of pain is not merely a twinge of pain. It is the message from a Father—'I would put this law in thy mind, which thou hast broken. I would write this law in thy heart which thou hast forgotten, for I have said that I would be your God and that you should be my people.

I do not forget any of my people, and I would not have any of them forget me.'

This seems to me very wonderful. And yet each day and night may show us that it is necessary for us. There is not one of us can do with any smaller blessing. If the laws stay outside of us they terrify us, we are sure we shall be punished for breaking them, but for all that, we cannot keep them. We are like people in a dream. There is a pit before us but we cannot help running into it. There is a robber behind us, but we cannot stir. And yet, as I said before, no man is able to force the laws inside of us; to make us love them instead of hating them; no man and no Angel; only God can do that for us. If He has not given us an assurance that He will, it is all over with us. We shall go wrong if we are ever so persuaded that it will lead to our ruin. Therefore I can imagine no better tidings for a man to hear than these, 'God has given this assurance. He has made this covenant with us in His Son who took the nature of us all, and died for us all, and rose again for us all, and is at the right hand of God for us all. "I will put my laws in your hearts, and in your minds will I write them."' That is the Gospel or good news we have received. And that is the Gospel Christ has bidden us preach to all nations. You were told this morning of a society which undertook, on behalf of us English, to spread this Gospel in the lands in which our countrymen settle; to keep alive the remembrance of it in those who have heard it and confessed it to be true, to make it known to those who have not received it. I shall say nothing of the countries in which the society is at work. You have been told of them already. But I will say to you a few words on the name which this society bears, then you will see what kind of task it has to perform.

It is a Society for the Propagation of the Gospel, or good news concerning God, of the Gospel or good news which God sends forth concerning Himself. What that is you have been hearing out of the Lesson of this afternoon. The nations of the earth have accepted bad news concerning their Creator and Ruler. They have supposed Him to be a Tyrant over men—governing them according to His fancies, One from whom they have need to seek deliverance. He proclaimed Himself to the Israelites as their Deliverer out of the house of bondage. He commanded them not to do the things which would bring them into bondage. The Israelites broke these commandments, made gods for themselves who enslaved them; then they cried to the God of their Fathers and He brake their bonds asunder. These Israelites, as you heard in the Lesson this morning, were to bless all the families of the earth. They were to tell all men, 'This Deliverer, whom we worship, is your God; there is no other.' But before they could do that fully and perfectly, God gave a higher sign of what He was than the signs which He gave the Israelites when He brought them out of the

T

land of Egypt. He sent His only begotten Son to deliver those who had rebelled against Him from sin; to deliver them from death and from him who had the power of death. The new covenant tells of this Deliverer. And the new covenant declares that He who is our Redeemer does not merely give men a good law to warn them of the things which shall make them slaves, but that He gives them His Spirit that they may love His law and obey it and be free.

Here is the good news which this society engages to tell first to English citizens and then to all other men whom its voice can reach. First, English citizens; for though they have heard these things in their infancy, and have been baptized into the Holy Name, they are as prone as any men can be to forget what they have been told, and to drop into dark thoughts of God, and to live as if He were their enemy and not their Redeemer. Next, all other people; for all have the same right to the message which God has sent by His Son to all. It cannot be true for us if it is not true for them. If God would put His laws into our minds He would put them into theirs. If He would write them on our hearts He would write them on theirs.

And so we understand what is meant by the next words: "And they shall not teach every man his neighbour," "saying, Know the Lord." For a moment you might say, 'Such language is inconsistent with the command to preach the Gospel to every creature; if it is true we need no societies like that which we have been asked to support to-day.' But if you think what the Gospel is which we profess to preach or propagate, you will not hold that opinion. We do not teach our Christian neighbour, or our Heathen neighbour, " Know the Lord." We say to him, 'We cannot teach you to know Him; but He can teach you to know Him. He knows your minds and hearts. He bids you lay them open to Him with all their ignorance and sin. He will make them sound minds and clean hearts. He will write His laws in them.' That is a very different message from the other; much less presumptuous, much more consolatory. There is no man, let him be ever so far fallen into evil, ever so little able to raise himself out of it, who may not hearken to that news and live.

And see, we are told that one day all shall know Him from the least even to the greatest. The words sound too amazing for our belief. Yet I do not suppose any of us would dare to say, 'They are not Divine words, I do not believe them.' We all of us have a hope that they must come to pass, let them go ever so far beyond our understanding. Yes, and let us cherish that hope. It will not make us ashamed at the last. And in the meantime it will strengthen us to be patient in well-doing; for we shall reap if we faint not. There were no signs of a harvest when you cast the seeds into the ground, nor for weeks and months after that. But you believed it would come; your belief helped you to work and to wait, and you have the fruit of it. So will it be with every word of God which is cast into the hearts of men. He who is the great Husbandman has long patience for the precious fruit of His Son's travail and suffering. He calls you to the high honour of being His fellow-workers and fellow-waiters; that you may enter into His joy when He shall bring back his sheaves with Him. Do not refuse that honour; there is none that can be compared with it.

SERMON XXXII.

THE LAST SUPPER.

Preached at Burnham, Morning of the 11th Sunday after Trinity, August 12, 1866.

"And as they were eating, Jesus took bread, and blessed it, and brake it, and gave it to the disciples, and said, Take, eat; this is my body. And He took the cup, and gave thanks, and gave it to them, saying, Drink ye all of it: for this is my blood of the New Testament, which is shed for many for the remission of sins."—
ST. MATTHEW xxvi. 26-28.

You know why I have chosen these words to-day. They speak of the Lord's Supper. They tell us when that feast was first kept, and who first kept it; what it meant to them, what it means to us when we keep it now. I shall speak to you on each of these points. May God enable us to think of them!

I. When it was first kept and who kept it. *As He was eating*, Jesus took bread. He was eating unleavened bread and drinking wine at the Feast of the Passover in the city of Jerusalem. The Jews held that feast once every year. It reminded them that their fathers had been slaves to the King of Egypt. It reminded them that the Lord God of their fathers had brought them out of their slavery. It reminded them that He was King over them as He had been over their fathers.

Each family slew a lamb and ate it with bitter herbs. For each family was to recollect what the misery was of being under a tyrant, and what the blessing was of having the gracious God for their King.

The Lord Jesus Christ had gone forth among the Jews and preached the Kingdom of Heaven. He said that in this Kingdom the greatest of all was the servant of all. He made these words good by His acts. His whole life was a service, a service to the poorest people. He healed the sick among them. He delivered them from evil spirits. He said that they, as much as the rich, were citizens of His Kingdom. He called out His twelve Apostles to tell men of the Kingdom of Heaven, and to give the same proofs as He had given, that it was a Kingdom of blessing and deliverance to the sons of men.

He had come into Jerusalem just before the great Feast. The people had cried, 'This is the Son of David. This is the King who is come in the name of the Lord.' The rulers of the Jews heard these words. They thought He was going to set Himself up as King during the Passover. Numbers were gathered together there; they fancied it was just the time He would choose for such a purpose. They determined that it should not be. They must, if possible, seize Him and give Him up to their masters the Romans. They were afraid to do it, for they thought the people were on His side. Just then one of His own Apostles came to them, and said, 'Give me money and I will betray Him to you.' No one else knew that he had done it. But our Lord Jesus knew it. He knew that Judas would sell Him, that the priests would have their way, that He should be delivered to the Romans, that He should be condemned, that He should bear the punishment of a slave.

This was on His mind on that night when He and His Apostles were sitting at the Passover Supper. He said He had greatly desired to eat it with them before He suffered. As soon as they were seated, He said, "Verily I say unto you one of you shall betray me." His words went home to each of them. Not one said, 'Is it you who will do it?' but each asked, "Is it I?" None could tell that the wicked thought might not come to him; that he might not do the deed. At last Judas said, "Master, is it I?" And the answer came straight to his ear and his heart, "Thou hast said."

And, while they were eating, Jesus took bread, and blessed it, and brake it, and gave it to them, and said, "Take, eat, this is my body." And He took the cup, and gave it to them, saying, "Drink ye all of it; for this is my blood of the New Testament, which is shed for many for the remission of sins." That was the Lord's Supper. It was first eaten at the Passover Supper of the Jews. It was first eaten by Jesus and his twelve Apostles the night that He was betrayed.

II. But now, secondly, what did these words mean to those who first heard them? The Apostles did not know what they meant. Jesus was with them at the feast. They could see His body, touch it. His blood was not poured out. But they knew that He spoke no words in vain. The bread was a token from Him. They could but eat it as He bade them. The wine was a token from Him. They could but drink it as He bade them.

But He went forth from that feast. The officers of the chief priests seized Him. The High Priest condemned Him as worthy of death because He said He was the Son of God. He was delivered to wear the purple robe and the crown of thorns, and then to be crucified for speaking of His Kingdom. All had turned out as He said it would. He was actually buried. The women anointed Him and wept over Him. It seemed as if He had been proved to be no prince or Saviour, as if death had swallowed up all their hopes. Then, on the third day, One stood among the Apostles, and said, "Peace be unto you." He showed them His Hands and His Side. They believed that death had not conquered Him, that He had conquered death. He said that He was going to His Father and their Father; but that He would send His Spirit that they might be able to tell Jews and Gentiles of this Lord who had risen and ascended, and that in His name they might preach remission of sins to all, beginning at Jerusalem.

Then the Apostles began to know a little what was meant by the words which were spoken at the feast. Then they understood that in the body of the Lord

Jesus Christ, God was united to men and men to God. Then they understood that His blood was poured out, not for a few disciples, but for all men in all lands. That blood was the seal of a new covenant between God and men that He would blot out their sins and give them a new Life, the Life of Him who died unto sin once, over whom death has no dominion.

The Apostles were to carry this good news of God's Redemption and Reconciliation of the world everywhere. They were to say to men in all lands, 'Christ, and not death, is your Lord. His Father has taken you to be His children, and has given you His Spirit.' But how were they to make people know that they were not merely talking about a Redemption and Reconciliation, that it was an actual real Reconciliation and Redemption for men who could not understand hard words, for men of all tongues and kindreds who used different words? They took the bread and the wine. They said, 'These our Lord gave to us at the Passover on the night on which He was betrayed. He said to us then, "This is my body which is given for you. This is the New Testament in my blood which is given for many for the remission of sins." Now that He has given up His body on the Cross; now that He has poured out His blood, now that He has risen from the dead and ascended to His Father's right hand, now that we are permitted to claim you all as the children of His Kingdom, now we know how mighty these words are, now we can bid you one and all receive these simple pledges and witnesses of what He is, and of what He has done for you all, and how He is the elder brother and Head of the whole family in Heaven and earth, how He delivers you from all your Tyrants; how He gives you His Spirit that you may be His free servants.'

III. You see, then, that the Sacrament of the Lord's Supper meant very little to the Apostles when they were sitting alone with our Lord at the feast, and His body was visibly with them; and that it meant everything to them when He was gone to His Father, and they could treat all men everywhere as His brethren and their brethren. And this is what it means to us who are invited to partake of it to-day. It is the assurance of the Redemption and Reconciliation which God has made for us and all mankind in the body and blood of His Son; it is the assurance that we are very members incorporate in the body of His Son; it is the assurance that He will give us His Spirit to enable us to do the good works which He has prepared for us to walk in. All this you are told in the Communion Service. I can only repeat its words and say, 'Verily they are true words;' we may all believe them and act upon them, we may in the strength of God's Sacrament defy the enemies that try to divide us from Him; our own lusts, all mortal tempters, all evil spirits. We may claim our place as the servants and children of His Kingdom, we may ask Him to give us power each day to do His will. And then it will be indeed a higher and better feast to us than the Passover was to the Jews; a feast like that which tells us of a God who has broken our bonds asunder; a feast like that which tells us that He is the King over us; but a feast which is not limited to one people but which is intended for all, because our Lord Jesus Christ is, as St. Paul said, the Head of every man, the Author and giver of Salvation and Life to those who have been most tied and bound by the chains of sin and death. I am not afraid to bid you one and all to it. I know, indeed—the Gospel tells us so—that there was at the first of these Lord's Suppers a Traitor, one whose soul was full of darkness, and who went forth when he had received the sop to do the darkest deed ever done. But that sop was itself a token of Christ's love to him; because he would not receive it as such a token, because he would not trust that love, he first sold his Master and then hanged himself. That is, indeed, a lesson to us all. Every one may say, should say, "Lord, is it I?" But every one who does say so should say also, 'Lord, if it is I, by Thy Cross and Thy precious blood, by Thy own infinite Love, raise me out of my selfishness and despair. I will not distrust Thee because I distrust myself. I am one of that family for which Thou didst offer Thyself. I claim no higher honour. I covet no separate place. Thou didst give Thy body and blood for the life of the world, let me partake of them as one of that world. Let me be united to Thee now that I may have Thee as my portion for ever.'

SERMON XXXIII.

THE LAW OF LIBERTY.

Preached at Burnham, Afternoon of the 11th Sunday after Trinity, August 12, 1866.

"So speak ye, and so do, as they that shall be judged by the law of liberty."—St. James ii. 12.

My friends, do you think it is liberty for a man to be left to do what he likes? I do not know any slavery so hard as that. A drunkard does what he likes, and so he becomes utterly unable to govern himself. He does the maddest things. He ruins his wife and children. That comes of a man having his own way. He is dragged along into courses that he knows to be utterly vile. He says in his misery, 'I could not help it; my inclinations had the mastery over me.' That is to say, he did what he liked to do, and his likings were the cruellest tyrants over him. There are none so bad, none that treat a man so unmercifully, that beat him and trample upon him so terribly.

Do you wish to know how we may get the better of these tyrants, let them be ever so savage, even when they have brought us down ever so low? I believe the

Gospel which St. Paul preached to us this morning tells us the secret. I believe we may learn it from what is said about the law of liberty by St. James this afternoon.

St. Paul told us that he had a gospel or good news to preach about our Lord's Resurrection. Christ, he says, has risen from the dead; He won the victory over sin and over death; He won it for us. If we trust in Him, the battle may be a very sharp one, but we shall prevail in it; He will be found mightier than all our enemies, yes, mightier than our own inclinations, mightier than death, mightier than hell and the devil. That was the good news which this apostle proclaimed to the people of Corinth who lived in a very loose corrupt city. That is his good news to all of us.

St. James has good news for us too, though he speaks in a somewhat different way, though he seems as if he were using harsher language. He tells us of a law—a law which God has made for us, a law which it was destruction to disobey. He puts the case very strongly. He says that if we break one part of God's law, we break it all. We cannot make a bargain that we will keep the sixth commandment if we are only allowed to break the seventh or the eighth. That plea, St. James says, will not answer. The same God who bids us not commit murder, bids us not commit adultery; He will have us submit to Him altogether if we submit at all. But then St. James calls the law which God requires us to obey a law of liberty. How is that? Because the God who commands us not to kill will enable us to overcome the desire to kill, the brutal savage anger that might set us on to plot against a neighbour's life. Because the God who commands us not to commit adultery or to steal would break the desires that lead us to ruin the character and peace of a neighbour or the goods of a neighbour—that is to say, God will deliver us from the chains that are strongest upon us, and that bind us most closely, and that no man is able to undo; God would make us free. Has not St. James then a right to call this law a law of liberty?

"Now," he says, "so speak and so do, as those who shall be judged by this law of liberty." Let us consider how it is possible to follow that precept.

I. What does the apostle mean by saying that we shall be judged by the law of liberty? He means that God will not say this to a man, 'Why hadst thou such and such a bad desire,' but this, 'Why didst thou not ask Me to set thee free from the desire, to give thee power over it? That is what I promised when I told thee not to do this thing and that thing. I know what evil tempers and inclinations are in thee. I know thou canst not prevail against them by any strength which is in thee. But I wanted thee to trust in Me; to seek My strength when thou wert weakest; to hope in My power of raising thee when thou wert most utterly down. I did not give thee My law to frighten thee away from Me, but to draw thee to Me, that thou mightest find out what need My children have of Me, that thou mightest understand how near

I am to them all.' Then thou wilt cry, as David cries in the Psalms, "Judge me, Oh God, and plead my cause against my enemies." 'Thou seest how these bad desires press upon me, how this evil spirit tempts me. Thou understandest my dangers much better than I understand them. But I belong to Thee. Thou hast created me; Thou hast redeemed me by Thy Son; Thou lovest me for His sake. Support me then against those that rise up against me. Be upon my side, Thou Judge of the whole earth, when I am ready to yield to those oppressors of mine. They are not my lords; Thou art my Lord. Oh, put them down!' If we pray thus, and believe thus, we shall find that we are under a law of liberty; we shall find that it is a great and blessed thing to have One who sees into the depths of our hearts, and judges righteously.

II. Then, secondly, St. James bids us *speak* as if we were to be judged by this law of liberty. Speak to your own hearts as if that were so. Speak to your neighbour as if that were so. Do not say to your heart, 'There is no great harm in yielding to this bad habit; in making myself a beast; in saying hard, cruel, blasphemous words; God is so merciful that He will not mind it much.' But say, 'God is so merciful, so good to me, that He will not have me make myself a beast; He will not have me use hard and cruel and blasphemous words. He loves me too well not to forbid my doing that—not to punish me for doing it, not to give me help that I may not do it.' And speak to your neighbour and your child in the same way. Do not revile him for the wrong tempers you see in him, for the evil acts which you see him committing. Own to him that there is in you the same evil which there is in him. Own that you might do just as bad things as he does. But say to him, 'My friend! God wishes you and me to be free from our evil tempers; to prevail against them. He has put us under a law of liberty; He would have us be true men. Let us turn to Him, and He will make us true men. He will enable us to hate the things which He hates, and which are for our ruin, and to love the things which He loves, the things which are for our peace and blessing.'

That is *speaking* as those who are to be judged by the law of liberty. But St. James adds, "So *do* as those who are to be judged by it." That he tells us is less easy. We may talk wonderfully well about the goodness of God and our sinfulness, but when the moment comes which shows us how sinful we are, we may not be at all ready for it; we may stumble miserably, just as if there were no good God to hold us up. We do not come here to the church that we may say a great many prayers, but that we may find out what we are to do in those sharp times when no mortal is near, to put us in mind what we should do, when it would be little aid to us if any mortal were near. We come to be told of a very present Helper in our need; of One who knows our necessities before we ask, and our ignorance in asking; of One who declares His almighty power most chiefly in showing mercy and pity. If there is such an One, if He is the judge of the whole earth and the judge of each of us, we may so do as if there were. When we are not taught that God is our Friend and our Deliverer, we are very apt to think of Him as our enemy and our oppressor; we fancy it would be a good thing to be out of His way; a good thing to be hidden from Him; a good thing that He should not be our judge. We learn in church what kind of Being He is; that He is one in whom we may take refuge; that we have got very cruel enemies, who are bent upon destroying us, but that He is the God of salvation; *that* always; *that* to all people. Instead then of turning from Him, our wisdom at every moment is to turn to Him. We may be sure that He does not change, however we may change. We may be sure that we never need a protector against Him; that we need His protection every moment against a spirit of malice and cruelty that is seeking to devour us. St. James in his first chapter—the one before that we read this afternoon—says a very wonderful thing; that we are to count it all joy when we fall into different temptations. And he gives the reason for that strange sentence—that by these temptations we are taught faith or trust in God; we find that He makes a way for us to escape from our temptations. In the lesson we have heard this afternoon, he teaches us that by this faith in God we are enabled to do what is right and good; he teaches us that our faith is not worth anything, that it is not really faith in the living God unless it leads us to do those things which He works in us to do.

So you understand what he means by bidding us *do* as those who shall be judged by the law of liberty. He bids us believe in a God who is without variableness, or the least shadow of a turning; a God from whom all good and perfect things come; a God who is always ready to be our Deliverer in every dark hour. He bids us ask what we have asked to-day in the Litany, 'In the hour of death, in the day of judgment, good Lord deliver us.' Never doubt that when we prayed so, we prayed according to the will of our Father in heaven. When we prayed so, we gave up all right to judge other men, we asked God to judge us all; we asked Him to give us grace that we might be delivered from our own darkness and come into His light. If we pray that prayer truly we shall not wish that the Lord should not come forth to judge us, we shall cry as the writer of the ninety-eighth Psalm—which we often use in our afternoon service—cries, "Let the floods clap their hands, and let the hills be joyful together before the Lord; for He cometh to judge the earth. With righteousness shall He judge the world, and the people with equity."

SERMON XXXIV.

THE SURE AND CERTAIN HOPE.

Preached at Burnham, 13th Sunday after Trinity, August 26, 1866.

"For He must reign, till He hath put all enemies under His feet. The last enemy that shall be destroyed is Death."—1 CORINTHIANS xv. 25, 26.

SOME of you have heard these words already, perhaps more than once, during this week. You have heard them in a way that explains them, as no words from a pulpit can explain them. You have seen the coffin in the church. You have known that it contained what was mortal of one whom you had seen lately among you, who has exchanged kind greetings with you, whom you have respected and cared for. You saw those mortal remains put into the grave, and you heard the words "earth to earth, dust to dust," pronounced over them. But these came first—"He must reign till all His enemies are put under His feet. The last enemy that shall be destroyed is Death."

Yes; they could not be mere words out of a book when they were spoken then; they must have concerned actual things which you had to do with, actual persons whom you had conversed with. They were human words, words about men and women; they were Divine words, words coming from the Living and Eternal God.

They were not less human words because they were Divine, not less Divine because they were human, for they speak of Him who is one with God and one with man; of Him in whom God and man are reconciled. It is said of Him, "He must reign till all His enemies are put under His feet." It is said of Him that death is one of those enemies.

My friends! we often wish—each of us has wished —that we could know what has happened to some one whom we have loved; where he or she is: what he or she is doing or feeling when we cannot talk with them any longer, when the veil has dropped between our eyes and them. Would it not be comforting to have some tidings of this person and that? would it not strengthen us for our work? should we not be encouraged to follow them? should we not have some fellowship with them which we have not now? I do not know, but I think not. I suspect that we have the best tidings about them which we can have, when we hear the assurance in this text; the greatest strength for all work; the best encouragement to follow those who have been better than we are; the most real fellowship with them and with all just men made perfect.

For I do not find that they fed themselves with dreams of what might come to pass some time or other. They lived upon realities. They liked to think of what had come to pass. They got from the Gospel their most clear and bright hopes of that which would be, which must be, in the days to come, ay, in the ages to come. They lived upon the thoughts which St. Paul sets before us in this chapter. "Christ has risen from the dead; Christ is become the first-fruits of them that slept. As in Adam all die, so in Christ shall all be made alive. Christ must reign till all enemies are put under Him."

Here was their consolation. It did not rest upon guesses or chances, it rested upon One who is, and was, and is to come; it rested upon a work which He has accomplished, upon a victory which He has won. It grew up in the hearts of those who were conscious of great sins, of manifold weaknesses; who did not feel less aware of their sins or of their weaknesses as they grew older and nearer the end of their pilgrimage, but more aware of them; who were therefore obliged to depend more upon the Deliverer from sin, more upon Him in whom is perfect righteousness and strength. They felt their enemies more cruel and harder to overcome every day, but they believed more in Him who was mightier than their enemies, who would put them under His feet. They learnt more and more that all their confidence must be in Him who had trodden the winepress alone; that all their life was in Him who had tasted death for all men, who had gone into the grave and had risen out of it.

Therefore if we would be partakers of their fight, or share in their victory, we should not be asking, 'Where are they? what are they doing?' but we should be remembering this. Wherever they are, whatever they are doing, that which they believed when they were with us, remains true now; this must be their comfort and ever increasing delight now that they have cast off the burden of mortality.

So St. Paul thought; for it is this he dwells upon throughout this chapter, when he is telling us the source of his own comfort, and when he is most trying to comfort his fellow-men. He does not talk of any special blessings that should come to him because he was an apostle; because he had laboured more abundantly than all; because he had been carried into the third heaven. He talks of that which was common to him with the Corinthians; common to him with all of us. He speaks of Christ's battle and Christ's victory. *That* is more to him than anything which he could imagine about himself, after all his visions and revelations. And yet that, he says expressly, is for the Corinthians, though he complains bitterly of them; he reproves them for not claiming this victory as theirs; for not assuring themselves that Christ's resurrection was their resurrection, that by it they might rise out of their sins, that by it they might set death at defiance.

We need not be afraid of following St. Paul, my brethren; we need not suspect that he will betray us or lead us into foolish confidence. If he encourages us to trust in Christ, we may be sure that trust is safe, that it will not disappoint us; that it is what we want, to make us right and true men.

Believe that Christ who died and was buried, is reigning over us and over the whole creation; believe that He will put all His enemies under His feet; believe that death—the death which we see sweeping away multitudes at once, the death which takes away one and another of those we have known, and which will take you and me—will be destroyed by Him; believe this, I say, really, seriously, and you will find that you have a bond to all those whom you see, and to those whom you do not see, which nothing else can give; you will not indulge in sin because you have such a hope, but the hope will purify you from sin; you will not lose your fear of God, you will change the fear of death, which hath torment, for the fear of God, in which there is rest and peace.

It is this belief, this sure and certain hope, which the Church in its Burial Service seeks to cultivate in us. When people try to rob us of those words which we repeat at the grave of all whom we commit to the dust, or when they would leave it to our poor miserable judgment, whether we should use them or not, they know not what they are doing. It is not the wrong they would cause to poor mourners which I complain of; it is not even the temptation they would cause us to break our Lord's commandment, "Judge not that ye be not judged." It is that we should teach you to disbelieve St. Paul's words, to doubt that Christ has actually risen and is actually reigning; to measure His victory by our low and feeble standards. If we are wise we shall never do that. We shall believe that His work exceeds all which we can ask or think; we shall not shrink from the strange and wonderful words, that these vile bodies of ours shall be made like to His glorious body, because we shall know that there is a power in Him which can subdue even all things to itself. Yes, if He can subdue our stubborn wills to Himself; if he can by His discipline bring our hard unbelieving hearts to trust in Him, it is not too much to think that these frames which are so curiously and marvellously made shall be delivered from their disease and death; that "this corruptible shall put on incorruption," that this "mortal shall put on immortality." But as St. Paul teaches us so continually in this chapter, that which sustains all these expectations is the recollection of Christ, of His death and resurrection—His union with the Father—His union with us His brethren upon earth. If we try to fashion this world or the world to come without Him, both will be very solitary and dreary; if we look to Him as our fellow-sufferer and our Lord, as our advocate and forerunner, the earth which He has trodden, which He has redeemed, will be full of delight and beauty amidst all its sorrows. And the world unseen into which He has entered will be filled with the brightness of His presence, with the brightness of that innumerable company which cast their crowns at His feet, and hail Him as the Lamb that was slain, and that has brought them out of every kindred and tribe into His Father's house.

SERMON XXXV.

THE BAPTISM OF REPENTANCE.

*Preached at Burnham, Morning of the 14th Sunday after Trinity,
September 2, 1866.*

"Then went out to him Jerusalem, and all Judæa, and all the region round about Jordan, and were baptized of him in Jordan, confessing their sins."—St. MATTHEW iii. 5, 6.

OUR Lord once asked the Jews why it was that they went in such multitudes into the desert. 'It could not be,' He said, 'to see reeds shaking in the wind; it must have been to see or hear some man. But what sort of man? Was it,' He asked, 'one clothed in soft raiment? Such a man,' He said, 'you might have found in kings' courts, but not in a wilderness. Was it then a prophet,' He said, 'whom you looked for? Did you think that the man who was clothed in camel's hair and with the leathern girdle about his loins was that? If you did,' our Lord said, 'you were not mistaken; he was a prophet—he was more than a prophet; of him it is written—"I will send my messenger before my face; he shall prepare my way before me."'

Let us try then to understand how this plain man showed himself to be a prophet, and how he prepared the way for a greater than he was.

He did no strange or wonderful act. He had lived alone in the deserts; the people in the towns and in the country knew nothing of him. His speech was plain like his dress, and he did not change it to suit the tastes of different people; he did not speak in one way to the rich, and in another to the poor; he had the same message for all—" Repent, for the Kingdom of Heaven is at hand."

What did he mean by saying "Repent"? He meant, 'Turn round to a God whom you cannot see, but who knows you; who knows what you have been doing; who knows all your bad ways. Turn to a righteous God, for you have been unrighteous men.'

Does that sound like a voice which men of all kinds and classes, in all different places, would like to hear? If John the Baptist had brought the tidings of some wonderful thing which they might gaze at or handle, they might have been curious to know what it was, if they even half believed that it was worth seeing. If they were told of a person who was very benevolent, and would give them some treasures, each according to his taste, *that* might have been a reason for crowds to gather, and to go some distance; but to hear of One whom they could not see—of One who had not found out some good in them which deserved rewards, but had found out the evil that was with them all—would not they be likely to shrink away from such words; to go as far as possible from the man who spoke them?

But perhaps the other words which he spoke made

up for what was hard and painful in these. He said—
"The Kingdom of Heaven is at hand." What did that sentence mean? It meant that the King of Heaven was very near to them, that He was coming to them; that He would know all that they were thinking as well as what they had been doing. "His fan," said John the Baptist, "is in His hand, and He will thoroughly purge His floor; He will gather the wheat into His garner, the chaff He will burn up with unquenchable fire." The words—"The Kingdom of Heaven is at hand," then, do not sound more cheering than the command "Repent."

And yet both were cheering; both were what men in that day wanted to hear. 'What?' you say; 'did murderers, and adulterers, and false-swearers want to hear of One who knew all their secrets; from whom they could not hide themselves any longer?' Yes, my friends. It is a very intolerable thing for a man to hide a bad secret in his heart, to feel that he is a liar. It is the best news, and what you want, to hear you may get rid of that burthen; you may throw it off; you may make a clean breast; you may become a straight and honest man again. If people felt that they might in very deed throw off the load which is on their hearts —the load of falsehood, the load of treachery—they would be more glad to do it than to get much corn and wine or stores of gold; for what good do the corn and the wine and the stores of money do a man if he carries a heavy heart within him, if he cannot quit himself of that? If he can, these things may give much pleasure, or he may go on very well without them. The only question is this—can any one take this burthen from us? Is there any one who is willing to take it?

Now John the Baptist did not pretend that he could take any single man's burthen from him, that he knew the secret of any man's heart. If he had spoken in his own name some might have heeded him; but those who did would have gone away disappointed, he would have given them no relief; they would have heard him preach, and they would have admired him, perhaps, but the preaching would have passed out of their minds; they would have been the same men as before. But he spoke in the name of the Lord God. He believed Him to be a real Being; a real searcher of the hearts of the children of men. He believed that God was able to take away the burthen from men's hearts, and that He was willing as well as able to take it away. When he said "Repent," he did not doubt that God was saying it; that God was in very deed calling men to repent and turn to Him; that He desired to send away the sins from them which were burthening them and hindering them from being His true servants. John believed that if God called men to repent, He would give them repentance, that He would draw them to Himself. He may have been astonished when he saw such crowds swelling around a poor man like him. He may have said—'What have I done to move people whom I do not know, whom I never heard of, like this?' He may have been astonished, but he will have known very well, 'I did not bring them; I had no charm to make them follow me. It is God's word that has entered into them. *That* has laid bare the secrets that they kept hidden; *that* has showed them that what they want is light, not darkness, that they want God to be near them, and not far from them. And now He has taught them that He is near them, and not far from them; that He is not their enemy, but their friend; that He does not desire their death, but their life; that He does not wish to destroy them for their sins, but to save them from their sins. He has taught them this, and therefore they have come to my baptism.' Here, my friends, are the signs of a prophet—a man who does not speak his own words, but the words of the Lord. But John not only spoke words, he baptized, we are told, for the remission of sins. He gave them a clear sign, a simple sign, that God actually sent away their sins; that when they turned to Him to make them clean, He did make them clean. It was a sign. The water washed their bodies, God washed their hearts within them; He took away that which was defiling their hearts, as He had appointed water for taking away that which defiled their bodies. If you ask me what it was that most defiled their hearts, I should answer it was distrust. They had not trusted God, therefore they disobeyed Him. Now they trusted Him, they told Him of their disobedience; they asked Him to make them what He wished them to be. So they became different men; their whole mind was changed. The baptism was God's assurance to them that He designed to purify them. When they received it they said—'That is what we need; we want that above all things.'

And so the news which John the Baptist brought about the Kingdom of Heaven became good and comfortable news to them, though he spoke of One coming after him who would purge His floor, and gather His wheat into the garner, and burn up the chaff. They had begun to know that they needed this kind of winnowing and threshing; that they had chaff in them which ought to be burnt up; that if there was any wheat in them, God Himself must nourish it and cause it to grow. And, therefore, if there was One coming who could do what John could not do; who could baptize them with His Holy Spirit; who could make all that was good in them to spring up and flourish, and with a fire could destroy all that was bad in them—they might indeed welcome Him as their Prince and Deliverer —the Prince from Heaven—the only one who could set things right on earth.

John's message, 'You may repent and turn to God; God calls you to repent and turn to Him;' was a comfortable message. The assurance, ' He sends away your sins,' was a comfortable message. But the message, " There is One coming who will baptize you with the Spirit and with fire," was a more wonderful and divine message still; it took in both the former. It said— 'There is One at hand who will prove that He has come from God, by ruling your hearts and turning them to

God. There is One coming who will show you how thoroughly God sends away sins.' But it said also—'There is One coming who by His Spirit will enable you to love God and love your brethren; to fight against all that makes you turn from God and hate your brethren; yea, to bring forth the fruit of good works with which God will be well pleased.'

Thus it was that John the Baptist prepared the way for the great King—for the Lord Jesus Christ.

My friends, when our Lord had described John as a prophet, yes, as greater than a prophet, He added—"Nevertheless he that is least in the Kingdom of Heaven is greater than he." John had said to them, 'The Kingdom of Heaven is at hand. The King of Heaven is coming to baptize with the Holy Spirit and with fire.' Those who lived after the King of Heaven had appeared, after He had begun to baptize with His Spirit and with fire—would have blessings which John the Baptist had not, which he only expected. And who are those that lived after the King of Heaven had appeared, after He had begun His baptism of the Spirit and of fire? We are of that number. We say that the Son of God has appeared; that He has walked and lived among men; that He has died for them. We say that He has ascended on high; that He has baptized with His Holy Spirit. We are baptized ourselves, our children are baptized, into the Name of the Father, and the Son, and the Holy Ghost. We ask in Christ's name that the Holy Spirit may be renewed in us day by day, that God will not take His Spirit from us; that His Spirit may in all things direct and rule our hearts. We ask this for the whole congregation, for the least and the greatest. We live therefore under that wonderful sentence—" He that is least in the Kingdom of Heaven is greater than John the Baptist." We have a greater assurance that God will give us repentance; we have greater encouragement to confess all our sins to Him. We have proofs which John the Baptist did not know, that He will put them away and give us a clean heart and a right mind. But oh, my friends, what madmen shall we be if, with all these pledges and encouragements to trust our Father in heaven, we distrust; if, with the certainty that He wills to take away our sins, we hug our sins and let them eat into our souls and destroy them; if, when we might have the Holy Spirit dwelling in us and reigning over us, we open our hearts to the Evil Spirit, and let him be our master. We are all tempted to do that; if our blessings are greater than those of the men in the old times our dangers are greater. The only deliverance is in coming to God and asking Him to search us and to try us, to see if there be any wicked way in us, to guide us in the way everlasting. From every town and village in England people may come and confess their sins to God, and ask Him to make them right; but if they choose their sins instead of His righteousness and truth, they choose misery instead of peace, death instead of life, the kingdom of hell instead of the Kingdom of Heaven.

SERMON XXXVI.

GOD'S COVENANT WITH THE NATIONS.

Preached at Burnham, Afternoon of the 14th Sunday after Trinity, September 2, 1866.

"And many nations shall pass by this city, and they shall say every man to his neighbour, Wherefore hath the Lord done thus unto this great city? Then they shall answer, Because they have forsaken the Covenant of the Lord their God, and worshipped other gods, and served them."—JEREMIAH xxii. 8, 9.

WE have read two chapters of this prophet Jeremiah to-day. You will have perceived that the man who wrote them was a very sorrowful man; one who was full of grief for what he saw and for what he expected. Why was he in grief for what he saw? He was an Israelite, one of the race of Abraham. He believed that God had chosen his Nation to be a blessing to all Nations. He believed that it was to tell all Nations, 'There is a righteous Lord governing us and you, and all the world. We cannot see Him, but He has promised to be with us and with our children. He delivered our Fathers out of bondage. He gave them commandments to warn them against the bad acts which would bring them into bondage again. He is ruling over us and watching over us day by day, as a husband watches over his wife. And we, who are His people, have been forgetting Him; we have loved things that we can see, and taste and handle, better than Him. We have broken His laws.' Jeremiah saw signs all about him that men were breaking God's laws. They were adulterers; they were drunkards; they were false-swearers. And Jeremiah did not say, 'That is nothing to me. I am not as other men are. I am not an adulterer, a drunkard, a false-swearer.' He did not say that. It was God's great mercy if he had not yielded to all the temptations to which some of his countrymen yielded. But he felt that his country, the country which he loved, was polluted by the evil things that were done in it. They were dragging it down. They were separating it from God. They were dividing the members of it from each other. So Jeremiah the prophet, however pure he might be himself, felt that these sins were his sins. He could not tear himself from his nation. He was tearing himself from God if he did. God's covenant was with Israel. He was in God's covenant because he was an Israelite. Whatever calamities befell Israel must befall him.

And what calamities did he expect would befall Israel? He might not know exactly what they would be. But he knew for certain such evil as Israelites were committing, would bring their land into misery. The heart was going out of his people. They were losing their courage. They would not be able to face any enemies that came against them. They were become distrustful of each other, for they did not trust God. They were become lazy and restless. They would soon not think it signified much whether they worked or were idle. They were losing hope. So at last they would not care to sow their ground; for all who sow must sow in hope of a harvest. They would trust to chance to supply them with food. The land, therefore, would go to decay. And, above all, they were losing care for each other. Each felt as if he had an interest against his neighbour. The rich man coveted his neighbour's wife. The poor man coveted his neighbour's ox or his ass. Children did not honour their parents; parents did not care for their children. What would come of that? Why, if that was so, they were not a people any longer. And therefore when some strong king came upon them with his armies, they would become his prey. For his army would hold together and do its work; and his people did not hold together, and would not do their work. This, then, was what Jeremiah expected. He knew there was a very powerful king, the king of Babylon, who was watching to swallow up the nations. He was sure that he would come down on the nation of Israel and would swallow it up.

The thought of what the children of Israel were doing, pressed heavily on Jeremiah's mind when he wrote the words which we read this morning; the thought of what they were about to suffer, pressed heavily on his mind when he wrote the words we have read this afternoon. Much had happened between these times. They were in danger from two great monarchs. One of their kings had been carried into Egypt. Very soon a large portion of the people as well as their king would be taken to Babylon. At last the city of Jerusalem and the Temple would be destroyed. When all these things had come to pass, Jeremiah supposes that people of other countries would walk through the land of Israel, and see its capital city in ruins, and would say, " Wherefore hath the Lord done this to this great city ?" And this, he says, would be the answer, " Because they have forsaken the Covenant of the Lord, and have worshipped other gods and served them." The unseen God had bound them to Him; they had not believed Him, they had chosen the gods they could see instead of Him. There was no strength in these things to save them from their enemies. He who was their true Lord would let them learn by hard punishment what was the fruit of their wilful ways, what comes of forgetting His Commandments.

And now, my friends, let us ask ourselves why these chapters have been read to us. They speak of things that happened long ago; they tell us about a people who lived in quite a different part of the world from that in which we live. Why should we in this country, poor as well as rich, hear of what the people of Judæa and Jerusalem did in the days of the prophet Jeremiah, and of what befell them? It would be the idlest thing in the world to read such chapters in this September, 1866, to dwellers in the county of Buckingham, if the Lord God of Israel were not also the Lord God of England; if His commandments to Israelites in the old time were not His commandments to Englishmen in this time; if He were not our King as He was their King; if He were not the same yesterday, to-day, and for ever. It would be quite idle to read these chapters to you, if you were not tempted to do just what the Israelites did; to forget the Lord your God, the righteous God of your land; to break His commandments which they broke. It would be idle to read these things to you if these transgressions of God's law did not threaten to ruin the good land which the Lord our God has given us, as much as they threatened to destroy the good land which the same Lord God gave to the children of Israel. But if that is so, then we ought to give good heed to the words of the prophet, and to consider whether we should not do just what he bade them do; just what—as you heard this morning—John the Baptist bade them do many hundred years after.

My friends, you will ask what covenant the Lord our God has made with us in England which answers to the covenant which He made with the Jews. I told you what this was a few Sundays ago, or rather the Epistle to the Hebrews told you. It is said that this is God's new covenant, "I will put my laws in your hearts, and in your mind will I write them, and you shall be my people, and I will be your God." It is a new covenant; a better covenant than that which God made with the Jews, because God does not merely say to us, 'Keep my commandments;' but He says, 'I will give you my Holy Spirit that you may keep them.' But the commandments which He bids us keep are the very same. He bids us worship Him who is the Deliverer out of bondage, and Him only. He bids us set up no likenesses of things in heaven or earth, or under the earth, but worship Him. He bids us not take His Holy name in vain. He bids us keep His days of rest and work. He bids us honour our fathers and mothers. He bids us not kill, or commit adultery, or steal, or bear false witness, or covet. The commandments are the same as ever. And every neglect of these commandments by Englishmen defiles England, makes the country weaker and more slavish; separates us from God, and separates us from each other. And when people grow indifferent to these commandments; when they think, 'God is not really speaking to us, He does not care whether we obey Him or not, He does not care whether we do right or wrong,' then it fares with us as it fared with the Jews; we cease to be a strong people, a united people, a wise and understanding people in the sight of the nations; we become weak and divided and foolish. And though none of us may know in what way God will bring us down, and show us what the misery is of breaking His commandments and trampling upon His law, we may be sure

He will take some way. And whatever it is, we must all share the suffering together. It is very bad for any of us who says, 'I am not my brother's keeper, I am not a sharer in his wrong doing. My hands are clean.' It is very bad, because if we understand that we are all Englishmen, all God's people, all under His righteous and gracious government, we should feel that we could not divide ourselves from our countrymen, that God has meant us to be one people, and that we cannot be serving Him or doing righteously when we do not bear each other's burdens, and grieve for each other's sins, and feel that they are in very deed our own. None of us feel that as we ought; but the more we feel it the more we shall have of the mind of Christ, the more we shall understand what it means that He bore the sins of us all in His own body on the tree; the more we shall understand that in Him we are united to all the members of our Nation, and to all mankind. It is not a hard sentence that we should bear other men's griefs and feel their sins in a little measure, if that was what He did, who is the Head and Brother of us all; if so He did His Father's will, and performed His Father's work. But if we feel each other's sins, we ought to be desiring to raise each man out of his sins; to make him a true Englishman and a true man. We ought to be telling him that he need not be a drunkard, need not be a liar, need not let corrupt communications go out of his mouth, that there is a Lord who died and rose again to set him free from all his sins, and that there is a Holy Spirit who will help him to conquer them all. We should be asking for ourselves and all our people, what we have asked to-day, that God will give us the increase of faith, hope, and charity; that is to say, that He will teach us to believe in Him our righteous Lord and Saviour, to hope in Him who has promised to give us His righteousness and His Eternal Life; to be charitable with that infinite charity which His Spirit is willing to shed abroad in our hearts. Then we shall 'love the things which God commands;' we shall feel how good it is for us all to be under His government; how holy and wise His laws are; then we shall obtain that which He doth promise; for He promises that we shall know Him and be like Him.

That is the covenant which He has made with us in Christ. If we hold fast to that covenant, it will go well with us and with our seed after us. We shall be true citizens of our land, and God will bless our land and cause His face to shine upon it. But if we refuse His covenant, if we will not let Him govern us, people hereafter will say of this good and glorious land, 'Wherefore has all this evil and misery and ruin come upon it?' and then the answer will be, 'Because they have forsaken the covenant of the Lord their God, because they have worshipped other gods, their money, their pleasures, their malice, and served them.''

SERMON XXXVII.

LIFE AND RAIMENT.

Preached at Burnham, 15th Sunday after Trinity, September 9, 1866.

" Therefore I say unto you, Take no thought for your life, what ye shall eat, or what ye shall drink ; nor yet for your body what ye shall put on. Is not the life more than meat and the body than raiment ? "—ST. MATTHEW vi. 25.

OUR Lord spoke these words to His disciples who were poor men, men that had to work for their livelihood. Do you think He told them that they need not work, that they might fold their hands and go to sleep, that God would take care of them if they did ? Do you think He meant to say, 'You need not provide for your children; may spend what you have got, just as you like'? No, my friends, He meant nothing of this kind. He wished these poor people to work more diligently than before. He wished them to be less hindered in their work. He wished them to think more of their children than they had ever thought; to be wise men and not spendthrifts. Let us consider what He had said just before. He spoke of their food and their clothing, their lives and their bodies—you heard me read it a few moments ago.

"Ye cannot," He said, "serve two masters;" that is, two masters of opposite minds, two masters that bid you do different things. And He tells them who the two masters are that had two opposite minds, and would bid them to do different things. "You cannot serve God and Mammon."

He had been declaring to them the great message, 'God is your Father.' When you pray to Him, say, "Our Father which art in Heaven."

He said they must trust Him for all that they wanted. They might ask day by day for their daily bread. They might ask Him to forgive them their sins. They might ask Him not to lead them into temptation. They might ask Him to deliver them from evil. He was willing to do all these things for them; they should not doubt or fear that He was.

And what made them doubt or fear that He would do these things? They did not really believe Him to be their Father. They did not give Him credit for feeling to them as a Father feels to His children. They thought He had a grudge against them. How came they to have such a notion? Because they were in their hearts worshipping Mammon; that is to say, a covetous god; a god who wants things for himself, a god who seeks to get and not to give. What made them dream of such a god as that and worship him? They dreamt of him because he was like themselves; they were covetous; they wanted to get and not to give. So they made a god who was such an one as they were. They might make no image nor picture of him; but they worshipped him in their hearts all the same.

Now our Lord said, 'This you cannot do if you worship your Father in Heaven. You cannot have both these Gods for your masters. You will hate one if you love the other; if you will hold to the one you will despise the other. You will hate the covetous god if you love the good and gracious Father. If you will hold to the covetous god you will despise the true God.'

But what is it to serve the covetous god? It is this. If I am fretful and anxious about what I shall eat and drink, and how I shall be clothed, I fancy that I am his subject. I act as if he, this grudging covetous god, were my master. And what is it to serve the Father in Heaven? If I work without fear or anxiety, believing that there is One over me who knows what I am doing, and takes an interest in it, and desires that my work should be healthy and profitable, then I am serving my Father in Heaven; then I am acting as if He were my Master.

Now, you all know very well that men do not work better for being fretful and anxious; they work much worse; after a time they are not able to work at all. Then instead of being more decently clothed they become ragged; instead of having more tidy houses, and more wholesome food, the houses become dirty and the food bad; instead of providing more for their children, their children starve. Our Lord wished to save His disciples from this. He wishes to save us from this. And so He says to them and to us, 'Remember Who your true Master is. Let no one persuade you that you have any other than my Father in Heaven; than Him Who sent me on earth to deliver you from all bad gods; than Him of Whom I—who go about doing good—am the perfect likeness; than Him Whose will is at all times and in all places to do you good.' Assure yourselves every morning when you wake, 'He and He only is my master.' Say to yourselves, 'We will not have the covetous god for our Lord. This is our Lord. He will be our Lord for ever and ever. He is our children's Lord. He will be their Lord for ever and ever.'

That is the purpose of all our Lord's teaching in the Sermon on the Mount, of which you have heard a part to-day. He made known to His disciples, He makes known to us, what He is Who created us, what He is Who governs us. They were apt to say, and we are apt to say, 'Oh no, that cannot be our Master. That is too good news to be true. It cannot be that we have actually, at all times, a Father in Heaven Who does not forget us, Who never becomes indifferent to us, Who never ceases to desire our good, and to contrive good for us.' And our Lord answers, 'Yes, but it *is* true, wonderful as it is; true to the very letter, more true than words can tell you or than you can imagine.' But then you may say, 'Yes, perhaps He cares about great things, but not about little. He may care that we should be wise and good, but He will not care whether we have food and raiment.' He does care, no doubt, first of all, that you should be wise and good. Doubt not that He does. And doubt not that He will enable you to be what He wishes you to be. Ask for that and you will have it; seek and you will find it. 'But why,' says our Lord, 'should you fancy that He does not care about your food? Look at these birds that are flying in the air. Could they get food if He did not provide them food? if He did not give them power to seek the food, and did not make them fit to receive the food? Why should you fancy He does not care about your clothing? Look at these lilies in the gardens, or at any of the flowers in the hedgerows. Would they, any of them, have their beautiful clothing—so much more beautiful than any that man ever weaves, or than any king has ever worn —if He did not clothe them? See what care He takes of the commonest of His creatures. And do you think He does not care more for men, whom He has formed in His own likeness; whom He has sent His own Son to claim as his brethren?'

That will explain why He bids you take no thought for your life. If we are fidgety and restless about it, we shall do ourselves no good. But if we trust it with God, then we shall go manfully forth to do all that we have to do, knowing that we are safe in His hand. Then we shall say to ourselves, 'Well, He has given us this wonderful life within us. How much more that is than the food which nourishes it! But since our life wants food to support it, He will surely let us have that. He will give us strength to labour for it, which is better than if it dropped into our mouths. He has given us these curious bodies; how much more curious they are than the very finest clothes we can put on them! But since they want clothing, He will enable us to obtain that. He has greater designs for us than for the birds and the lilies, so He will not treat us as He treats them; He will treat us more generously, more considerately. He will call out a faith, and hope, and love in us, which they cannot have. He will bring us often in what seem very hard ways, by great sorrows, to this trust and hope and love. It is worth while. We shall find it so at last. The clothes and food will have done their work and will perish. The faith and hope and love will abide for ever. They will bind us to those that have gone before us, and to those that shall come after us. They will bind us to the Lord Jesus Christ, and to God our Father through all ages.' And it is, my friends, that God Who invites us this day to eat of that food which sustains our spirits. He wants them to live and not die. He wants them to believe Him and trust Him and love Him. And thus He enables them to do it. He says, 'I have given My Son to suffer and die for you all, for the whole world. Remember that love of Mine, that love which He showed forth in His death.' Feed upon that in your hearts. There is nothing like it. Angels and Archangels feed upon it. Poor men and women may feed upon it with them. It will never wear out. And you need not take thought or be anxious about this food more than the other. We cannot earn it. God gives it. He sends you this simplest sign and token how real it is, and that He would have all partake of it together. He bestows it freely; we receive when we give Him thanks for it.

SERMON XXXVIII.

THE HOUSE OF GOD.

Preached at Stoke Bishop.

"Make not My Father's house an house of merchandise."
St. John ii. 16.

You have heard these words in the lesson for this morning. If you understand them I think they will tell you what this Church testifies of, why it has been set apart from the buildings round about it, what it may do for those who worship in it, and even for those who see it as they pass.

Every Nation had its temples; these temples spoke to the Nation of a Being higher than themselves; these temples said that men might hope by prayers and sacrifices to approach these Beings, to make them hear their prayers and do what they desired. The Jewish temple said to those who worshipped in it—'The God who made the heaven and earth; the God whom no man hath seen or can see, has chosen your fathers to know Him, and to bear witness of Him. You did not seek for Him, He sought for you. He has desired you to know that He is not like the things which you see and handle; that these are given you to rule and to use; that He is the Lord your God, the Lord of your hearts and reins; the guide of your thoughts, desires, hopes; He who shows you what is right and what is wrong; He who gives you hands to war and fingers to fight; He who puts down the oppressor and exalts the oppressed. In that character above all others He reveals Himself to you. He brought your fathers, when they were a set of poor slaves, out of the land of bondage. He led them through the wilderness. He gave them the land in which they dwelt. And ever since, when they have remembered Him, the unseen God, and have trusted in Him as their Redeemer and their King, they have been a brave, free, united people; though they have been insignificant in their numbers and in outward power, they have been able to teach the Nations round about them who the Lord of the whole earth is, and to raise their thoughts above those idols to which they were bowing down, and to show them that Righteousness is supreme over all, and that all unrighteousness must be put down at last.

'And when they have forgotten Him, when they have thought that they were not His people and that He was not their Redeemer and King, or that He was only the Redeemer and King of their forefathers, and had ceased to care for them, then they have become weak, cowardly, divided, superstitious; then they have begun to bow down like the other people before the works of their own hands, and to think they could bribe the beings they worshipped to deal falsely, to let transgressions go unpunished, to favour the ill-doers, and to make good evil and evil good; and so instead of being teachers of the Nations, they have caused God's name to be blasphemed among the Nations. And the Nations have despised them, and trampled upon them, and they have become slaves as they were before in the land of Egypt.'

The temple had borne this testimony to past generations of Jews. The testimony was all the stronger to the Jews who were living in the days of Herod, because that was not the temple which Solomon had built. The unbelief and corruption of the people had caused the destruction and overthrow of that. The goodly building in which they were worshipping then, reminded them that no building could do anything for them if they did not understand the purposes for which it existed, if they were insincere and heartless. They thought they had learnt the lesson, for they were not bowing to foreign idols as their ancestors had done. They gloried in their separation from the other peoples of the earth. They rejoiced that they knew the true God, and the way of serving Him. But they did not know the true God, and they were not serving Him.

There was an idol in that very temple—an idol which they had with them in their houses and by the wayside. They were worshipping their gold. That was dearer to them than all things in heaven and earth. And, therefore, they could not believe in an unseen God who had redeemed them from the service of visible things, and had made them His people. Visible things had dominion over them—more complete dominion than they had over any generation of those who had gone before them—and the necessary effect had followed. They were not instruments of good to the heathen people, they were instruments of evil. These people found them more grasping, more covetous than themselves. They thought their religion taught them to be grasping and covetous. The people saw that their religion did not unite them, but set them quarrelling with each other; that they were divided into sects and parties; that they had no strength to resist wrong or to do right. And so the same consequences followed as of old. These Jews had fallen into slavery. They had first become slaves in their own hearts, then the Romans took from them all their outward freedom.

The oxen and cattle and sheep, and the changers of money who were sitting in the temple, were signs of this state of things. They were tokens how the trade spirit had got the mastery over them, and how little they were able to get rid of it even when they came into the building which they counted the most sacred of all. But now One stood up in that building, One whom they were told was a Galilean, who walked about the streets with fishermen for His friends, who went among publicans and sinners. And He made a scourge of small cords, and drove the oxen, and the sheep, and the changers of money out of the temple, saying— "Take these things hence; make not my Father's house an house of merchandise."

"My Father's house!" Think how these words must have sounded in the ears of those who were assembled there! This man of Nazareth dares to call the Maker of heaven and earth, the God of Abraham, and Isaac, and Jacob, His Father. But we do not speculate about the way in which such language may have affected the Jewish people. We know how it did affect them. The gospels—this gospel of St. John especially—tell us that. They called Him a blasphemer. This was what made what He did and said so dreadful in their eyes. He declared that He had come down from heaven to do a Father's Will. He was showing them by His own acts and words what that Father was; what His mind was; what His purposes to men were. In every message to publicans and sinners, in every warning to Scribes and Pharisees, in every parable, in every miracle for the hungry or the sick, this great pretension was involved. He had come to claim men as His brethren. He had come to redeem them from the service of the world and of their own lusts, that they might be the children of the living and righteous and eternal God. For this He was arraigned before Caiaphas; for this He was condemned to die. The other charge, 'He has made Himself a King,' was the plea on which He was delivered to the Romans. That was the charge which caused him to be crucified instead of being stoned. But].the chief priests and scribes regarded the first as the real crime ; the other as consequent upon it.

We believe that the Jewish temple fell again, fell finally, because those who worshipped in it would not acknowledge that there was One upon earth, born of a woman, who had a right to say, ' This is my Father's house. This house exists to testify that the God of all has sent me to redeem you into the state of children.' We believe that when the Jewish priests had refused this message for their nation, it went forth to all nations; that Greeks, Romans, Germans, Gauls, Britons, were told, ' God has sent His Son, made of a woman, made under the law, that you may receive the adoption of sons.' We believe that when the temple of their own nation had fallen, the churches in all the different nations rose up to proclaim this as the great gospel to mankind. And every new church that is reared in any neighbourhood, carries this testimony with it to that neighbourhood. It repeats Christ's own proclamation. It says this is His Father's house; the Father of the Son of Man; therefore, O sons of men, it is the house of your Father ! In Him God looks upon you as His children. In Him you may one and all say, " Our Father."

My brethren, it is this witness and no other, which this church is meant to bear unto you. For this work it was consecrated, or set apart from ordinary houses. It was not that those houses, the houses in which you dwell, the houses in which your fathers dwelt, in which your children may dwell after you, might be less dear and sacred in your eyes. It was that they might be more dear and sacred; that you might understand how blessed they are. The father of the family, the hearth, and the household, receive a fresh consecration where there is a house in which the great Father, the Father of the whole family in heaven and earth is worshipped. Each English household belonging to the richest man and the poorest man, becomes then not a mere isolated house; but all its own holy memories, all its trials, and sorrows, and joys, all that binds it to the past and to the future, become joined to those of every other. The family relations and affections which are so apt to become isolated, to cut us off from those who have been brought up in circumstances and under an education different from our own, all are so many ties of common citizenship and common fellowship. We cannot spare one of them. Our Heavenly Father has ordered each one of these human relationships; they are images of His divine relationship. He has inspired every one of these human affections. They come forth out of His universal and all-embracing love. So again, the consecration of churches is the consecration of all that we call our national duties and obligations. I have shown you how the Jewish nation fell into debasement and slavery. At one time, as much as at another, the cause was the same. The visible things which were given them to use as their servants, became their masters. In the earlier ages of their commonwealth, the temptation came through the sun and the stars which showed them the seasons when they were to sow and reap, through the animals which worked for them. They supposed that God must be like some of these. In the later times of the commonwealth, it came from the trade spirit. Their buying and selling absorbed their whole souls. To both periods the description of their own prophet is equally applicable "They forgat God their Redeemer." And in forgetting Him they forgot their manhood. The nobleness and freedom which belongs to men cannot remain when they are busy only about things that are beneath them, things that they can hold and grasp, things that are changing and perishing every hour, things that one man has and another wants. When these things get the mastery over us, when our thought is how we can get the most of them, how we can best exchange one of them for another, we do not lose our religion, but it becomes a trading, bargaining religion; a religion like that we read of in the Bible, of the nations who worshipped at hill altars, who cried and cut themselves with stones to make their gods hear. It ceases to be the worship of a Deliverer and a Father; it becomes the worship of superstitious slaves, not of courageous men. Every church stands up to bear witness against such a religion as this. It stands up to say to prince and peasant, to him who has no house and to him who has one, 'The Father who is rich in grace and goodness, who so loved the world that He sent His only begotten Son to save it, has given this land to you all to keep it and till it and improve it for Him. All your works and toils as professional men, tradesmen, or handicraftsmen, are given you by Him. All are honourable and precious in His sight. There is nothing so great, nothing so mean, but that He cares for it, and will make it minister for your good. Evil and misery and baseness come when your Father's house comes to be regarded as a house of merchandise. Evil and misery and baseness come when you forget that the God of heaven and earth cares that you should be right and true men, that you should know His name and show forth His image.'

Brethren! for the sake of the houses of merchandise—for the sake of that trade and commerce with which God has blessed this land, and which may be unspeakable blessings to it—I rejoice to see these houses rising up which are not houses of merchandise, but witnesses of a Father. Our trade and commerce have grown up through the toil and suffering of enterprising noble men, who have had courage to face dangers and wisdom to guard against them. Do not think that such courage and wisdom will remain to us if we become mere money worshippers. That worship makes us fear where no fear is. It gives men no nerve in hours of peril. It takes away their foresight and makes them reckless gamblers. But what can take away fear and cowardice, but this belief that you cannot go out of the reach of His government who walked the waves, and healed sicknesses, and delivered from death; that death and the grave and hell have been visited by Him who gave Himself for us, and that He came back the conqueror of them all, to say, " I ascend to my Father and your Father, to my God and your God "? What can be a motive and encouragement to men to plant colonies in new lands, or to work as the servants of the Queen in governing, educating, civilising any races who have been committed to our sceptre, like this, that wherever we go we may bear witness of a Father who claims men of every tribe and colour as His children, that wherever we go we may bear the good news that the earth is His and the fulness thereof; and that He is not a Destroyer but a Redeemer and Lifegiver; not the favourer of any caste or nation but the Righteous Judge of all? Every act of mercy which our higher science is able to accomplish for sufferers from sickness, becomes a witness for God; so the work of every magistrate becomes a witness for Him equally; so commerce as it extends the bonds of fellowship between lands, and shows how one can give what another lacks, bears a witness no less mighty and effectual. And those who have been doing works in distant lands may return to their own, and find again that which has told them in infancy of a Father, still telling of Him in their manhood or old age, reminding them that they were signed with the sign of the Cross and marked out as God's children and servants; giving sacredness to their early lives and their marriage vow, giving them a sure and certain sign that there is a resurrection to Eternal Life for them that have fallen asleep, and whose places on earth know them no more. So all the stages of our earthly life on to the last are consecrated; so every beautiful spot in nature as well as all the forms of art share in the same consecration, and have that one name of 'Father' illuminating them all.

My brethren, I have not thought it necessary to show you that the church in which we worship has any distinctive claim to your affection, because I believe that I am but recalling to your memories what has made it dear to you, when I dwell on the great universal characteristic. When you enter the church the first words tell you of a Father to whom you arise and go; the next tell you that you may come to Him though you have forgotten that you are His children, and have erred and strayed from His ways; the next how He pardons and absolves you, to the intent that you may join with His whole family in heaven and earth in saying "Our Father." That Name meets you everywhere, goes through every prayer and thanksgiving and act of adoration. There is not a sentence but declares to us the love of Him who sent His only begotten Son to take our nature, and through that Son bestows on us His Spirit, that we may know and worship the Father and the Son in the unity of that Spirit, world without end. These are the signs that we meet not to glorify our own opinions or our own sect, but to claim all the citizens of the land, rich and poor, as the children of one Father, heirs of one Hope; to warn them that all their misery now, all their misery hereafter, will come from not trusting Him, from not believing that He has reconciled them, from living as exiles and strangers when He has brought them nigh; from selling themselves to be slaves when He has redeemed them to be freemen.

I believe that this is a testimony which the great merchant city that is so near us needs, which the whole land needs, which mankind needs, which each of us needs. Therefore, I beseech you that you will bring some of the fruits of that merchandise which may else turn to the injury of your civic life and your national life, which may be a canker to eat up your nobler inward life, which may make you less of Englishmen, less of men, to the support of this house which speaks of a Father who will make the gold and silver, and the stone and the iron and wood, all to serve for the good and glory of His creatures, and who will make those creatures themselves into a more glorious temple in which He Himself will dwell for ever and ever.

SERMON XXXIX.

ST. JOHN THE EVANGELIST'S DAY.

"And now, little children, abide in Him, that when He shall appear we may have confidence and not be ashamed before Him at His coming."—1 ST. JOHN ii. 28.

THESE words are fit for St. John's Day if any in the Bible are. They were written by St. John; they were meant for those among whom St. John dwelt. They show us the very mind and heart of St. John, and they belong to Christmas time if any words in the Bible belong to it. They tell us what the meaning of Christmas day is; how we have and may have the blessing for which we ask in the collect that we repeated on Friday, and have been repeating again this evening; and they are words for the last Sunday in the year if any in the Bible are. They make known to us what has been the error of one and of all of us in the year that is going; they make known to us what we want and may have in the year that is coming, and in all the years that we are to spend on earth, and when we have left the earth.

St. John was a very old man when he wrote these

words. They sound like the words of a father, and no doubt he felt like a father to all who were about him—rich and poor—to all to whom he had spoken concerning Christ, to all who had been baptized into Christ's Name.

Sometimes he says 'my little children,' but he does not say so here. I am not sure that he meant it; I think it was far more in his mind that all to whom he was speaking were God's children, redeemed by Him from their enemies, owned by Him as His sons and daughters.

St. John was soon to go out of this world; most of his friends had gone already. Those who had heard his voice were to hear it no more; those who had looked up at his venerable face, and loved to see him smile, were to see him no more. But his words were to live on; he himself was to live on. His words were to be heard in distant parts of the earth, in countries which he did not know, in languages very unlike that which he spoke. And the words would not be mere words in a book; he himself would speak the words; he, the man who leaned on Christ's breast at supper; he, the man who heard Christ saying after he had ascended on high, "I am the first and the last, the beginning and the end."

Wherever in any part of the world there is a congregation of Christian men met together on this day, he is saying to them, 'You are God's little children.' Some of them may be grown men, some of them may be stepping into their graves full of years. Still they are in the sight of God little children. How few the years of the oldest of them have been in comparison with the ages in which the world has lasted, and how few in comparison with the ages upon ages in which He has lived. They would be little children just beginning a life that was to go on through His ages. So it was with those who saw St. John; so it is with us who are here to-day. God speaks to us all as little children, and we ought all to like the name, and to desire, as our Lord bids us, to become little children, that we may indeed enter into His kingdom.

Well!—that is the name by which we are addressed —remember it when you see infants brought to the font in this church, and signed with the Name of the Father, and the Son, and the Holy Ghost. Remember that they are taken into the congregation of Christ's flock, that they are members of His body. And recollect that you are members of His body, one and all of you, just as they are, and that you only live because you are so.

We say this again and again. You listen to the sounds. Oh, do not fancy them to be idle sounds which mean nothing; they mean everything. Let us try and find out what they mean. Nothing will help us to do so better than the sentence which I have just read to you—" And now little children, abide in Him, that when He shall appear we may have confidence, and not be ashamed before Him at His coming."

I. A little child who is told by its father or mother to abide or stay in a house where it has been left, understands very well what the command means. Some of its playfellows may ask it to come out into the street, or to go into their house, but that is not to be. The child may yield to them, but it knows if it yields that it is doing wrong. But what is the house in which St. John says we are to abide? We want a home for our hearts, just as much as we want a home for our limbs. Every one of us is looking for such a home. We need something, as we say, to set our hearts upon, and we try a number of things. Some you know try money. They set their hearts upon that; they long for it. When they succeed in getting it, their hearts become shut up in it; they seem as if they could never get away from it; they abide in it. But it is a poor dwelling-place. They become uneasy and restless in it; they say it is not large enough; they must have much more money, or they have not room enough to breathe. Young men sometimes complain of old men for liking this money so much. They see other things which they like better to abide in; they try various pleasures, some good, some bad, but none last long enough, none will give a man space to rest in, and those which suit one do not suit another. And some desire to have some possession which they cannot enjoy together, so they have to struggle each one to drive out the other. Could there not be a home for all? Could there not be something in which we might abide together? Could not there be something in which we might abide for ever? What we are told at our baptism is that there is such a home for us all. The home is a Person, is a Friend. We are baptized into Jesus Christ; we put on His Name; we claim Him as the Lord and Friend and Brother of us all. We say that He took the nature of us all; that He died for us all. We say that He has risen for us all, and is at the right hand of God for us all. That is what we start from before we can speak or think. 'And now,' says St. John, 'when you can speak and think, act as if this were so; act as if you had this Friend; let your hearts stay in this home; do not go out of it; when you have gone out of it, return to it as quickly as possible.'

But how, you will say, have we not our different works to see after? Must we not each in his own place be getting bread for ourselves and our children? Can the carpenter be neglecting his tools, and the shoemaker his last, and the physician his patients, and the lawyer his clients, that he may be seeking after this home?

No, verily; if the carpenter does neglect his tools, or the shoemaker his last, or the physician his patients, or the lawyer his clients, he will not find this home; he will not know what need he has of it; he will not be able to abide in it. The harder a man works, the more he learns that he cannot let his thoughts go astray. They must be fixed somewhere. They must be turned to some one who will show him how he must pursue his business heartily, not lazily; honestly and not like a rogue; as a freeman, not as a slave. Abide in this Lord of your hearts; set your heart upon Him and you will get this help. I am not speaking about coming to church. That is a good and blessed thing to do, because there you may get strengthened and may learn what you have to do with each other, and who is with you at your right hand that you may never be moved. You may learn *that* in the Psalms, and in the prayers and the Lessons; and sometimes our sermons may teach you a little about it. But I am speaking about our common week-day life, about that which comes to us every hour. There come to us ten thousand little trials continually. We are tempted to lose our temper; to be very angry with that which happens to ourselves; to lay the blame upon our neighbours; to cheat just a little when no one can find it out; to make ourselves beasts instead of men. Now whenever such base thoughts and desires surprise any man, whether they come to him from other people, or out of his own heart, a man may say boldly, 'I belong to Christ; I am a member of His body; I know He is on my side; I know the devil is against me; but Christ has overcome the devil; therefore will I call upon Him. I will say, 'Son of God, I am very weak, but thou art very strong. Let not these enemies prevail over me. Thou hast said, I shall be more than conqueror because thou lovest me. Oh! conquer for me now; I need Thee now.' That is abiding in Christ. That is what St. John bids us do, because we are God's little children. And when we have not done this, when we have forgotten Christ, and let the devil prevail with us, then the message to repent and turn is not a sad one, but is very cheering and comfortable. "My little children," says St. John, "these things write I unto you, that you sin not. And if any man sin, we have an advocate with the Father—Jesus Christ the righteous; and He is the propitiation for our sins, and not for ours only, but for the sins of the whole world." I do not see how there can be better tidings than these. They are the tidings which were brought to us when we were invited to eat the bread and drink the wine in remembrance of him who had taken our nature upon Him, and had purified it from all sin. We were taught that He has united us to God our Father in Heaven. He does not change, though we change; He abides always the same. Therefore we may abide in Him, if we are ever so weak, if we have stumbled and fallen ever so many times.

II. And then the words go on—"That when He shall appear we may have confidence in Him." When He shall appear! You see he takes it for granted that Christ will appear. The apostles never have the least doubt upon that point. They tell those of their own day that he would be seen by every one of them; they tell us, who read their letters now, that He will be seen by every one of us. Men had longed for One who should come and show them what God was; who should come and rule over them in his Name. We believe that Christ did come in great humility; that He was laid in a manger; that He did show what God His Father is; that He did show himself to be the ruler over men. Therefore we believe that He will put His enemies—Death, Sin, and Hell—under His feet; that He will claim the earth which He has redeemed. Do you think it is hard to believe this? Very hard indeed it is for a sick person who is tossing on his bed and can find no rest, for a lonely man who has lost himself on the hills at night, to believe that the sun will ever rise. But the sun does rise, and fill the world with his light. So when we feel our own evils, and when we look on all the wrongs and oppressions of the world, we cannot help fancying that the Deliverer is very far away, and has forgotten us. But He is not far away; He has not forgotten us. And St. John tells every sufferer, and every man who feels the burden of his sins, how he may find that out. 'Abide,' he says, 'in Christ. Hold fast by Him, though he seems to be far away, that you may have trust and confidence in Him when he does appear; accustom yourselves to believe in this righteous Lord and Friend; get into the way of asking His help in your troubles; get into the way of asking Him to keep you from doing wrong things, and to help you to do what is right. When you are puzzled, ask Him to teach you what is wrong and right. And then you will be always wishing to know Him more; you will long for the day when He shall scatter all the darkness away from the earth; you will cherish the hope of his appearing as the best of all hopes.'

III. But he speaks also of "not being ashamed before Him at His coming." You know how ashamed we have sometimes been when a dear friend—someone who cared for us, and for whom we had a great respect—came suddenly and found us doing things that we ought not to be doing, thinking thoughts that we ought not to be thinking. It is not because this person is our enemy that we are afraid of him; it is not because he is wont to be hard with us. We were afraid because he was so good and so kind. We dared not let Him see how hard and unkind and wicked we were. So the New Testament speaks of our Lord's appearing. It says that we may be ashamed before Him, just because He has been so good and gracious to us, and we have cared so little for His goodness and graciousness, because we have had such cruel thoughts of Him, because we have been so unlike Him in all our ways and works. A fearful thing that is to think of, that because Christ is so gentle, and cares for us all, and never forgets us for a moment, and is always seeking to make us like the things which He likes, we may be ashamed to meet Him. But then this need not be. If you determine not to think of Him as your enemy, but as your best friend, who has given you all you have; who renews His gifts day by day; who gives you the power of enjoying what he sends you—if you recollect that when He denies you anything, or takes anything from you, it is to prepare you for something better; to prepare you for being with Him; if you are sure since He gave Himself for you He is always ready to do more for you than you can ask or wish—then you will wait for his appearing and long for it, then you will mourn that you have spent this old year so little trusting in His help, so little hoping for more knowledge of Him, so little trying that your fellow-men should trust Him and know Him. Then you will ask that the new year may find you claiming your rights as new-born men, as God's own children. Then you will desire that each day of the coming year you may grow more to confide in Him, and to be like Him; then you will pray that whichever of us is taken this year out of the sight of his brethren on earth, may not really be removed from fellowship with them; you will pray that we may meet him, though we cannot see him, whenever we are met here to pray and praise. Then you will desire that when next Christmas comes we may be really able to join with sufferers on earth, and with Angels and Archangels round His throne, in that great Christmas hymn which St. John has taught us—"Glory to Him that sitteth on the throne, and to the Lamb for ever and ever."

SERMON XL.

SUFFERING AND GLORY.

Preached at Eversley, 4th Sunday after Trinity, July 10th, 1870.

" I reckon that the sufferings of this present time are not worthy to be compared with the glory which shall be revealed in us."—ROMANS viii. 18.

THE Epistle which we have just heard is very wonderful. It sounds more wonderful to me every time I read it. There are words and thoughts in it which baffle me; they point to things which I can hardly conceive of, or ask for, and yet I am sure that it is all true—and what is more, I am sure that it is written for all of us who are here to-day. To us—not to some very wise people, not to some great saints—are these words about suffering and glory, about groans and redemption, addressed. Our Father in heaven speaks them to us, and He has given all of us the power of understanding them.

What do you think the apostle meant by the sufferings of this present time? He meant the pains which he saw men and women suffering wherever he travelled. He dwelt in a different country from ours; he spoke a different language from ours. But men suffered in his country, and in his time, as they do here in this year 1870. They had palsies in their limbs, they had fevers, they tossed on sick-beds; they often felt as if their bodies were a torment to them of which they should like to be rid. Then they had pains in their minds like ours; they lost dear friends; they had hard words spoken about them; sometimes those whom they trusted most proved false to them. And they had deeper cause for groaning still. They knew that they had done wrong. There was a voice which said to each of them, 'Thou hast sinned.' It was with them, then, as it is with us. St. Paul speaks of all these sufferings; he knew them all. He knew the pains of body; he knew the pain of losing friends and being hardly spoken of—even of being cruelly treated by those whom he loved, and to whom he had done good. He knew most of all the pain of hearing a word saying in his heart, 'Thou hast sinned; thou hast rebelled against the righteous and true God.'

It was just this pain—the worst of all—which led him to cry for a deliverer or redeemer. He had thought very well of himself; he had fancied he was very zealous for God. Then it was shown him that he was doing just the thing which God would not have him do; that he was fierce and cruel, while God was full of mercy and love. How was that? He must have yielded himself to a bad spirit; the bad spirit must have got the mastery over him. Who could deliver him from this tyrant? It was shown him that the Son of God was not far from him ; that He could break the yoke of the Evil Spirit; that He could give him His own gracious and good Spirit. Was that discovery for him only ? No, when this Spirit began to work in him he felt that he was to go forth into all lands with these tidings—" God in Christ has reconciled the world unto Himself, not imputing their trespasses unto them;" and these, 'God hath sent forth His Son, born of a woman, that they might receive the adoption of sons; and because you are sons, He hath sent forth the Spirit of His Son into your hearts, that you may call Him "Father;" and these, 'He has delivered us from the powers of darkness, and has translated us into the kingdom of His dear Son.'

I have said that he who was sent with this message to men was not more free from sufferings than they were; few men ever suffered so much, and he found that it was good for him to suffer. In former days he had been inclined to think himself different from other men, and better than other men. Now, he rejoiced to know that he was one with them, for that was what his Master had been. Jesus Christ, as it is written, " took our infirmities and bare our sicknesses." And again, 'He tasted death for all men.' Now if St. Paul had said, 'I am not of the same flesh and blood with these poor men and women about me, I have a better lot than theirs,' that would have been like saying, ' The Lord Jesus Christ is not my Lord and my brother ; His Father is not my Father.' But when he said within himself, 'What misery there is in the world! how men, and not only men but all creatures, are groaning under the burthen of death,' then he gave thanks that the Son of God had borne this burthen, that He had given His flesh and blood for the life of the world. When he believed in Christ, he could enter into the sufferings of men; he could feel with them as he had never felt before. And yet he could see a hope and a promise in their groans. They were, as he says in the Epistle, travailing pangs; they were the anguish of death, but they were leading on to a glorious birth.

My friends, it is easy for any of us to talk about the troubles and sorrows that men pass through in body and mind and spirit. But we shall only sympathise with them, as St. Paul did, when we have his faith and his hope. But the troubles and sorrows remain, whether I take heed of them or not. I look into any poor man's cottage, and I know that pain and death have been there, and will be there. I look into any prince's palace, and I know that pain and death have been there, and will be there. The face of the oldest and of the youngest testify 'they will be with us.' The animals feel them as well as men; and the trees and the flowers, though they do not suffer pain, yet wither and die, so that we have all clear proofs that St. Paul is right in half of what he tells us. But is it true that Death is the lord of any man or woman or child; of any beast or any insect; of any tree or flower? No. Death did not make them; and He who did make them, He who gave them life, He by whom their life has been renewed every hour, He has proved that He is stronger than Death. When I say, 'I believe in Jesus Christ the Son of God, our Lord, who was crucified, dead and buried, who rose again from the dead,' I say, 'Not death, but the conqueror of death is my master; not death, but He that destroyed death—the Prince of Life.' I say all things have been shown to be His; all His enemies will be put under His feet. I declare then —you and I have declared to-day—that we claim for ourselves that redemption which St. Paul says all God's creation is waiting for and expecting; that glory with which he says the sufferings of this present time are not to be compared. When we say Christ is our Saviour, or our Redeemer, we mean that He has died and risen again to deliver our bodies from their slavery as well as our spirits. Our spirits have fallen under the power of sin; our bodies have fallen under the power of death. Christ, our true king, has shown that he is mightier than both; that he is the Deliverer from both. And if I turn to Him as the Deliverer out of my slavery to sin, if I say to the Evil Spirit, 'Thou art not my lord at all, Christ has claimed me as His servant and His brother,' then I shall be able to say to death also, 'I defy thee; thou hast had power to rack this body of mine which is so curiously and wonderfully made; the breath will go out of it, as it went out of the body of the Lord Jesus; my dead body will be put into the grave, as His was; what is dust will return to dust; but He will take care of the life which He has given me. I can commit that to Him. I know He will accomplish the purpose for which He came upon earth and submitted to death. I know He will not leave any part of His work unfinished.' That is the ground for St. Paul's language about the redemption of the body. We all groan together; we say men, women, children—all God's creatures—are under the burden of death. We who have felt the power of God's Spirit in our spirit, do not groan less than others. We wait for the Deliverer of these bodies from their aches and torments; we wait for the day when Christ shall set them free from the bondage of death; when He shall make them like His glorious body. And as we hope for ourselves, so we hope for all those creatures who not for their own fault have been made subject to misery and death, who are not sinful as we have been. We hope that the curse of death shall be taken off the whole of this beautiful earth, that wherever there has been woe and death, there shall be the triumph of peace and life.

St. Paul hoped this because he believed that Jesus Christ, the crucified, had ascended on high in the glory of His Father. He hoped it because he believed that His glory is to fill the earth. Just as the sun rises out of the night, and brings everything that had been hidden and dark into light, so he believed that Christ, the true Lord of all, would be manifested, and that His light would enter into every dark corner of the earth, that nothing would be hidden from it. That is the glory with which he thinks the sufferings of this present time are not to be compared. It was not some glory of his own. He had desired such glory once; when he began to trust in Christ he gave up the thought of it. Then it was His glory which he desired to behold hereafter, which he desired that all should behold. For he welcomed it as the common glory, the glory that had risen upon all men as well as upon him; the glory which had been coming forth through all man's own darkness; the glory that must at last shine out fully, and which nothing should quench.

Now, I said before, and I say again, that these words are quite beyond me, that there is a height and depth and breadth in them which I cannot measure. I said before, and I say again, I believe them to be all true, and I think that there are ways by which every one of you may find them out to be true. The chief way is this. Suppose any of us has fallen into some evil habit—suppose a man has become a drunkard, or has taken a great spite against any of his neighbours, or is often giving way to bad temper, or feels very indifferent about the good of the people around him—he says, 'I cannot get out of this bad custom; it is too strong for me.' He is right; it is too strong for him. He has a master over him who will not let him go, but this master is not too strong for Christ. Christ, when upon earth, set men free from such masters; He is not less mighty now. Call upon Him as a Redeemer from this evil spirit. Ask that the good Spirit may come and dwell with you, and take possession of you, and then you will begin to understand what the sufferings of the body and the mind are for; you will find that they have been your schoolmasters to bring you to Christ the Deliverer. Then you will all say, 'Surely He who has broken my bands asunder is the king and Lord of the whole earth. Surely it must be His will and His Father's will that all His creatures should be brought out of the bondage of corruption. Surely it is His glory that we are all to long for and hope for. There must be a day when that glory shall appear, and all flesh shall see it, for the mouth of the Lord hath spoken it.'

SERMON XLI.

REPENTANCE AND CONVERSION.

Preached at Carisbroke.

"Repent ye therefore and be converted, that your sins may be blotted out."—ACTS iii. 19.

ST. PETER had been telling his countrymen that the Jesus whom they had crucified was their Lord and Christ. Strange words! They expected a King, who was to reign over them and to put down all other people; they were doubting and debating how He would show forth His glory to men; how He would begin His conquests over the world. And now a poor fisherman stood up in the midst of them and said, 'He *has* shown forth His glory to us, He *has* begun His conquest. And you have been yourselves helping to bring forth that glory. You have been preparing the way for His victory. For you have given Him up into the hands of the Romans, and they have hanged Him upon a tree. There in His death upon that Cross He has manifested the glory of God. And because He could not be holden of death, because He was the Son of God, He has risen from the dead, He has ascended on high. There is the beginning of His victory over all nations.'

St. Peter said, 'This crucified Man is *Lord*,' that is to say, 'He is the Ruler over men, over their spirits and over their bodies. He is the Ruler over the earth which He has given men to replenish and subdue.' And St. Peter said further, 'He is *Christ*.' That is to say, 'He is anointed with the Spirit of the Eternal God. That Spirit dwelt in Him while He was upon earth without measure. That Spirit, since He has ascended on high, He pours forth upon men, that they may know Him and know His Father, and that they may bear His image and His Father's image on their hearts.'

I. On this ground the Apostle rests the exhortation in the text, "Repent, therefore, and be converted;" these two words do not mean the same thing. But they commonly are found together in the Scriptures; one is not perfect without the other. To *Repent* is to change our minds; to think quite otherwise of some matter or some person than we have been used to think. St. Peter knew what the people he was speaking to thought about God. He knew what he himself had thought about God. They thought of Him as an enemy from whom they were to fly if they could, and whom, if they could not escape, they must persuade by all arguments and bribes not to destroy them. Now it was this mind of theirs which St. Peter desired that they should change. These were the thoughts from which he wished to deliver them. But he could not work this change or deliverance. He had not been able to work it in himself; he certainly could not produce it in anyone else. If they merely listened to his arguments, or to the arguments of any man or any Angel, they would go on suspecting God; they would suspect Him more every day, because every day they would be doing more wrong acts, speaking more wrong words, thinking more wrong thoughts, which He must hate. But St. Peter was not using his own arguments or the arguments of any Angel, he was using God's arguments. He was speaking as His messenger. He was declaring that Jesus Christ in dying and rising from the dead had shown forth God's mind to His creatures. Christ had shown how God felt to those who were feeling estranged from Him. Christ had revealed Him as a Shepherd seeking after the sheep who had wandered from Him; as a Father watching over the prodigal who had gone out of his Father's house into a far country, and had wasted his substance in riotous living. He had set forth this Father not only in His words but in His deeds; going about doing good, healing the sick, casting out devils. He had set Him forth most of all in His own sufferings; entering into the death of all men, bearing their sorrow and their sin. He had shown that there is a Living Power proceeding from the Father and the Son which could change the minds and hearts and wills of men, which could turn them from evil to good.

St. Peter, then, preaching of this Lord and Christ, affirming Him to be the Son of God, could say to these Jews, 'Repent, change your minds about God. He is not, He cannot be, such a One as you have taken Him to be; He must be just the opposite of this. All your suspicions of Him must be wicked and false suspicions; which an Evil Spirit, a slanderer, has sown in your hearts. I bid you—because He bids you—cast them aside.'

II. And if you do cast them aside, if you do repent or change your minds about God, then you will turn or be converted to Him. You have been turning away from Him. He has been with you when you rose up, when you lay down. He has been your Protector, the Giver of your life, the Renewer of your life. He has been speaking to you continually. Every tree and flower; every sunrise and sunset; the voices of friends who are with you and who are gone from you—all have brought messages to you from Him. He has been conversing with you in lonely hours when there was none else beside you. He has been bringing deeds you did, thoughts you thought long ago, to your minds. He has made you see how evil they were, though at the time you might think nothing of them, or find them pleasant. He has sent you blessed memories and recollections of days gone by; of lessons you learnt on your mother's knee, or out of holy books, or through the lives of good men. Yet you have turned away from Him. You have been seeking treasures here and there, in the earth at your feet, or at the end of some rainbow which you could never reach. You have been always in want of something, you could not exactly say what, which would make you happy, which would perfectly content you. And all the while the good you wanted, the Being who would have satisfied you, was close to you, and you turned from Him. But now that you know what He is, now that you know His face is turned to you, turn yourselves to Him. Let Him who has not spared His own Son, but given Him up for you all, bind you to Him. Let Him hold you fast. Do not struggle to separate yourselves from an Everlasting Friend. Yield yourselves to Him. Suffer Him to rule over you, for to be His servants is to be perfectly free.

III. You will see that St. Peter could not call upon his countrymen to repent without also calling on them to be converted, to change their minds concerning God; to act as if He were a Friend and not an enemy, to trust Him instead of distrusting Him. This was in fact to turn to Him. This was to recollect the Father who had given all His creatures bread enough and to spare, while His own children through their own fault and folly were perishing of hunger. This was to arise and go to Him, saying, 'Father, we have offended against Thee and before Thee, and are not worthy to be called Thy children.' For now first they would feel that they had *sinned*. Before, they might have felt uncomfortable in a thousand ways, restless, desponding. They might have accused others of doing them great injuries; they might have accused themselves of great foolishness; they might have had both remorse and shame for acts which had been done and could never be undone, but they will not have said, *We have sinned.* No one says that till he feels that he has been disbelieving, distrusting, disobeying a *Father*; that he has been fighting against One who was always caring for him and doing him good. Then comes the sense of sin; then comes the confession of sin. And the confession, though it may be full of sadness, is also full of joy; because it is throwing off a weight too heavy to be borne, because it is to return to One who more wishes to take the load from us than we wish to be rid of it.

IV. And so St. Peter might well add to the exhortation, "Repent and be converted," those other words, " that your sin may be blotted out." Remember, I pray you, to whom he spoke these words. Many of those who heard him will have joined in the shout *Crucify Him!* when Jesus was standing before the Roman governor and Pilate wished to let Him go. Some may have bowed the knee to him in mockery when He wore the purple robe and the crown of thorns; some may have imitated the priests who said, " Let Him come down from the Cross; He saved others, Himself He cannot save." To one and all, whoever might be there, whatever they might have been, St. Peter addresses the same words, he holds out the same hope: ' Your sins may be blotted out. You may be made new and pure creatures.' The Jews were not unused to this language. They knew that their great King David, after he had committed his terrible sin, after he had been an adulterer and murderer, had prayed, "Make me a clean heart, Oh God! renew a right spirit within me. Purge me with hyssop and I shall be clean, wash me, and I shall be whiter than snow." They were certain that what he prayed for was granted; that he was fearfully punished for his transgressions, but that his heart and spirit did become right and true; that he did rise up a new man. This blessing which had been given to David, St. Peter said was bestowed upon all men who would receive it. God owned them in Christ as His children. He promised to put the evil which had become part of themselves far from them. He said that the new and pure and holy mind of Christ should be their mind. They might sink lower and lower into the dark and selfish and separate nature—the stagnant pool out of which all foul odours had come, which had bred all fevers and pestilences. They might continue selfish creatures, foes to God and to each other. But they might claim to be members of Jesus Christ, to have that true human nature which is in Him who is one with the Father, and in whom the Father sees all and loves all. Thus their sins could be blotted out. I do not say they would not be haunted continually by the spectres of evil they had done in past time. I do not say they would not be continually reminded of a flesh and a world and a devil, that would drive them into deeper evil still. But they would have a right to say, 'Jesus our Lord and Christ has died to set us free from those dark shadows of the past, and from you our present seducers. He has risen again, and lives to put you under His feet. Married to Him, trusting in Him, we can defy you. We know that He will overcome you altogether at last. In that hope we can live and work with Him for your extirpation in ourselves and in our fellow-men.'

Brethren! I said the first words of St. Peter—those in which He declared a crucified Man to be both Lord and Christ—were strange and startling words to those men who heard them first. You cannot be surprised that many of them cried, 'What! Are we to believe such tidings—such monstrous tidings—on the word of an ignorant Galilean, a mender of nets?' The surprising thing is not that so many rejected his word, but that so many believed it. The surprising thing is that it made its way beyond the limits of Judea and Palestine, that it reached Greece and Italy, that it came over to Britain, that at last the most civilised and powerful nations of the earth received it as the very ground of their existence. You are here to-day, this church stands in this village, because our fathers confessed, because our nation confessed, that the Jesus who was crucified on Calvary is both Lord and Christ, is the Son of Man and the Son of God.

This is indeed marvellous. Others may account for it as they can. I believe it came to pass because the message was a true message ; because it was what all nations were craving for; because it was what God had stirred them up to crave for ; because it was what the Lord created them to receive. Therefore, though they had a thousand motives without, and ten thousand within, *not* to receive it, though it contradicted all the feelings and notions respecting God which belong to our evil nature—though it turned the policy of the world upside down—yet peoples and races and kingdoms bowed before it; the Cross proved itself mightier than all the powers in earth or hell.

Well! But those words of St. Peter which follow these, what of them ? He said "Repent, therefore, and be converted, and your sins shall be blotted out." Is *that* sentence worn out ? Has that nothing to do with Englishmen as well as with Jews ? Brethren, I do not think we any of us know the least what it had to do with the Jews, if we have not learnt by experience what it has to do with ourselves. I do not think we could tell how the Jews thought of the God who had made a covenant with them and chosen them to be His people, if we were not bitterly aware how we have thought of Him who has made the better covenant with us, and chosen us to be witnesses of His Truth and Love to all the families of the earth. Are you astonished when you hear how stiff-necked the Israelites were, how they refused to believe in the God who had led them through the Red Sea, who had borne them as on eagles' wings across the wilderness ? Does it not strike you? We have been the sharers in a greater Redemption than that—we have been borne, we are borne day by day, through greater perils. And do we believe the more for that? Do we trust Him who has taken us to be His children, who has declared that we belong to the body of His own Son, who has sealed us with His Spirit? Do we not continually believe this God, this Father, this Deliverer, to be our foe; One whom it would be well if we could banish from us for ever? Do we not act as if we wished that there were no such Being; as if we only acknowledged Him because we dare not deny Him? Oh! Brethren, must not the message come to us also, 'Repent! change your minds altogether respecting Him whom it is Eternal Life to know, Eternal Death to lose? Do not maintain a perpetual war with Him who has made peace with you in the blood of His Son! Do not treat that blood as if it were a common unholy thing, not a witness and pledge—as Apostles declared, as our fathers believed—of His love to men, of His reconciliation of the world.' All of us have need of this repentance—none more than we who preach it to others. How continually do our hearts accuse us of repeating the words which record the greatest wonder in heaven and earth—of arguing about them—of condemning those who do not receive them—whilst the faith, the hope, the love, which they express is hidden from us, is as though it were not. How often the message of the Angels—when it is uttered from our lips—comes darkened by the thought that we have not given glory to God in the highest, or helped the cause of peace on earth, or done deeds of good will towards men! What a knell of death rings in our ears, along with the promise of Eternal Life.

What do such lessons teach us? Is it that we should doubt the might and efficacy of God's Word? Is it not rather that we should always recollect ourselves, always declare to you that this call to repentance comes from Him and not from us; that as there are none who do not need it, so there are none who may not profit by it; that it is addressed to the drunkard and the harlot as well as to the most religious; that the sin of all is the same—unbelief in God, distrust of His Goodness and Truth—that the remedy for sin is the same for all, the Love of God manifested in His only begotten Son, shed abroad in our hearts by the Divine Spirit?

And so the command, 'Convert or turn yourselves to God,' is for us also inseparable from the command, 'Repent or change your minds respecting God.' 'This is the name,' said the Prophet, 'whereby the child of the virgin shall be called—Emmanuel, that is to say, God with us.' It is the promise of all the Scriptures, that God shall come nearer to men, that He shall dwell among them. But it is our inclination to think that instead of being nearer to us, in closer converse and communion with men than He was in the old times, He has gone further from us; that then He revealed Himself with open face, that we can only behold him through a veil. Oh! Brethren, it is our wish that is father to this thought. We desire that God should be at a distance from us—therefore we persuade ourselves that He is. We do not like to retain Him in our knowledge; therefore we do not think it is possible for us to know Him. But the Light is about us, however we may shut our eyes to it. And when we believe that God is not the tyrant we have taken Him to be—that He is that Father of whom Christ said: "He that hath seen Me hath seen the Father"—when we believe this, we turn to the Light from which we have been turning away; we desire to come to it that our deeds may be made manifest; if it is ever so searching we are sure that it is blessed; if the darkness invites us ever so much, we are sure it is deceitful, bewildering, accursed.

Oh, let us cherish this belief more and more. Let us act upon it more and more. For then we shall find that the Apostle's last words are fulfilled to us, as much as to the people of any former generation. We, too, may have our sins blotted out. We, too, may have clean, free, purified consciences. We, too, may know how the blood of Christ cleanseth from all sin. When we turn to God, not that we may obtain indulgence for our sin, but that we may be delivered from it; not that we may gain some blessing for ourselves from which others are excluded—but that we may partake of that perfect sacrifice, oblation, and satisfaction, which was made for the whole world; we shall find that every promise of God in Christ is Yea and Amen, that the fulfilment does not fall short of the expectation, but exceeds all that we can ask and think. For then we shall look forward to that time of refreshing from the presence of the Lord, of which the Apostle speaks at the end of this verse. We shall expect the appearing of the Lord Jesus Christ, that restitution of all things which God hath promised by the mouth of all His holy Prophets, since the world began. We shall wait for this Revelation and hasten towards it, because it is the Revelation of Him who is the perfect Light of the world: because before His brightness all that is false and corrupt and evil must for ever flee away.

www.ingramcontent.com/pod-product-compliance
Lightning Source LLC
Chambersburg PA
CBHW020220240426
43672CB00006B/371